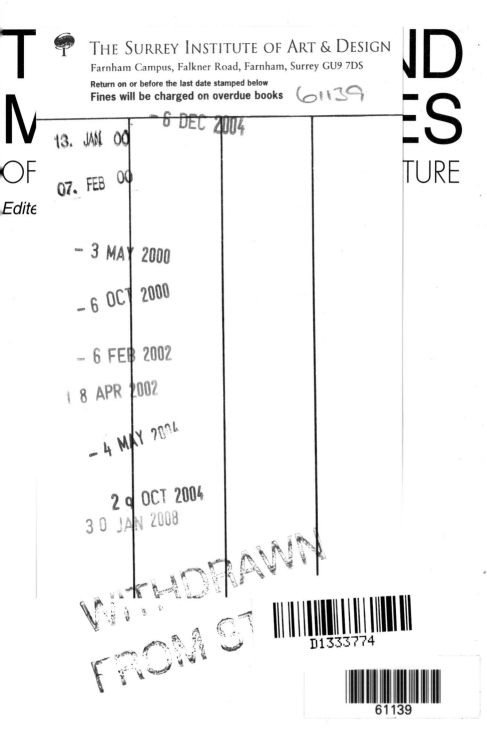

THE SURREY INSTITUTE OF ART & DESIGN
Farnham Campus, Falkner Road, Farnham, Surrey GU9 7DS

Return on or before the last date stamped below
Fines will be charged on overdue books   61139

- 6 DEC 2004
13. JAN 00
07. FEB 00
- 3 MAY 2000
- 6 OCT 2000
- 6 FEB 2002
1 8 APR 2002
- 4 MAY 2004
2 9 OCT 2004
3 0 JAN 2008

WITHDRAWN
FROM ST

D1333774

61139

ACADEMY EDITIONS

61139

ACKNOWLEDGEMENTS

Every attempt has been made to locate the sources of all material used in this publication to obtain full reproduction rights but in the very few cases where this process has failed to find the copyright holder, apologies are offered.

Individual copyright clauses are noted at the end of each section of text.

Picture credits: all images are courtesy of the individual editors, authors and architects unless otherwise stated: Charles Jencks: pp12, 13, 29, 39, 46, 51, 58, 64, 87, 120, 132, 195, 206, 238, 253, 284; Paul Raftery p300

First published in Great Britain in 1997 by
ACADEMY EDITIONS
a division of John Wiley & Sons,
Baffins Lane, Chichester,
West Sussex PO19 IUD

Copyright © 1997 Academy Group Ltd. All Rights Reserved. No part of this publication may be reproduced, stored in a retrieval system, or transmitted, in any form or by any means, electronic, mechanical, photocopying, recording, scanning or otherwise, except under the terms of the Copyright, Designs and Patents Act 1988 or under the terms of a licence issued by the Copyright Licensing Agency, 90 Tottenham Court Road, London, UK WIP 9HE, without the permission in writing of the publisher and the copyright holders.

Other Wiley Editorial Offices
New York • Weinheim • Brisbane • Singapore • Toronto

72 0 . 1 JEN

ISBN 0-471-97687-3

Printed and bound in the UK by Bookcraft (Bath) Ltd, Midsomer Norton

THE LIBRARY

 THE SURREY INSTITUTE OF ART & DESIGN

CONTENTS

CHARLES JENCKS
The Volcano and the Tablet

Why do politicians and architects write manifestoes? When Karl Marx wrote *The Communist Manifesto* he was not trying to produce a piece of literature – nor interpret the world, as he said, but change it. Our century, as Ulrich Conrads has shown in his book *Programmes and Manifestoes on Twentieth-Century Architecture* (1964) has turned the architectural manifesto into a predictable event. Unable or unwilling to advertise, an architect must become well known in other media besides buildings. Other professionals use the manifesto for the same reason and the surprising thing is that, although politicians, theologians and artists all write them – constantly – they do not give the genre much thought. It is a curious art form, like the haiku, with its own rules of brevity, wit and *le mot juste*.

The first architectural manifesto, or rules for decorum, was God's Ten Commandments. Plato called God 'the architect of all things', and architects play God when they make arbitrary decisions and adopt one theory rather than another. In the Bible the ultimate creator had several distinct personalities which He used effectively, in opposition to each other: abstract creator, warrior-Lord, law-giver and personal friend. As Jack Miles shows in his psycho-history, *God, A Biography* (1995), the warrior type, the Lord, inspires fear and awe, like a cosmic force, a hurricane or flood. He does this as a prelude, just before he shows compassion and tells people what kind of buildings they should construct. The good manifesto mixes a bit of terror, runaway emotion and charisma with a lot of common sense.

In *Exodus*, when Moses is leading the Israelites out of Egypt, He is full of genocidal declarations which are meant to frighten followers into monotheism. 'I will utterly blot out the memory of Amalek from under heaven', He predicts, and also announces a scorched earth policy against the unfortunate Canaanites, who worship other gods. As Nietzsche and then Le Corbusier quoting Nietzsche were later to proclaim in their manifestoes: 'burn what you love, love what you burn'. The genre demands blood – although you will find that Robert Venturi writes 'a gentle manifesto'.

The motives for destruction – to inspire fear in order to create unity and orthodoxy – are fairly transparent and they lead to the first declaration of architectural Minimalism in the famous Decalogue of Commandments. Moses, braving much cosmic terror of lightening and thunder, takes his tablets up Mount Sinai, on which are inscribed the rules against representation. 'Thou shalt not make unto thee any graven image, or any likeness of any thing that is in heaven above, or that is in earth beneath . . . ' Why this injunction against icons and images? Because 'Thou shalt have no other gods before me. Thou shalt not bow down thyself to them, nor serve them: for I the Lord thy God am a jealous God . . . ' Just to prove the point He destroys the architecture and cities of those who fall into idolatry, even those of the Israelites.

Enforcing purity and orthodoxy, we will see, is still a tactic of Modernists, Late Modernists and Prince Charles, with his Decalogue of Ten Principles. These were delivered, as a religious leader might do, in a manifesto called *A Vision of Britain*. Those who write manifestoes are jealous prophets who call the class to order by damning other teachers. If God first appears to Moses in fire and thunder as He lays down the great moral code of 'thou shalt and shalt not', then his final presence in architecture is equally threatening. Moses gives the laws a monumental setting and puts the tablets in 'the ark of the covenant'. Then, 'When Moses had finished his work, the cloud covered the Tent of Meeting, and the Presence of the Lord filled the Tabernacle . . . Over the Tabernacle a cloud of the Lord rested by day, and fire would appear in it by night, in the view of all the house of Israel throughout their journey'.

The image of God is arresting. What is a cloud by day and fire by night? A volcano. It is this irresistible display of violence and strength which makes the manifesto memorable and psychologically impressive. There is one more important aspect to the genre: the personal element. 'The Lord used to speak to Moses face to face, as one speaks to a friend', and there are many other passages which personalise the message, to both Moses and the chosen people. The most effective manifestoes, such as Le Corbusier's *Towards a New Architecture* (1923) constantly address the reader as 'you' and reiterates the joint 'we' until an implied pact is built up between author and convert. A manifesto must manifest its message to you, personally.

The volcano (the explosion of emotion), the tablet (the laws and theories) and the personal voice; to these three tropes and strategies have been added a few more. AWN Pugin, in the beginning of the nineteenth century, gave architecture the good/bad comparative drawings in his *Contrasts* and, ever since the lecture with two slide projectors caught on in the 1920s, it has been the stock-in-trade of polemicists. All four strategies are evident in Coop Himmelblau's *Architecture Must Blaze*, a New Modern manifesto of 1980. Here we find The Bad – Biedermeier – versus The Good – an architecture that 'lights up' – and the two are distinguished in the first person plural ('We are tired of seeing Palladio and other historical masks'). Here is the Tablet of Virtues – architecture that is 'fiery, smooth, hard, angular' etc. And the volcanic violence – 'architecture must blaze' and 'bleed, whirl, even break'.

Violence and the irrational are hallmarks of the New Modern manifesto, as one can see with the writings of Tschumi, Kipnis, Wigley, Woods and others. Often critical of Modernist humanism as too anthropomorphic, it proffers a type of anti-humanism. This was Peter Eisenman's reading of Foucault and the new paradigm coming out of France, and in 1976 he ushered in the break from Late Modernism. His article 'Post-Functionalism' was also opposed to the incipient Post-Modernism. So, again, polemical positions have to be jealously asserted in opposition to each other, in order to keep the tribe pure, and it is no accident that Eisenman – the master theorist and polemicist – inscribed his tablets in the pages of his magazine, called significantly, *Oppositions*.

Eisenman is the Le Corbusier of the late twentieth century, at least with respect to formulating new theories. Theory is a kind of congealed manifesto, its violence subtracted to become acceptable in the groves of academe. Since there are more academic architects alive than ever before, there is more theory produced, much of it written in a turgid and impenetrable style. Still, as Le Corbusier and Eisenman prove, theory is an engine of architecture and, like the *concetto* in the sixteenth century, the machine which invents new types of building, new responses to the city. Ours is an age of theories responding to a changing world, to the global economy, ecological crises and cultural confusions. In effect, these are a second type of volcano and they disrupt normal architecture and provoke the response of Rem Koolhaas, Ian McHarg and Christian Norberg-Schulz, to mention only three of the theorists reprinted here. Eisenman, with his 'Cardboard Architecture' of 1972, and his work, also shows that theory can keep architecture honest as well as inventive. This is no small matter in a period which has seen most architects succumb to the comfort industry.

The fact that Eisenman should write a Late Modern manifesto in 1972, defending the autonomy of form, and then four years later jump to a New Modernism that 'displaces man away from the centre of his world' brings out a surprising aspect of contemporary architecture. At least it surprised me, after Karl Kropf and I forced the contributors into the four main pigeonholes you will find. The classification system we used reveals that a few architects jump between traditions. For instance, sometime after 1980, Leon Krier slid from Post-Modern to Traditional; Kenneth Frampton, usually attacking Post-Modernism, produced his highly influential essay supporting it – 'Critical Regionalism' – in 1983, before jumping back to

Late Modernism, with his writings on tectonics in 1989. From the seventies to the eighties, Robert Stern moved from Post-Modernism to Traditional, Christopher Alexander from Late to Post-Modernism, and so it goes. There are interesting reasons for these jumps which may tell us something important about the period.

First of all, the protean creator, like Michelangelo, may go through four periods simply because he is so creative – in his case from Early to High Renaissance and then from Mannerism to Baroque. Eisenman is an example of this restless self-transformation. Secondly, the maverick, like Philip Johnson, may jump back and forth because, as Johnson says, he and his audience get bored. Third, and most important, a change may signify a shift in culture and the development of an architect. It often represents a response to new pressures, explosive non-architectural growths: in short, the second type of volcano.

The fact that most architects stay loyal to one approach is quite obvious and it allows traditions to grow in opposition to each other – dialectically – and thus produce a varied environment, a maximum choice for society. Yet there are a few architects who not only cut across categories in time but do not fit happily into any tradition. With these, the more unclassifiable ones, there is always the temptation, as with those such as Frank Gehry and Eric Moss, to invent *sui generis* labels. Here the strategy would become unwieldy and lead to confusion. Hence we have limited ourselves to four major approaches, classified by the most prevalent definer, and placed the fifth, the ecologists, within the expansive Post-Modern tradition. Why? Because their attacks on overdevelopment, the mechanistic paradigm and economism are all critical of Late Modernism.

Capsule Definitions

It is always reductive to define growing, complex movements, always foolhardy because it can never be done satisfactorily, and always necessary – in order to clarify the issues at stake. Thus the following four:

Traditional architecture, whose greatest exponents here are Leon Krier, Demetri Porphyrios and Prince Charles. This movement backwards quite obviously builds on past models, often classical, which are modified piecemeal with an attention to context and the elaboration of construction and the vernacular. The ideals of traditional architecture are a classical proportion that reflects an ordered cosmos, harmony, a seamless integration of past and present and the use of timeless, Platonic forms. Traditional architecture, although it never completely died, reasserted itself in the mid-seventies as it, like Post-Modernism, reacted to urban dissolution and the housing failures of Modernism.

THE LIBRARY

Late Modern architecture is pragmatic or technocratic in its social ideology and, from about 1960, takes many of the stylistic ideas and values of Modernism to an extreme in order to resuscitate a dull (or clichéd) language. A pronounced emphasis on technology and the autonomy of form, the exaggeration of a previous rhetoric, characterises the architecture, as often happens in 'Late' periods. Late Modern architecture, also facing the popular rejection of the 'dumb box', developed after 1965 in a sculptural direction – the articulated box – and towards an elaboration of structure, services and joints: High Tech.

New Modern architecture is deconstructive of Modern forms and ideas, hermetic in coding, often fragmented and dissonant in form, self-contradictory by intention, anti-humanist and, spatially, explosive. Often the intention is to weave opposites together and deconstruct traditions from the inside, in order to highlight difference, otherness and our alienation from the cosmos. Beginning in the late 1970s as a reaction to both Modernism and Post-Modernism, it has been influenced by the philosophy of Derrida and the formal language of the Constructivists – hence its most visible manifestation, Deconstructivism.

Post-Modern architecture is doubly-coded – the combination of modern techniques and methods with something else (often traditional building) in order for architecture to communicate with both the public and a concerned minority, usually other architects. Since post-modernists wish to restitch the fragmenting city, without being traditional, and communicate across the classes and professional divides, they adopt a hybrid language – even foreground architecture as a language itself. Post-Modern ecologists also adopt a double-agenda which criticises Modernism and Traditionalism while, at the same time, selecting elements from both of them. Post-Modernism as a rainbow coalition of those who resist or criticise Modernism started in the 1960s; as a movement it only came together in the mid-1970s with my article, reprinted herein.

Manifesto Logic

Those definitions, however, are academic, theoretical, bloodless – not something to leave home for (the ultimate aim of a good manifesto). They are necessary for cool ratiocination and comparison, which is why they are included, but I defy you to repeat them verbatim, without looking. Manifestoes, however, are jack-hammered into the mind, like a painful experience (and only recently have neurologists found the painful mechanisms that cement old horrors into our brains). They are repetitive, incantatory, responding to the imperatives of history, hoping to ward off catastrophe with magic or logic. They are like first grade recitation, responses in church:

Post-Modern is paradox – After Now, Post-Present
Post-Modern is 'posteriority', after all time
Post-Modern is the desire to live outside, beyond, after
Post-Modern is time-binding of past, present, future
Post-Modern is the continuation of Modernism and its transcendence.

If they scanned and rhymed, such verses could be set to music and be more memorable. At best, the propositions of a manifesto verge on self-parody and are funnier when serious.

Post-Modernism is crossing boundaries, crossing species
Post-Modernism is operating in the gap between art and life
Post-Modernism is Cambozola Cheese (illicit hybrid with the best genes
    of Mrs Camembert and Mr Gorgonzola)
Post-Modernism is the rabbi's advice to his son: 'Whenever faced with
    two extremes, always pick a third'.
Post-Modernism revisits the past – with quotation marks
Post-Modernism revisits the future – with irony
Post-Modernism is acknowledging the already said, as Eco has already
    said, in an age of lost innocence.

Manifestoes use any rhetorical tools available – rhymes, bad jokes, puns, outrageous untruths (think of Baudrillard) – and they always mint new metaphors, in an attempt to persuade. *When the Cathedrals were White*, Le Corbusier's polemical book of the 1930s, was meant to instil the new white spirit into the 'land of the timid', that is, Americans, New Yorkers – but a moment's cogitation would have revealed that the cathedrals were never white. Like the Parthenon, and Greek temples which always looked white to the purist's wishful gaze, they were, originally, painted (which does not sound right to the Minimalists and the jealous God).

Manifestoes are poetry written by someone on the run (like Trotsky's polemic after the Revolution written while fighting the Whites, jumping on and off his militarised train). They have an hysterical, telegraphic quality (or today an Internet truncation) as if the sender did not want to pay for extra syllables. Architects, such as Aldo van Eyck, are adept at these gnomic utterances, wordtrunks that collapse space-time into neologisms such as 'builtform'. These are directed at other architects, to hypnotise them. The general public would stop reading – but that does not deter the polemicist, who is looking to tantalise a sect. To read a polemic, you already have to want the expected outcome since the manifesto is made more to keep an audience united than to convert the heathen.

As you read the following manifestoes and theories, note this logic and the way ideas unfold in time, as if there were a *Zeitgeist* at work. The section on Post-Modernism reveals an impending sense of crisis within Modernism, or within the environment due to Modernism, and each of the following traditions also shows a similar mood. Crisis, or the feeling of imminent catastrophe, is one more reason why the 'volcano' is as deep a metaphor as the 'tablet' – pure theory – for without the motive to change the world the manifesto would not be written. In our time, we might reflect with irony, as opposed to the Christian or Modernist time, that a collection of manifestoes and theories must show difference: ie, show the pluralism and dialectic between manifestoes which each one denies. This is why a purified, Modernist collection, such as that of Ulrich Conrads, mentioned at the outset, is no longer possible.

Madelon Vriesendorp, St Jerome reading Rem Koolhaas, S,M, L, X-L, 1997

POST-MODERN

James Stirling and Michael Wilford, Neue Staatsgalerie, Stuttgart, 1977-84

1955   JAMES STIRLING

From Garches to Jaoul: Le Corbusier as Domestic Architect in 1927 and 1953

*The two following reviews by James Stirling (b 1926, Glasgow, d 1992)
show both the reverence Le Corbusier commanded and the confusion
he inspired with his later buildings. By apparently repudiating his earlier work, Le Corbusier seemed to throw into question the entire programme of Rationalist and Functionalist Modernism. Yet, as Stirling
and Gowan's Leicester Engineering Building (1964) demonstrates,
the doubts led to a new kind of functionalism, one that openly represented function and used simple, industrial materials in a straightforward way. Stirling carried the notion of representation – the expression
of function and symbolic forms – into his later and essentially Post-
Modern work such as the Staatsgalerie, Stuttgart (1983) and the
Clore Gallery, London (1985).*

Villa Garches, recently reoccupied, and the houses for Mr Jaoul and his son, now
nearing completion, are possibly the most significant buildings by Le Corbusier
to be seen in Paris to-day, for they represent the extremes of his vocabulary: the
former, rational, urbane, programmatic, the latter personal and anti-mechanistic.
If style is the crystallization of an attitude, then these buildings, so different even
at the most superficial level of comparison, may, on examination, reveal something of a philosophical change of attitude on the part of their author.

Garches, built at the culmination of Cubism and canonizing the theories in
'Towards a New Architecture', has since its inception been a standard by which
Le Corbusier's genius is measured against that of the other great architects of
this century . . .

If Garches appears urban, sophisticated and essentially in keeping with the
'l'esprit Parisian', the Jaoul houses seem primitive in character, recalling the
Provençal farmhouse community; they seem out of tune with their Parisian environment . . .

Maison Jaoul is no doubt dimensioned according to 'Le Modulor', a development from the application of the golden section by regulating lines as at Garches,
where it is possible to read off the inter-relations of squares and sections as the
eye traverses the façade and where, internally, every element is positioned

according to an exact geometrical hierarchy. In fact, Garches must be considered the masterpiece of Neo-Palladianism in modern architecture . . .

Garches is an excellent example of Le Corbusier's particular interpretation of the machine aesthetic . . .

There is no reference to any aspect of the machine at Jaoul either in construction or aesthetic. These houses, total cost £30,000, are being built by Algerian labourers equipped with ladders, hammers and nails, and with the exception of glass no synthetic materials are being used; technologically, they make no advance on medieval building . . .

To imply that these houses will be anything less than magnificent art would be incorrect. Their sheer plastic virtuosity is beyond emulation. Nevertheless, on analysis, it is disturbing to find little reference to the rational principles which are the basis of the modern movement, and it is difficult to avoid assessing these buildings except in terms of 'art for art's sake' . . .

As homes the Jaoul houses are almost cosy and could be inhabited by any civilized family, urban or rural. They are built by and intended for the status quo. Conversely, it is difficult to imagine Garches being lived in spontaneously except by such as the Sitwells, with never less than half a dozen brilliant, and permanent, guests. Utopian, it anticipates, and participates in, the progress of twentieth-century emancipation. A monument, not to an age which is dead, but to a way of life which has not generally arrived, and a continuous reminder of the quality to which all architects must aspire if modern architecture is to retain its vitality. (pp145-151)

Extracts. Source: *The Architectural Review*, vol 118; no 705, September 1955. © *Lady Mary Stirling*.

1956 JAMES STIRLING

Ronchamp: Le Corbusier's Chapel and the Crisis of Rationalism

With the simultaneous appearance of Lever House in New York and the Unité in Marseilles, it had become obvious that the stylistic schism between Europe and the New World had entered a decisive phase. The issue of art or technology had divided the ideological basis of the modern movement, and the diverging styles apparent since Constructivism probably have their origin in the attempt to fuse Art Nouveau and late 19th-century engineering. In the USA, functionalism now means the adaptation to building of industrial processes and products, but in Europe it remains the essentially humanist method of designing to a specific use. The post-war architecture of America may appear brittle to Europeans and, by obviating the hierarchical disposition of elements, anonymous; however, this academic method of criticism may no longer be adequate in considering technological products of the 20th century. Yet this method would still appear valid in criticizing recent European architecture where the elaboration of space and form has continued without abatement; and the chapel by Le Corbusier may possibly be the most plastic building ever erected in the name of modern architecture . . .

It may be considered that the Ronchamp chapel, being a 'pure expression of poetry' and the symbol of an ancient ritual, should not therefore be criticised by the rationale of the modern movement. Remembering, however, that this is a product of Europe's greatest architect, it is important to consider whether this building should influence the course of modern architecture. The sensational impact of the chapel on the visitor is significantly not sustained for any great length of time and when the emotions subside there is little to appeal to the intellect, and nothing to analyze or stimulate curiosity. This entirely visual appeal and the lack of intellectual participation demanded from the public may partly account for its easy acceptance by the local population . . .

With the loss of direction in modern painting, European architects have been looking to popular art and folk architecture, mainly of an indigenous character, from which to extend their vocabulary. An appreciation of regional building, particularly of the Mediterranean, has frequently appeared in Le Corbusier's books, principally as examples of integrated social units expressing themselves through form, but only recently has regional building become a primary source of plastic incident. There seems to be no doubt that le Corbusier's incredible powers of observation are lessening the necessity for invention, and his travels round the world have stockpiled his vocabulary with plastic elements and *objets trouves* of considerable picturesqueness. If folk architecture is to re-vitalise the movement, it will first be necessary to determine what it is that is modern in modern architecture. The scattered openings on the chapel walls may recall de Stijl but a similar expression is also commonplace in the farm buildings of Provence . . .

Since the Bauhaus, the fusion of art and technology has been the lifelong mission of Gropius, and yet it is this aspect which denotes his least achievement. The Dessau building itself presents a series of elevations each of which is biased towards either art or technology. The suggestion that architecture has become so complex that it needs to be conceived by a team representing the composite mind may partly account for the ambiguity which is felt with buildings generated in this manner. On the other hand, Maillart, who evolved his aesthetic as the result of inventing theories of reinforcing to exploit the concrete ribbon, achieved in his bridges an integration of technique and expression which has rarely been surpassed. The exaggerated supremacy of 'Art' in European Architecture probably denotes a hesitant attitude towards technology, which itself has possibly been retarded by our derisive attitude towards the myth of progress, the recent belief that true progress lies in charity, welfare, and personal happiness, having replaced the Victorian idea of progress as the invention and perfection of man's tools and equipment . . .

The desire to deride the schematic basis of modern architecture and the ability to turn a design upside down and make it architecture are symptomatic of a state when the vocabulary is not being extended, and a parallel can be drawn with the Mannerist period of the Renaissance. Certainly, the forms which have developed from the rationale and the initial ideology of the modern movement are being mannerized and changed into a conscious imperfectionism . . . (pp155-161)

Extracts. Source: *The Architectural Review*, vol 119; no 711, March 1956. © *Lady Mary Stirling.*

1960   KEVIN LYNCH
The Image of the City

The Image of the City was published at a time when the aridity of Modernist theories of urbanism had reached an extreme. In that environment, Kevin Lynch's (b 1918, d 1989) pragmatic, perceptually based approach to urban form was all the more readily absorbed. His concern for the legibility of cities countered the abstract rationalism of CIAM as well as the unavoidable reality of suburban sprawl. Lynch taught planning and urban design at the Massachusetts Institute of Technology and published extensively, including What Time is This Place? *(1972),* Managing the Sense of a Region *(1976) and* A Theory of Good City Form *(1981).*

The City Image and its Elements

There seems to be a public image of any given city which is the overlap of many individual images. Or perhaps there is a series of images, each held by some significant number of citizens. Such group images are necessary if an individual is to operate successfully within his environment and cooperate with his fellows. Each individual picture is unique, with some content that is rarely or never communicated, yet it approximates the public image, which, in different environments, is more or less compelling, more or less embracing.

This analysis limits itself to the effects of physical, perceptible objects. There are other influences on imageability, such as the social meaning of an area, its function, its history, or even its name. These will be glossed over, since the objective here is to uncover the role of form itself. It is taken for granted that in actual design form should be used to reinforce meaning, and not to negate it.

The contents of the city images so far studied, which are referable to physical forms, can conveniently be classified into five types of elements: paths, edges, districts, nodes, and landmarks. Indeed, these elements may be of more general application, since they seem to reappear in many types of environmental images . . . These elements may be defined as follows:

1   *Paths*. Paths are the channels along which the observer customarily, occasionally, or potentially moves. They may be streets, walkways, transit lines, canals, railroads. For many people, these are the predominant elements in their image.

People observe the city while moving through it, and along these paths the other environmental elements are arranged and related.

2 *Edges*. Edges are the linear elements not used or considered as paths to the observer. They are boundaries between two phases, linear breaks in continuity: shores, railroad cuts, edges of development, walls. They are lateral references rather than coordinate axes. Such edges may be barriers, more or less penetrable, which close one region off from another; or they may be seams, lines along which two regions are related and joined together. These edge elements, although probably not as dominant as paths, are for many people important organizing features, particularly in the role of holding together generalized areas, as in the outline of a city by water or wall.

3 *Districts*. Districts are the medium-to-large sections of the city, conceived of as having two-dimensional extent, which the observer mentally enters 'inside of', and which are recognizable as having some common, identifying character. Always identifiable from the inside, they are also used for exterior reference if visible from the outside. Most people structure their city to some extent in this way, with individual differences as to whether paths or districts are the dominant elements. It seems to depend not only upon the individual but also upon the given city.

4 *Nodes*. Nodes are points, the strategic spots in a city into which an observer can enter, and which are the intensive foci to and from which he is travelling. They may be primarily junctions, places of a break in transportation, a crossing or convergence of paths, moments of shift from one structure to another. Or nodes may be simply concentrations, which gain their importance from being the condensation of some use or physical character, as a street-corner hangout or an enclosed square. Some of these concentration nodes are the focus and epitome of a district, over which their influence radiates and of which they stand as symbol . . .

5 *Landmarks*. Landmarks are another type of point reference, but in this case the observer does not enter within them, they are external. They are usually a rather simply defined physical object: building, sign, store, or mountain. Their use involves the singling out of one element from a host of possibilities . . .
(pp46-48)

City Form

We have the opportunity of forming our new city world into an imageable landscape: visible, coherent, and clear. It will require a new attitude on the part of the city dweller, and a physical reshaping of his domain into forms which entrance the eye, which organize themselves from level to level in time and space, which can stand as symbols for urban life.The present study yields some clues in this respect.

Most objects which we are accustomed to call beautiful, such as a painting or a tree, are single-purpose things, in which, through long development of the impress of one will, there is an intimate, visible linkage from fine detail to total structure.A city is a multi-purpose, shifting organization, a tent for many functions, raised by many hands and with relative speed. Complete specialization, final meshing, is improbable and undesirable. The form must be somewhat non-committal, plastic to the purposes and perceptions of its citizens.

Yet there are fundamental functions of which the city forms may be expressive: circulation, major land-uses, key focal points.The common hopes and pleasures, the sense of community may be made flesh. Above all, if the environment is visibly organized and sharply identified, then the citizen can inform it with his own meanings and connections. Then it will become a true *place*, remarkable and unmistakable . . .

As an artificial world, the city should be so in the best sense: made by art, shaped for human purposes. It is our ancient habit to adjust to our environment, to discriminate and organize perceptually whatever is present to our senses. Survival and dominance based themselves on this sensuous adaptability, yet now we may go on to a new phase of interaction. On home grounds, we may begin to adapt the environment itself to the perceptual pattern and symbolic process of the human being . . .

To heighten the imageability of the urban environment is to facilitate its visual identification and structuring. The elements isolated above – the paths, edges, landmarks, nodes and regions – are the building blocks in the process of making firm, differentiated structures at the urban scale . . . (pp91-95)

Form Qualities

These clues for urban design can be summarized in another way, since there are common themes that run through the whole set: the repeated references to certain general physical characteristics. These are the categories of direct interest in design, since they describe qualities that a designer may operate upon. They might be summarized as follows:

1 *Singularity of Figure-Ground Clarity*: sharpness of boundary . . .

2 *Form Simplicity*: clarity and simplicity of visible form in the geometrical sense, limitation of parts . . .

3 *Continuity*: continuance of edge or surface (as in street, channel, skyline, or setback) . . .

4 *Dominance*: dominance of one part over others by means of size, intensity, or interest, resulting in the reading of the whole as a principle feature with an associated cluster . . .

5 *Clarity of Joint*: high visibility of joints and seams (as at major intersection, or on a sea front) . . .

6 *Directional Differentiation*: asymmetries, gradients, and radial references which differentiate one end from another . . .

7 *Visual Scope*: qualities which increase the range and penetration of vision, either actually of symbolically. These include transparencies . . . overlaps . . . vistas and panoramas . . .

8 *Motion Awareness*: the qualities which make sensible to the observer, through both the visual and the kinesthetic senses his own actual or potential motion . . .

9 *Times Series*: series which are sensed over time, including both simple item-by-item linkages . . . and also series which are truly structured in time and thus melodic in nature . . .

10 *Names and Meanings*: non-physical characteristics which may enhance the imageability of an element . . . (pp105-108)

Extracts. Source: Kevin Lynch, *The Image of the City*, MIT Press (Cambridge, Mass), 1960. © 1960 by The Massachusetts Institute of Technology and the President and Fellows of Harvard College.

1961   N JOHN HABRAKEN
Supports: An Alternative to Mass Housing

Largely on the strength of Supports, *N John Habraken (b 1928, Bandung, Indonesia, of Dutch parents) was Director of the Stichting Architecten Research (SAR) from 1965 until 1975. SAR was a working party of Dutch architects created to explore the possibilities of support structures and infill building as an alternative to mass housing. Working primarily through research, writing and teaching, Habraken has maintained the view that the built environment is a living thing and that change within a durable pattern is one of its primary characteristics. He was Head of Department and Professor of Architecture at the Massachusetts Institute of Technology from 1975 until 1995 and continues to work in private practice.*

. . . The new landscape we survey is still shrouded in mist, but clear orientation points can be discerned. Support structures make a new orientation possible.
–   They enable the occupants to be involved via the independent dwelling.
–   They distinguish between industrial production and site labour.
–   They distinguish between the general and the particular, thus allowing industrial development to take place, but at the same time they gather both together by an all-embracing industrial apparatus.
–   They make possible the living, evolving town.
–   They offer, as the framework of a town, great opportunities in town planning terms.
–   They bring to an end artificial aspects of the way in which society is housed.
–   They distinguish between the field of the architect and that of the town planner.
–   They encourage the growth of a new society.
The idea of support structures and support towns is the idea of a world based upon the realities of human relationships. *No thoughts directed toward a better future can be fruitful unless they couple confidence in human nature with a full exploitation of all useful means.*

   If in housing we wish to restore human relationships, but mean to exclude today's technical possibilities, we are following a road to the past, a road we cannot follow. If we wish only to develop the technological potential without touching human relationships, we end up with something like mass housing. Support towns are to some extent inherent in today's activities. Technology has developed to such a point that a serious study of the notion of support structures is feasible. The impoverishment of human society in mass housing towns is becoming generally recognised. Like a caterpillar in a cocoon, we have surrounded ourselves with a technical potential which, as yet, has not found its proper purpose. The time has come to free ourselves and regain the initiative.

The continuing development of the present situation will inevitably lead to some kind of support-structure system. There is no question of invention here, but rather of a certain insight. That is why it is necessary to discuss it. We must not allow new forms to overcome us in the way mass housing came upon us like a natural disaster. Our task is to try and understand what we are doing as clearly as possible, and not to explain and interpret it only after it is done. We must see what the future holds so that we may judge it, come to terms with it, or fight it.

If new forms of human housing offer new opportunities, we must be able to say why they are preferable to old ones. To do that a clear insight is needed into what dwelling really means. Once we agree that it is necessary to introduce the inhabitant or active force into the housing process, we can face the future with confidence. Building has always been a matter of confidence and to make this a reality we must be clear and unequivocal about the nature of man's housing needs. (pp 92-93)

Extracts. Source: N John Habraken, *Supports: An Alternative to Mass Housing*, translation by B Valkenburg, The Architectural Press (London), 1972. © N John Habraken. Originally published as *De Dragers en de Mensen*, Scheltema and Holkema NV (Amsterdam), 1961. © Schelterma and Holkema NV.

1961 JANE JACOBS
The Death and Life of Great American Cities

The simmering discontent with Modernist urbanism that began after the Second World War came to a boil around 1960. Jane Jacobs (b 1916), a journalist and activist, stoked the fire with The Death and Life of Great American Cities, one of the first books to take the issue out of the closed world of the professionals and expose it to the general public. Most if not all of the principles she set out are still relevant and are only now being applied in actual planning and urban design. Jacobs has written extensively on urban issues, her other works including, The Economy of Cities (1969) and Systems of Survival (1992).

This book is an attack on current city planning and rebuilding. It is also, and mostly, an attempt to introduce new principles of city planning and rebuilding, different and even opposite from those now taught in everything from schools of architecture and planning to the Sunday supplements and women's magazines . . . (p3)

The Peculiar Nature of Cities

The Uses of Sidewalks: Safety

Streets in cities serve many purposes besides carrying vehicles, and city sidewalks – the pedestrian parts of the streets – serve many purposes besides carrying pedestrians. These uses are bound up with circulation but are not identical to it and in their own right they are at least as basic as circulation to the proper working of cities . . . (p29)

A city equipped to handle strangers, and to make a safety asset, in itself, out of the presence of strangers, as the streets of successful neighborhoods do, must have three main qualities:

- First, there must be a clear demarcation between what is public space and what is private space . . .
- Second, there must be eyes upon the street, eyes belonging to those we might call the natural proprietors of the street . . .
- Third: the sidewalk must have users on it fairly continuously . . . (p35)

The Uses of Sidewalks: Contact

Lowly, unpurposeful and random as they may appear, sidewalk contacts are the small change from which a city's wealth of public life may grow . . . (p72)

A sidewalk life . . . arises only when the concrete, tangible facilities it requires are present. These happen to be the same facilities, in the same abundance and ubiquity, that are required for cultivating sidewalk safety . . . (p70)

The Uses of City Neighborhoods

The lack of either economic or social self-containment is natural and necessary to city neighborhoods – simply because they are parts of cities . . .

But neighborhoods in cities do need to supply some means for civilized self-government. This is the problem.

Looking at city neighborhoods as organs of self-government, I can see evidence that only three kinds of neighborhoods are useful: (1) the city as a whole; (2) street neighborhoods; and (3) districts of large, subcity size, composed of 100,000 people or more in the cases of the largest cities . . . (p117)

The Conditions for City Diversity

The Generators of Diversity

To understand cities, we have to deal outright with combinations or mixtures of uses, not separate uses, as the essential phenomena . . . (p144)

The Need for Primary Mixed Uses

Condition 1: The district, and indeed as many internal parts as possible, must serve more than one primary function, preferably more than two. These must insure the presence of people who go outdoors on different schedules and are in the place for different reasons, but who are able to use many facilities in common . . . (p152)

The Need for Small Blocks

Condition 2: Most blocks must be short; that is, streets and opportunities to turn corners must be frequent . . . (p178)

The Need for Aged Buildings

Condition 3: The district must mingle buildings that vary in age and condition, including a good proportion of old ones . . . (p187)

The Need for Concentration
Condition 4: The district must have a sufficiently dense concentration of people, for whatever purpose they may be there. This includes people there because of residence . . . (p200)

When we deal with cities we are dealing with life at its most complex and intense. Because this is so, there is a basic esthetic limitation on what can be done with cities: *A city cannot be a work of art* . . . (p372)

The Kind of a Problem a City is . . .
Cities happen to be problems in organized complexity, like the life sciences. They present 'situations in which a half-dozen or even several dozen quantities are all varying simultaneously *and in subtly interconnected ways*'. Cities, again like the life sciences, do not exhibit *one* problem in organized complexity, which if understood explains all. They can be analyzed into many such problems or segments which, as in the case of the life sciences, are also related with one another. The variables are many, but they are not helter-skelter; they are 'interrelated into an organic whole' . . . (p433)

Why have cities not, long since, been identified, understood and treated as problems of organized complexity? If the people concerned with the life sciences were able to identify their difficult problems as problems of organized complexity, why have people professionally concerned with cities not identified the *kind* of problem they had? . . .

The theorists of conventional city planning have consistently mistaken cities as problems of simplicity and of disorganized complexity . . .

These misapplications stand in our way; they have to be hauled out in the light, recognized as inappropriate strategies of thought and discarded . . . (pp434-435)

Because the life sciences and cities happen to pose the same *kinds* of problems does not mean they are the *same* problems . . .

In the case of understanding cities, I think the most important habits of thought are these:
1   To think about processes;
2   To work inductively, reasoning from particulars to the general;
3   To seek for 'unaverage' clues involving very small quantities, which reveal the way larger and more 'average' quantities are operating. (pp439-440)

Extracts. Source: Jane Jacobs, *The Death and Life of Great American Cities*, Jonathan Cape (London), 1962. © 1961 by Jane Jacobs. Reprinted by permission of Random House, Inc.

1962 ALDO VAN EYCK
Team 10 Primer

*Team 10 was originally formed as a working group of younger archi-
tects to prepare for CIAM X, the tenth and last meeting of the Congrès
Internationaux d'Architecture Moderne, held in Dubrovnik in 1956.
Of the members, Aldo van Eyck (b 1918, Driebergen, The Nether-
lands) was perhaps the most poetic yet articulate in suggesting ways
past the dull, hygienic emptiness of Functionalism and the Athens
Charter. More concerned with architecture than urbanism, his work
combines Modernist idealism with a sense of multivalent reading and
surprise more characteristic of Post-Modernism. His buildings include the
Children's Home, Amsterdam (1960), Sculpture Pavilion, Arnhem (1966)
and Housing, Zwolle (1977).*

Space has no room, time not a moment for man. He is excluded.

In order to 'include' him – help his homecoming – he must be gathered into
their meaning. (Man is the subject as well as the object of architecture.)

Whatever space and time mean, place and occasion mean more.

For space in the image of man is place, and time in the image of man is occasion.

Today space and what it should coincide with in order to become 'space' – man
at home with himself – are lost. Both search for the same place, but cannot find it.

Provide that space, articulate the in-between.

Is man able to penetrate the material he organizes into hard shape between one
man and another, between what is here and what is there, between this and a
following moment? Is he able to find the right place for the right occasion?

No – So start with this: make a welcome of each door and a countenance of
each window.

Make of each place a bunch of places of each house and each city, for a
house is a tiny city, a city a huge house. Get closer to the shifting centre of
human reality and build its counterform – for each man and all men, since they
no longer do it themselves.

Whoever attempts to solve the riddle of space in the abstract, will construct
the outline of emptiness and call it space.

Whoever attempts to meet man in the abstract will speak with his echo and
call this dialogue.

Man still breathes both in and out. When is architecture going to do the same? . . . (p101)

Take off your shoes and walk along a beach through the ocean's last thin sheet of water gliding landwards and seawards.

You feel reconciled in a way you wouldn't feel if there were a forced dialogue between you and either one or the other of these great phenomena. For here, in-between land and ocean – in this in-between realm, something happens to you that is quite different from the sailor's nostalgia. No landward yearning from the sea, no seaward yearning from the land. No yearning for the alternative – no escape from one into the other.

Architecture must extend 'the narrow borderline', persuade it to loop into a realm – an articulated in-between realm. Its job is to provide this in-between realm by means of construction, ie to provide, from house to city scale, a bunch of real places for real people and real things (places that sustain instead of counteract the identity of their specific meaning) . . . (p99)

Awareness of this in-between (in-between awareness) is essential. The ability to detect associative meanings simultaneously does not yet belong to our mental equipment. Since, however, the meaning of every real articulated in-between place is essentially a multiple one, we shall have to see to it that it does.

Our target is multiple meaning in equipoise . . .

Awareness of the in-between creeps into the technology of construction. It will transform not only our ideas as to what we should make, but also as to how we shall make it – including our technological approach. It will be there in the body, the members and the joints of whatever we make . . . (p103)

Space and time must be opened – interiorized – so that they can be entered; persuaded to gather man into their meaning – include him.

By virtue of what memory and anticipation signify, place acquires temporal meaning and occasion spatial meaning. Thus space and time, identified recipro-cally (in the image of man) emerge humanized, as place and occasion.

Places remembered and places anticipated dovetail in the temporal span of the present. Memory and anticipation, in fact, constitute the real perspective of space; give it depth.

What matters is not space but the interior of space – and the inner horizon of the interior.

The large house-little city statement (the one that says: a house is a tiny city, a city a huge house) is ambiguous and consciously so. In fact its ambiguity is of a kind I should like to see transposed to architecture. It points, moreover, towards a particular kind of clarity neither house nor city can do without; a kind which never quite relinquishes its full meaning.

Call it Labyrinthian Clarity

Such clarity (ally of significant ambiguity) softens the edges of time and space and transcends visibility (allows spaces to enter each other and occasions to encounter each other in the mind's interior).

It is kaleidoscopic.

The In-between Realm is never without it . . . (p41)

Extracts. Source: Alison Smithson (ed), *Team 10 Primer*, Studio Vista (London), 1968. © Aldo Van Eyck. Originally published in magazine form in *Architectural Design*, December 1962. Reprinted in August 1965 in square paperback format by the Whitefriars Press.

Aldo van Eyck and Theo Bosch, Zwolle Housing, 1975-77

1965 CHRISTOPHER ALEXANDER
A City is not a Tree

*At a time of increasing concern over the adequacy of design methods,
'A City is not a Tree' broke open and reoriented the debate. It also
represented a fundamental change in Christopher Alexander's (b 1936,
Vienna of British parents) thinking. While retaining the mathematical
foundation underlying his* Notes on the Synthesis of Form, *'A City is
not a Tree' takes it in a very different direction. Where the one seeks
a crystalline logic to arrive at the notion of 'fitness' between form and
programme, the other points to a fundamental ambiguity and overlap in the relation of form to its uses. The one is an extreme extension of Modernist rationalism, the other a reaction against it.*

The tree of my title is not a green tree with leaves. It is the name for a pattern
of thought. The semi-lattice is the name for another, more complex pattern of
thought.

In order to relate these abstract patterns to the nature of the city, I must first
make a simple distinction. I want to call those cities which have arisen more or
less spontaneously over many, many years *natural cities*. And I shall call those
cities and parts of cities which have been deliberately created by designers and
planners *artificial cities*. Siena, Liverpool, Kyoto, Manhattan are examples of
natural cities. Levittown, Chandigarh, and the British New Towns are examples
of artificial cities . . .

Too many designers today seem to be yearning for the physical characteristics
of the past, instead of searching for the abstract ordering principle which the towns
of the past happened to have, and which our modern conceptions of the city have
not yet found.

*What is the inner nature, the ordering principle, which distinguishes the artificial
city from the natural city?*

You will have guessed from my title what I believe this ordering principle to
be. I believe that a natural city has the organization of a semi-lattice; but that
when we organize a city artificially, we organize it as a tree.

Both the tree and the semi-lattice are ways of thinking about how a large collection of many small systems goes to make up a large complex system. More
generally, they are both names for structures or sets . . .

The semi-lattice axiom goes like this: *A collection of sets forms a semi-lattice if and only if, two overlapping sets belong to the collection, then the set of elements common to both also belongs to the collection . . .*

The tree axiom states: *A collection of sets forms a tree if and only if, for any two sets that belong to the collection, either one is wholly contained in the other, or else they are wholly disjoint . . .*

Since this axiom excludes the possibility of overlapping sets, there is no way in which the semi-lattice axiom can be violated, so that every tree is a trivially simple semi-lattice.

However, in this paper we are not so much concerned with the fact that a tree happens to be a semi-lattice, but with the difference between trees and those more general semi-lattices which are *not* trees because they *do* contain overlapping units . . .

It is not merely the overlap which makes the distinction between the two important. Still more important is the fact that the semi-lattice is potentially a much more complex and subtle structure than a tree . . .

Whenever we have a tree structure, it means that within this structure no piece of any unit is ever connected to other units, except through the medium of that unit as a whole.

The enormity of this restriction is difficult to grasp. It is a little as though the members of a family were not free to make friends outside the family, except when the family as a whole made a friendship . . .

When we think in terms of trees we are trading the humanity and richness of the living city for the conceptual simplicity which benefits only designers, planners, administrators and developers. Every time a piece of a city is torn out, and a tree made to replace the semi-lattice that was there before, the city takes a further step toward dissociation.

In any organized object, extreme compartmentalization and the dissociation of internal elements are the first signs of coming destruction. In a society, dissociation is anarchy. In a person, dissociation is the mark of schizophrenia and impending suicide. An ominous example of a city-wide dissociation is the separation of retired people from the rest of urban life, caused by the growth of desert cities for the old such as Sun City, Arizona. This separation is possible only under the influence of tree-like thought.

It not only takes from the young the company of those who have lived long, but worse, causes the same rift inside each individual life. As you will pass into Sun City, and into old age, your ties with your own past will be unacknowledged, lost, and therefore broken. Your youth will no longer be alive and in your old age the two will be dissociated, your own life will be cut in two.

For the human mind, the tree is the easiest vehicle for complex thoughts. But the city is not, cannot and must not be a tree. The city is a receptacle for life. If the receptacle severs the overlap of the strands of life within it, because it is a tree, it will be like a bowl full of razor blades on edge, ready to cut up whatever is entrusted to it. In such a receptacle life will be cut to pieces. If we make cities which are trees, they will cut our life within to pieces.

Extracts. Source: *Architectural Forum*, vol 122; no 1, April 1965. © Christopher Alexander.

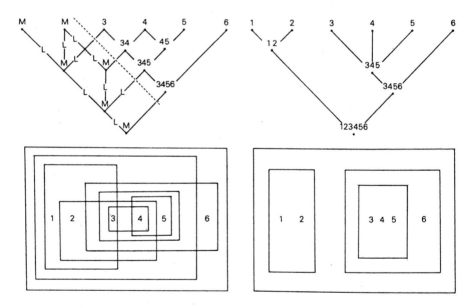

Christopher Alexander, Semi-Lattice Versus a Tree

1965 CHRISTIAN NORBERG-SCHULZ
Intentions in Architecture

Published within a few years of Aldo Rossi's Architecture of the City *and Robert Venturi's* Complexity and Contradiction, *Christian Norberg-Schulz' (b 1926)* Intentions in Architecture *is equally a reaction against Modernism, in particular as realised after the War. Norberg-Schulz begins the book with an extended argument suggesting that the perception of form has a cultural basis and meaning in architecture is the result of cultural intentions. The task of the architect is then to work within the network of those intentions.*

We are here faced with basic problems which involve a revision of the aesthetic dimension of architecture. How can architecture again become a sensitive medium, able to register relevant variations in the building tasks, and at the same time maintain a certain visual order? A new aesthetic orientation transcending the arbitrary play with forms is surely needed, although it is not claimed that the result should resemble the styles of the past. Undoubtedly we need a formal differentiation of the buildings corresponding to the functional differences of the building tasks. But so far we have not found any answer to the question of whether the differentiation should also acquire a symbolizing aspect by the assignment of particular forms to particular functions with the purpose of 'representing' a cultural structure. So far modern architecture has had the character of a 'belief' rather than a worked-out method based on a clear analysis of functional, sociological, and cultural problems . . . (p18)

The Problem

What we need is a conscious clarification of our problems, that is, the definition of our *building tasks* and the *means to their solution . . . What purpose has architecture as a human product? . . . How does architecture (the environment) influence us? . . .*

To give the questions about the purpose and effects of architecture a basis, it is necessary to inquire whether particular forms ought to be correlated with particular tasks. We thus have to ask: *Why has a building from a particular period a particular form?* This is the central problem in architectural history as well as in architectural theory. We do not intend that the study of history should lead to a new historicism based on a copying of the forms of the past. The information given by history should above all illustrate the relations between problems and solution, and thus furnish an empirical basis for further work. If we take our way of putting the problem as a point of departure for an investigation of architecture's (changing) role in society, a new and rich field of study is laid open . . .

On a purely theoretical level we gain knowledge about the relation between task and solution. But this knowledge may also be incorporated into a *method* which helps us in solving concrete problems, and which might facilitate the historical analysis going from the solution back to the task. The historical analysis orders our experience and makes the judgement of solutions possible. All in all we arrive at a theory treating architectural problems . . . (pp21-24)

Architecture is explicitly a *synthetic* activity which has to adapt itself to the form of life as a whole. This adaptation does not request that *every* work should be related to the total whole. The individual work concretizes secondary wholes, but because it belongs to an architectural system, it participates in a complete concretization. New concretizations can neither imitate the past, nor break completely with tradition. They are dependent upon the existence of symbol-systems which are capable of development. This implies that we should conserve the structural principles of tradition rather than its motives . . . (p188)

The modern movement is the only *true* tradition of the present because it understands that historical continuity does not mean borrowed motives and ideals, but human values which have to be conquered in always *new* ways . . .

Modern forms have developed through experimentation and the fight against borrowed motives. But they have never been ordered, they have never become a real formal *language*. This is the basic problem that the present generation of modern architects has to face, and it can only be solved through the formation of types. The types must be interrelated in such a way that they form a hierarchy corresponding to the task-structure. (pp206-207)

Extracts. Source: Christian Norberg-Schulz, *Intentions in Architecture*, MIT Press (Cambridge, Mass), 1977. © 1977 by The Massachusetts Institute of Technology. First published in 1965 simultaneously in Oslo, Norway, for Scandinavian University Books by Universitetsforlaget, in the United Kingdom by George Allen & Unwin Ltd, London, and in the United States by The Massachusetts Institute of Technology, Cambridge, Mass.

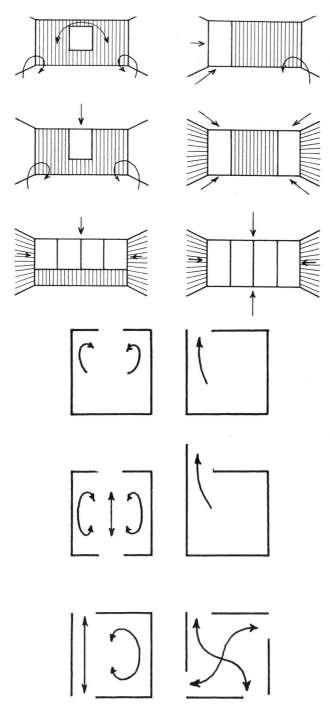

Christian Norberg-Schulz, Visual Forces Inherent to Form

1966   ALDO ROSSI
The Architecture of the City

The notion of typology was taken up generally in Italy after the Second World War, in large part as a critical response to Modernist urbanism. In the highly polarised realm of Italian architecture, however, it became a source of contention. Carlo Aymonino and Aldo Rossi (b 1931, Milan) saw type more as a subjective tool, as opposed to the objective view developed by Saverio Muratori and his followers. If both camps recognised the connection between the building and the city, Rossi's view became the more well known. The Architecture of the City *proved immensely popular, its compelling imagery and evocation of the richness of the urban environment making up for its lack of a clear methodology.*

Urban Artifacts and a Theory of the City

The city, which is the subject of this book, is to be understood here as architecture. By architecture I mean not only the visible image of the city and the sum of its different architectures, but architecture as construction, the construction of the city over time. I believe that this point of view, objectively speaking, constitutes the most comprehensive way of analysing the city; it addresses the ultimate and definitive fact in the life of the collective, the creation of the environment in which it lives . . .

Architecture came into being along with the first traces of the city; it is deeply rooted in the formation of civilization and is a permanent, universal, and necessary artifact.

Aesthetic intention and the creation of better surroundings for life are the two permanent characteristics of architecture. These aspects emerge from any significant attempt to explain the city as a human creation. But because architecture gives concrete form to society and is intimately connected with it and with nature, it differs fundamentally from every other art and science. This is the basis for an empirical study of the city as it has evolved from the earliest settlements. With time, the city grows upon itself; it acquires a consciousness and memory. In the course of its construction, its original themes persist, but at the same time it modifies and renders these themes of its own development more specific . . . (p21)

The changes in housing and in the land on which houses leave their imprint become signs of this daily life. One need only look at the layers of the city that archaeologists show us; they appear as a primordial and eternal fabric of life, an immutable pattern. Anyone who remembers European cities after the bombings of the last war retains an image of disembowelled houses where amid the rubble, fragments of familiar places remained standing, with their colors of faded wall paper, laundry hanging suspended in the air, barking dogs – the untidy intimacy of places. And always we could see the house of our childhood, strangely aged, present in the flux of the city.

Images, engravings, and photographs of these disembowelled cities, record this vision. Destruction and demolition, expropriation and rapid changes in use and [sic] as a result of speculation and obsolescence, are the most recognizable signs of urban dynamics. But beyond all else, the images suggest the interrupted destiny of the collective. This vision in its entirety seems to be reflected with a quality of permanence in urban monuments. Monuments, signs of the collective will as expressed through the principles of architecture, offer themselves as primary elements, fixed points in the urban dynamic . . . (p22)

I believe that the importance of ritual in its collective nature and its essential character as an element for preserving myth constitutes a key to understanding the meaning of monuments and, moreover, the implications of the founding of the city and of the transmission of ideas in an urban context. I attribute an especial importance to monuments, although their significance in the urban dynamic may at times be elusive . . . (p24)

Generally, the most difficult historical problems of the city are resolved by dividing history into periods and hence ignoring or misunderstanding the universal and permanent character of the forces of the urban dynamic; and here the importance of comparative method becomes evident . . . (p27)

There are people who do not like a place because it is associated with some ominous moment in their lives; others attribute an auspicious character to a place. All these experiences, their sum, constitute the city. It is in this sense that we must judge the *quality* of a space – a notion that may be extremely difficult for our modern sensibility. This was the sense in which the ancients consecrated a place, and it presupposes a type of analysis far more profound than the simplistic sort offered by certain psychological interpretations that rely only on the legibility of form . . . (p32)

Typological Questions

The first houses sheltered their inhabitants from the external environment and furnished a climate that man could begin to control; the development of an urban nucleus expanded this type of control to the creation and extension of a microclimate. Neolithic villages already offered the first transformations of the world according to man's needs. The 'artificial homeland' is as old as man. In precisely this sense of transformation the first forms and types of habitation, as well as temples and more complex buildings, were constituted. The type developed according to both needs and aspirations to beauty; a particular type was associated with a form and a way of life, although its specific shape varied widely from society to society. The concept of type thus became the basis of architecture, a fact attested to both by practice and by the treatises . . .

I would define the concept of type as something that is permanent and complex, a logical principle that is prior to form and that constitutes it . . .

As a constant, this principle, which we can call the typical element, or simply the type, is to be found in all architectural artifacts. It is also then a cultural element and as such can be investigated in different architectural artifacts; typology becomes in this way the analytical moment of architecture, and it becomes readily identifiable at the level of urban artifacts . . .

Ultimately we can say that the type is the very idea of architecture, that which is closest to its essence. In spite of changes, it has always imposed itself on the 'feelings of reason' as the principle of architecture and of the city . . . (pp35-41)

Critique of Naive Functionalism

We have indicated the principle questions that arise in relation to an urban artifact – among them, individuality, *locus*, memory, design itself. Function was not mentioned. I believe that any explanation of urban artifacts in terms of function must be rejected if the issue is to elucidate their structure and formation. We will later give some examples of important urban artifacts whose function has changed over time or for which a specific function does not even exist. Thus, one thesis of this study, in its effort to affirm the value of architecture in the analysis of the city, is the denial of the explanation of urban artifacts in terms of function. I maintain, on the contrary, that far from being illuminating, this explanation is regressive because it impedes us from studying forms and knowing the world of architecture according to its true laws . . . (p46)

Monuments and the Theory of Permanences

Clearly, to think of urban science as a historical science is a mistake, for in this case we would be obliged to speak only of urban history. What I mean to suggest, however, is that from the point of view of urban structure, urban history seems more useful than any other form of research on the city . . .

One must remember that the difference between past and future, from the point of view of the theory of knowledge, in large measure reflects the fact that the past is partly being experienced now, and this may be the meaning of permanences: they are a past that we are still experiencing . . . The most meaningful permanences are those provided by the street and the plan . . . (pp57-59)

The complex structure of the city emerges from a discourse whose terms of reference are still somewhat fragmentary. Perhaps the laws of the city are exactly like those that regulate the life and destiny of individual men. Every biography has its own interest, even though it is circumscribed by birth and death. Certainly the architecture of the city, the human thing par excellence, is the physical sign of this biography, beyond the meanings and the feelings with which we recognise it. (p163)

Extracts. Source: Aldo Rossi, *The Architecture of the City,* translated by Diane Ghirardo and Joan Okman, MIT Press (Cambridge, Mass), 1982. © 1982 by The Institute of Architecture and Urban Studies and The Massachusetts Institute of Technology. Originally published as *L'architettura della città,* Marsilio Editori, Padua, 1966.

Aldo Rossi (with G Braghieri), IBA Social Housing, Berlin, 1981-88

1966 ROBERT VENTURI

Complexity and Contradiction in Architecture

While most often glibly cited for his inversion of Mies van der Rohe's declaration 'less is more', Robert Venturi (b 1925, Philadelphia) made an indelible impression on Western architectural thinking with Complexity and Contradiction in Architecture. Stimulated in part by a stay in Rome as a Fellow of the American Academy in 1956-57, Venturi's polemic presented one of the most compelling arguments against Modernist functionalism at the time and paved the way for the development of Post-Modernism.

Non-Straightforward Architecture: A Gentle Manifesto

I like complexity and contradiction in architecture. I do not like the incoherence or arbitrariness of incompetent architecture nor the precious intricacies of picturesqueness or expressionism. Instead, I speak of complex and contradictory architecture based on the richness and ambiguity of modern experience, including experience which is inherent in art. Everywhere, except in architecture, complexity and contradiction have been acknowledged, from Gödel's proof of ultimate inconsistency in mathematics to TS Eliot's analysis of 'difficult' poetry and Joseph Albers' definition of the paradoxical quality of painting.

But architecture is necessarily complex and contradictory in its very inclusion of the traditional Vitruvian elements of commodity, firmness, and delight. And today the wants of program, structure, mechanical equipment, and expression, even in single buildings in simple contexts, are divers and conflicting in ways previously unimaginable. The increasing dimension and scale of architecture in urban and regional planning adds to the difficulties. I welcome the problems and exploit the uncertainties. By embracing contradiction as well as complexity, I aim for vitality as well as validity.

Architects can no longer afford to be intimidated by the puritanically moral language of orthodox Modern architecture. I like elements which are hybrid rather than 'pure', compromising rather than 'clean', distorted rather than 'straightforward', ambiguous rather than 'articulated', perverse as well as impersonal, boring as well as 'interesting', conventional rather than 'designed', accommodating rather than excluding, redundant rather than simple, vestigial as well as innovating, inconsistent and equivocal rather than direct and clear. I am for messy vitality over obvious unity. I include the *non sequitur* and proclaim the duality.

I am for richness of meaning rather than clarity of meaning; for the implicit function as well as the explicit function. I prefer 'both–and' to 'either–or', black and white and sometimes gray, to black and white. A valid architecture evokes many levels of meaning and combinations of focus: its space and its elements become readable and workable in several ways at once.

But an architecture of complexity and contradiction has a special obligation toward the whole: its truth must be in its totality or its implications of totality. It must embody the difficult unity of inclusion rather than the easy unity of exclusion. More is not less.

Complexity and Contradiction vs Simplification or Picturesqueness

Orthodox Modern architects have tended to recognise complexity insufficiently or inconsistently. In their attempt to break with tradition and start all over again, they idealized the primitive and elementary at the expense of the diverse and sophisticated . . .

But now our position is different: 'At the same time that the problems increase in quantity, complexity, and difficulty they also change faster than before.'

Ambiguity

. . . indeed complexity of meaning, with its resultant ambiguity and tension, has been characteristic of painting and amply recognized in art criticism . . .

In literature, too, critics have been willing to accept complexity and contradiction in their medium . . . and some, indeed for a long time, have emphasized the qualities of contradiction, paradox, and ambiguity as basic to the medium of poetry, just as Albers does with painting.

Contradictory Levels

The Phenomenon of 'Both-And' in Architecture
Contradictory levels of meaning and use in architecture involve the paradoxical contrast implied by the conjunctive 'yet'. They may be more or less ambiguous. Le Corbusier's Shodhan House is closed yet open – a cube, precisely closed at the corners, yet randomly opened on its surfaces . . .

Cleanth Brooks refers to Donne's art as 'having it both ways' but, he says, 'most of us in this latter day, cannot. We are disciplined in the tradition either–or, and lack the mental agility – to say nothing of the maturity of attitude – which would allow us to indulge in the finer distinctions and the more subtle reservations permitted by the tradition of both-and'. . .

Contradictory Levels Continued
The Double-Functioning Element
The 'double-functioning' element and 'both–and' are related, but there is a distinction: the double-functioning element pertains more to the particulars of use and structure, while both–and refers more to the relation of the part to the whole. Both–and emphasizes double meanings over double-functions . . .

Accommodation and the Limitations of Order
The Conventional Element
A valid order accommodates the circumstantial contradictions of a complex reality. It accommodates as well as imposes. It thereby admits 'control and spontaneity', 'correctness and ease' – improvisation within the whole. It tolerates qualifications and compromise. There are no fixed laws in architecture, but not everything will work in a building or a city . . .

The Inside and the Outside
Contrast between the inside and the outside can be a major manifestation of contradiction in architecture. However, one of the powerful twentieth century orthodoxies has been the necessity for continuity between them: the inside should be expressed on the outside . . .

The Obligation Toward the Difficult Whole
An architecture of complexity and accommodation does not forsake the whole. In fact, I have referred to a special obligation toward the whole because the whole is difficult to achieve. And I have emphasized the goal of unity rather than of simplification in an art 'whose . . . truth [is] in its totality.' It is the difficult unity through inclusion rather than the easy unity through exclusion.

Extracts. Source: Robert Venturi, *Complexity and Contradiction in Architecture*, 2nd edition, The Museum of Modern Art in association with the Graham Foundation for Advanced Studies in the Fine Arts (New York/Chicago), 1977. © The Museum of Modern Art. A version of this text was first published in *Perspecta: The Yale Architectural Journal*, no 9/10, 1965.

1969 CHARLES JENCKS
Semiology and Architecture

Over the 1950s and 60s, the study of language and signs was increasingly applied to areas outside linguistics, most notably by writers such as Roland Barthes, Umberto Eco and AJ Greimas. Charles Jencks (b 1939) was one of the first writers in English to apply it to architecture (he studied English Literature and Architecture at Harvard). As part of a critique of Modernism, Jencks' use of semiology laid the foundation for the Post-Modernism of which he was a principal champion.

Meaning, Inevitable yet Denied

This is perhaps the most fundamental idea of semiology and meaning in architecture: the idea that any form in the environment, or sign in language, is motivated, or capable of being motivated. It helps to explain why all of a sudden forms come alive or fall into bits. For it contends that, although a form may be initially arbitrary or non-motivated as Saussure points out, its subsequent use is motivated or based on some determinants. Or we can take a slightly different point of view and say that the minute a new form is invented it will acquire, inevitably, a meaning. 'This semantization is inevitable; as soon as there is a society, every usage is converted into a sign of itself; the use of a raincoat is to give protection from the rain, but this cannot be dissociated from the very signs of an atmospheric situation'. Or, to be more exact, the use of a raincoat *can be* dissociated from its shared meanings *if* we avoid its social use or explicitly decide to deny it further meaning.

It is this conscious denial of connotations which has had an interesting history with the avant-garde. Annoyed either by the glib reduction of their work to its social meanings or the contamination of the strange by an old language, they have insisted on the intractability of the new and confusing. 'Our League of Nations symbolizes nothing' said the architect Hannes Meyer, all too weary of the creation of buildings around past metaphors. 'My poem means nothing; it just is. My painting is meaningless. Against Interpretation: The Literature of Silence. Entirely radical.' Most of these statements are objecting to the 'inevitable semantization' which is trite, which is coarse, which is too anthropomorphic and old. Some are simply nihilistic and based on the belief that any meaning which may be applied is spurious; it denies the fundamental absurdity of human existence. In any case, on one level, all these statements are paradoxical. In their denial of meaning, they create it. (pp11-12)

The Sign Situation

The first point on which most semiologists would agree is that one simply cannot speak of 'meaning' as if it were one thing that we can all know or share. The concept meaning is multivalent, has many meanings itself; and we will have to be clear which one we are discussing. Thus in their seminal book *The Meaning of Meaning*, Ogden and Richards show the confusion of philosophers over the basic use of this term. Each philosopher assumes that his use is clear and understood, whereas the authors show this is far from the case; they distinguish sixteen different meanings of meaning . . . (p13)

In the usual experience, the semiological traingle, there is always a percept, a concept and a representation. This is irreducible. In architecture, one sees the building, has an interpretation of it, and usually puts that into words . . . In most cases there is no direct relation between a word and a thing, except in the highly rare case of onomatopoeia. That most cultures are under the illusion that there is a direct connection has to be explained in various ways. One explanation is neoplatonic; another is psychological. In any case, everyone has experienced the shock of eating a thing which is called by the wrong name, or would question the adage that a rose 'by any other name would smell as sweet'. It would not smell as sweet if called garlic.

But the main point of the semiological triangle is that there are simply *relations* between language, thought and reality. One area does not determine the other, except in rare cases, and all one can really claim with conviction is that there are simply connections, or correlations . . . (pp15-16)

Context and Metaphor

There are two primary ways to cut through the environment of all sign behaviour. For instance fashion, language, food and architecture all convey meaning in two similar ways: either through opposition or association. This basic division receives a new terminology from each semiologist, because their purposes differ: here they will be called context and metaphor.

It is evident, as a result of such things as Morse Code and the computer, that a sign may gain meaning just from its oppositions or contrast to another. In the simple case of the computer, or code, it may be the oppositions between 'off–on' or 'dot–dash'; in the more complex case of the traffic light each sign gains its meaning by opposition to the other two. In a natural language each word gains its sense by contrast with all the others and thus it is capable of much subtler shades of meaning than the traffic light. Still one could build up a respectable discourse with only two relations, as critics have found. The perennial question of whether a good, bad symphony is better or worse than a bad, good symphony is not as it appears an idle pastime – simply because one adjective acts as the classifier while the other acts as the modifier and vice versa . . . (p21)

The other dimension of meaning is conveyed through associations, metaphors or the whole treasure of past memory. This is often built up socially, when a series of words conveys the same connotations in a language. But it also occurs individually through some experience of relating one sign to another: either because of a common quality, or because they both occurred in the same context (which would *be* the common quality, *pace* behaviourists). Thus an individual might associate blue with the sound of a trumpet either because he heard a trumpet playing the blues in an all blue context (the expressionist ideal), or because they both have a common synaesthetic centre; they both cluster around further metaphors of harshness, sadness and depth. The behaviourist Charles Osgood (*Measurement of Meaning*) has thus postulated a 'semantic space' for every individual which is made up by the way metaphors relate one to another . . . (p22)

Multivalence and Univalence

When one sees an architecture which has been created with equal concern for form, function and technic, this ambiguity creates a multivalent experience where one oscillates from meaning to meaning always finding further justification and depth. One cannot separate the method from the purpose because they have grown together and become linked through the process of continual feedback. And these multivalent links set up an analogous condition where one part modifies another in a continuous series of cyclical references. As Coleridge and IA Richards have shown in the analysis of a few lines from Shakespeare, this imaginative fusion can be tested by showing the mutual modification of links. But the same should be done for any sign system from *Hamlet* to French pastry. In every case, if the object has been created through an imaginative linkage of matrices (or bisociation in Koestler's terms), then it will be experienced as a multivalent whole. If, on the other hand, the object is the summation of past forms which remain independent, and where they are joined the linkage is weak, then it is experienced as univalent. This distinction between multivalence and univalence, or imagination and fancy, is one of the oldest in criticism and probably enters any critic's language in synonymous terms . . . (p24)

To concentrate first on the univalence of the *Semantic Space* [see diagram overleaf], one can see how architects tend to cluster around similar areas, which to my mind constitute groups or traditions. Secondly, my preference for the technical school is shown by comparing it with my distaste for the formalists. The latter is shown on the negative side of all three poles, not because it does not make positive efforts, but because in my judgement it fails (this *is* a diagram of pre-judice). Lastly, Corbusier, Aalto and Archigram are far out on the positive side and thus explicitly show my preference. But this is not all. What is also indicates is that my experience of the latter inextricably links matrices which are normally dissociated.

Extracts. Source: *Meaning in Architecture*, Charles Jencks and George Baird eds, Barrie & Rockliff: The Crescent Press (London), 1969. © The Contributors and Design Yearbook Limited.

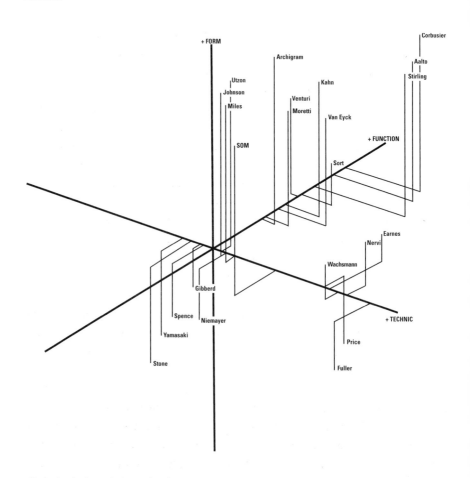

Charles Jencks, Semantic Space of Architects, 1968

1970   GIANCARLO DE CARLO
Architecture's Public

A sometime member of Team 10, Giancarlo de Carlo (b 1919, Genoa) was an early advocate of participatory design. Reacting against the reductive and authoritarian nature of Modernism, he sought to initiate a broader design process that took account of a wider range of people and ideas. This paper, originally delivered at a conference in Liege in 1969, first had the deliberately provocative title, 'Architecture, too important to be left to the architects?'

In reality, architecture is too important by now to be left to the architects. A real change is necessary, therefore, which will encourage new characteristics in the practice of architecture and new behaviour patterns in its authors: therefore all barriers between builders and users must be abolished, so that building and using become two different parts of the same planning process; therefore the intrinsic aggressiveness of architecture and the forced passivity of the user must dissolve in a condition of creative and decisional equivalence where each – with a different specific impact – is the architect, and every architectural event – regardless of who conceives it and carries it out – is considered architecture. The change, in other words, must coincide with the subversion of the present condition, where to be an architect is the result of power delegated in a repressive fashion and to be architecture is the result of reference to class codes which legitimate only the exception, with an emphasis proportional to the degree to which it is cut off from its context. The expedient of 'not reading the surroundings' (used so well by official criticism by means of the technique of uninhabited cut-outs or even trick photographs; or by the use of a linguistic analysis which excludes all judgement on the use and consumption of the event under analysis) corresponds, in fact, to an ideological, political, social, and cultural falsification which has no counterpart in other disciplines . . . (p210)

We cannot sit waiting . . . (in the cave of architecture-as-it-is waiting for the social palingenesis to generate automatically architecture-as-it-will-be) but we must immediately change the whole range of objects and subjects which participate in the architectural process at the present time. There is no other way, besides this one, to recover architecture's historical legitimacy, or, as we have said, its credibility . . .

The evolution of society toward the abolition of classes, the population explosion and technological development pose enormous problems of organization of the physical environment. In order to preserve its rôle, architecture must assume clear ideological positions and operative procedures with regard to these problems . . . (p211)

In reality, participation transforms architectural planning from the authoritarian act which it has been up to now into a process. A process which begins with the discovery of the user's needs, passes through the formulations of formal and organizational hypotheses, reaches a phase of use where, instead of coming to a close, the process is re-opened in a continuous interaction of controls and reformulations which feed back into the needs and hypotheses, soliciting their continual redefinition . . . (p212)

The growth and flexibility of an architectural organism are not really possible except through a new conception of architectural quality. And this new conception cannot be formulated except by means of a more attentive exploration of those phenomena of creative participation which are dismissed as 'disorder'. It is in their intricate context, in fact, that we will find the matrix of an open and self generating formal organization which rejects a private and exclusive way of using land and, through this rejection, delineates a new way of using it on a pluralistic and inclusive basis. In giving the user a creative role, we implicitly accept this basis, and in this way the morphological and structural conceptions and all the operative tools which have so far governed architectural production become open to question. The whole vast set of variables which institutional culture and practice had suppressed come back into play, and the field of reality in which architecture intervenes becomes macroscopic and complex. Thus only the adoption of clear ideological positions and the application of rigorously scientific procedures can guarantee a legitimate political and technical framework within which new sets of objectives can give rise, through the use of new practical instruments, to a balanced and stimulating physical environment. (p215)

Extracts. Source: Benedict Zucchi, *Giancarlo De Carlo*, Butterworth Architecture, (Oxford) 1992. © Giancarlo De Carlo. Based on a text first prepared for a conference held in Liège in 1969, then published as an article in *Parametro*, no 5, 1970, then in *Environnement*, no 3, March 1970, under the title, 'L'Architecture, est-elle trop importante pour être confiée aux architectes?'

1972 CHARLES JENCKS AND NATHAN SILVER
Adhocism

An outgrowth of both the Pop architecture of the 1950s and 60s and Jencks' investigations of semiology, his adhocism exploits the arbitrary relation between signifier and signified, between form and function. It represents a further polemic against Modernist purism and élitism but, compared to the extremes of Pop, is at once less consumed by technology and more pluralist.

The Spirit of Adhocism

Ad hoc means 'for this' specific need or purpose.

A need is common to all living things; only men have higher purposes. But these needs and purposes are normally frustrated by the great time and energy expended in their realization.

A purpose immediately fulfilled is the ideal of adhocism; it cuts through the usual delays caused by specialization, bureaucracy and hierarchical organization.

Today we are immersed in forces and ideas that hinder the fulfilment of human purposes; large corporations standardize and limit our choice; philosophies of behaviorism condition people to deny their potential freedom; 'modern architecture' becomes the convention for 'good taste' and an excuse to deny the plurality of actual needs.

But a new mode of direct action is emerging, the rebirth of a democratic mode and style, where everyone can create his personal environment out of impersonal subsystems, whether they are new or old, modern or antique. By realizing his immediate needs, by combining *ad hoc* parts, the individual creates, sustains and transcends himself. Shaping the local environment towards desired ends is a key to mental health; the present environment, blank and unresponsive, is a key to idiocy and brainwashing . . . (p15)

The Pluralist Universe, or Pluriverse

The man-made world is built up of fragments from the past.

We live in a pluralist world confronted by competing philosophies, and knowledge is in an *ad hoc*, fragmented state prior to some possible synthesis . . . (p29)

Mechanical, Natural and Critical Evolution

Contrary to some theories, both design and nature are radically traditional; they work with subsystems which have existed in the past. All creations are initially *ad hoc* combinations of past subsystems; 'nothing can be created out of nothing . . . '

Natural evolution and its few possibilities are not necessarily beneficial to men. We must project forward many possible trends, not just mechanical and natural ones, and then dissect apart their positive and negative consequences, recombining *ad hoc* those totalities we desire. Dissectibility is the essence of adhocism and critical evolution; contrary to the Romantic poets, we murder *not* to dissect . . . (p39)

Consumer Democracy

New techniques and a new strategy have emerged. The electronic techniques of communication now allow decentralized design and consumption based on individual desire. 'You sit there and need – we do the rest. Green Stamps given!' . . .

The Resource-Full Computer

The new strategy is latent within the do-it-yourself industry, Hippie consumer tactics and space program: the re-use of old parts, the recycling of waste . . . (p55)

Towards an Articulate Environment

Adhocism makes visible the complex workings of the environment. Instead of an homogeneous surface which smooths over all distinctions and difficulties, it looks to the intractable problem as the source of supreme expression. From problems, from the confrontation of diverse subsystems, it drags an art of jagged, articulated cataclysms that shouts out the problems from every corner.

By combining diverse subsystems *ad hoc*, the designer shows *what* the previous history was, *why* they were put together and *how* they work. All this articulation is pleasing to the mind and allows an experience of a higher order.

Meaningful articulation is the goal of adhocism. Opposed to purism and exclusivist design theories, it accepts everyone as an architect and all modes of communication, whether based on nature or culture. The ideal is to provide an environment which can be as visually rich and varied as actual urban life . . .(p73)

The *Ad Hoc* Revolution

The time is ripe for redefining the theory and practice of revolution – beyond the vulgar Marxism and liberal reaction of the present . . .

Two Proposals

First, the revolutionary interests should be recognized in their actual plurality rather than limited to one of class or group. Second, this plurality of *ad hoc* organization, which always occurs in popular revolution, should be preserved. The groups, or communes, or *Räte*, are the basic institutions of freedom and civil life; they must be allowed to spring into existence and thereafter be protected by institutions and law . . . (p89)   *Charles Jencks*

The Adhocist Sensibility

a) The pleasure of unexpected recognition . . . b) An appreciation of hybrid forms . . . c) Contrived spontaneity . . . d) An appreciation for 'function'. The word is in quotes because actual function need only be supposed . . . e) Nostalgia. Old things can be recognized. Old associations are respected, if perhaps confounded by new usage . . . f) Identification. Personal familiarity is evoked when ordinary things are recognized . . . g) The superiority of the perceiver. Caused by the supposed humility of the object . . . h) The principle you love to hate. One can admire the subversiveness of adhocism's impurity, or, indeed, the seductive allure of all of the above . . . (pp140-143) Ad hoc choices can be made consciously, for the sake of style, encouraging rhetorical confrontations and blunt semantic distinctions . . . Instead of accommodating conflict, adhocism can ignore it, permitting a plain facade to glide over multiple distinctions or leave disharmonies behind . . . (pp168-169)   *Nathan Silver*

Extracts. Source: Charles Jencks and Nathan Silver, *Adhocism*, Secker and Warburg (London), 1972. © Auricula Press Inc and Charles Jencks.

Charles Jencks, Madonna of the Future by Henry James plus Electric Heater, plus Mannikin, *London, 1971*

1972 ROBERT VENTURI, DENISE SCOTT BROWN AND STEVEN IZENOUR

Learning from Las Vegas

Significantly quoting Andy Warhol, Learning from Las Vegas *is in many respects a Pop document. The book began as a research project on symbolism and commercial architecture in 1967, the year Denise Scott Brown (née Lakofski, b 1931 'Nkana, Zambia) joined the firm of Venturi and Rauch. Taking the Las Vegas strip as an example, the authors argue for 'ugly and ordinary' architecture and urbanism, and introduced the often quoted distinction between the 'duck' and the 'decorated shed' – between building as symbol and building with applied symbols.*

A Significance for A&P Parking Lots, or Learning from Las Vegas

'Substance for a writer consists not merely of those realities he thinks he discovers; it consists even more of those realities which have been made available to him by the literature and idioms of his own day and by the images that still have vitality in the literature of the past. Stylistically, a writer can express his feeling about this substance either by imitation, if it sits well with him, or by parody if it doesn't.'[1]

Learning from the existing landscape is a way of being revolutionary for an architect. Not the obvious way, which is to tear down Paris and begin again, as Le Corbusier suggested in the 1920s, but another, more tolerant way; that is, to question how we look at things.

The commercial strip, the Las Vegas Strip in particular – the *example par excellence* – challenges the architect to take a positive, non-chip-on-the-shoulder view. Architects are out of the habit of looking nonjudgementally at the environment, because orthodox Modern architecture is progressive, if not revolutionary, utopian, and puristic; it is dissatisfied with *existing* conditions. Modern architecture has been anything but permissive: Architects have preferred to change the existing environment rather than enhance what is there.

But to gain insight from the commonplace is nothing new: fine art often follows folk art. Romantic architects of the eighteenth century discovered an existing and conventional rustic architecture. Early Modern architects appropriated an existing and conventional industrial vocabulary without much adaptation. Le Corbusier loved grain elevators and steamships; the Bauhaus looked like a factory;

Mies refined the details of American steel factories for concrete buildings. Modern architects work through analogy, symbol and image – although they have gone to lengths to disclaim almost all determinants of their forms except structural necessity and the program – and they derive insights, analogies, and stimulation from unexpected images. There is a perversity in the learning process: we look backward at history and tradition to go forward; we can also look downward to go upward. And withholding judgement may be used as a tool to make later judgement more sensitive. This is a way of learning from everything. (p3)

Some Definitions Using the Comparative Method

'Not innovating willfulness but reverence for the archetype.' *Herman Melville*
'Incessant new beginnings lead to sterility.' *Wallace Stevens*
'I like boring things.' *Andy Warhol*

To make a case for a new but old direction in architecture, we shall use some perhaps indiscreet comparisons to show what we are for and what we are against and ultimately to justify our own architecture. When architects talk or write, they philosophize almost solely to justify their own work, and this apologia will be no different. Our argument depends on comparisons, because it is simple to the point of banality. It needs contrast to point it up. We shall use, somewhat undiplomatically, some of the works of leading architects today as contrast and context.

We shall emphasize image – image over process or form – in asserting that architecture depends in its perception and creation on past experience and emotional associations and that these symbolic and representational elements may often be contradictory to the form, structure and program with which they combine in the same building. We shall survey this contradiction in its two main manifestations:

1 Where the architectural systems of space, structure and program are submerged and distorted by an overall symbolic form. This kind of building-becoming-sculpture we call the *duck* in honor of the duck-shaped drive-in, 'The Long Island Duckling', illustrated in *God's Own Junkyard* by Peter Blake.[2]

2 Where systems of space and structure are directly at the service of program, and ornament is applied independently of them. This we call the *decorated shed*.

The duck is the special building that is a symbol; the decorated shed is the conventional shelter that applies symbols. We maintain that both kinds of architecture are valid – Chartres is a duck (although it is a decorated shed as well) and the Palazzo Farnese is a decorated shed – but we think that the duck is seldom relevant today, although it pervades Modern architecture . . .

The Duck and the Decorated Shed

Let us elaborate on the decorated shed by comparing Paul Rudolph's Crawford Manor with our Guild House (in association with Cope and Lippincott). These two buildings are comparable in use, size and date of construction: both are high-rise apartments for the elderly, consisting of about 90 units, built in the mid-1960s. Their settings vary: Guild House, although freestanding, is a six-story imitation palazzo, analogous in structure and materials to the surrounding buildings and continuing, through its position and form, the street line of the Philadelphia grid-iron plan it sits in. Crawford Manor, on the other hand, is unequivocally a soaring tower, unique in its Modern, Ville Radieuse world along New Haven's limited-access Oak Street Connector.

But it is the contrast in the images of these buildings in relation to their systems of construction that we want to emphasize. The system of construction and program of Guild House are ordinary and conventional and look it; the system of construction and program of Crawford Manor are ordinary and conventional but do not look it. (pp87-90)

Heroic and Original, or Ugly and Ordinary

The content of Crawford Manor's implicit symbolism is what we call 'heroic and original'. Although the substance is conventional and ordinary, the image is heroic and original. The content of the explicit symbolism of Guild House is what we call 'ugly and ordinary'. The technologically unadvanced brick, the old-fashioned, double-hung windows, the pretty materials around the entrance, and the ugly antenna not hidden behind the parapet in the accepted fashion, all are distinctly conventional in image as well as substance or, rather, ugly and ordinary. (The inevitable plastic flowers at home in these windows are, rather, *pretty* and ordinary; they do not make this architecture look silly as they would, we think, the heroic and original windows of Crawford Manor.)

But in Guild House, the symbolism of the ordinary goes further that this. The pretensions of the 'giant order' on the front, the symmetrical, palazzo-like composition with its three monumental stories (as well as its six real stories), topped by a piece of sculpture – or almost sculpture – suggest something of the heroic and original. It is true that in this case the heroic and original facade is somewhat ironical, but it is this juxtaposition of contrasting symbols – the appliqué of one order of symbols on another – that constitutes for use the decorated shed. This is what makes Guild House an architect's decorated shed – not architecture without architects. (pp93-100)

Ugly and Ordinary as Symbol and Style

Artistically, the use of conventional elements in ordinary architecture – be they dumb doorknobs or the familiar forms of existing construction systems – evokes associations from past experience. Such elements may be carefully chosen or thoughtfully adapted from existing vocabularies and standard catalogs rather than uniquely created via original data and artistic intuition. To design a window, for instance, you state not only with the abstract function of modulating light rays and breezes to serve interior space but with the image of window – of all the windows you know plus others you find out about. This approach is symbolically and functionally conventional, but it promotes an architecture of meaning, broader and richer if less dramatic than the architecture of expression.

Against Ducks, or Ugly and Ordinary over Heroic and Original, or Think Little

We should not emphasize the ironic richness of banality in today's artistic context at the expense of discussing the appropriateness and inevitability of U&O architecture on a wider basis. Why do we uphold the symbolism of the ordinary via the decorated shed over the symbolism of the heroic via the sculptural duck? Because this is not the time and ours is not the environment for heroic communication through pure architecture. Each medium has its day, and the rhetorical environmental statements of our time – civic, commercial, or residential – will come from media more purely symbolic, perhaps less static and more adaptable to the scale of our environment. The iconography and mixed media of roadside commercial architecture will point the way, if we will look. (pp130-131)

To find our symbolism we must go to the suburban edges of the existing city that are symbolically rather than formalistically attractive and represent the aspirations of almost all Americans, including most low-income urban dwellers and most of the silent white majority. Then the archetype Los Angeles will be our Rome and Las Vegas our Florence . . .

High-Design Architecture

Finally, learning from popular culture does not remove the architect from his or her status in high culture. But it may alter high culture to make it more sympathetic to current needs and issues. Because high culture and its cultists (last year's variety) are powerful in urban renewal and other establishment circles, we feel that people's architecture as the people want it (and not as some architect decides Man needs it) does not stand much chance against urban renewal until it hangs in the academy and therefore is acceptable to the decision makers. Helping this to happen is a not-reprehensible part of the role of the high-design architect; it provides, together with moral subversion through irony and the use of a joke to get to seriousness, the weapons of artists of nonauthoritarian temperament in social situations that do not agree with them. The architect becomes a jester.

Irony may be the tool with which to confront and combine divergent values in architecture for a pluralist society and to accommodate the differences in values that arise between architects and clients. Social classes rarely come together, but if they can make temporary alliances in the designing and building of multivalued community architecture, a sense of paradox and some irony and wit will be needed on all sides. (p161)

1   Richard Poirier, 'TS Eliot and the Literature of Waste', *The New Republic*, 20 May, 1967, p21.
2   Peter Blake, *God's Own Junkyard: The Planned Deterioration of America's Landscape*, Holt Rinehart and Winston, (New York) 1964, p101. See also Denise Scott Brown and Robert Venturi, 'On Ducks and Decoration', *Architecture Canada*, October 1968.

Extracts. Source: Robert Venturi, Denise Scott Brown and Steven Izenour, *Learning from Las Vegas*, revised edition, MIT Press (Cambridge, Mass), 1977. © 1977 by The Massachusetts Institute of Technology. 'A Significance for A&P Parking Lots, or Learning from Las Vegas' was first published in *Architectural Forum*, March 1968.

1975 CHARLES JENCKS
The Rise of Post-Modern Architecture

In the 1970s, Critical Modernist views had gained sufficient currency and force to constitute a number of inchoate partial movements. Jencks, as both historian and advocate, was one of the first to identify the preoccupations and range of specific antidotes that were emerging. With this, the first essay on Post-Modernism, he drew these departures together into what was to become a major movement in architecture and the other arts and philosophy.

The title is evasive of course. If I knew what to call it, I wouldn't use the negative prefix 'post'. It is rather like defining women as 'non-men' – not a useful or complimentary definition. No doubt modern architecture has ended as a serious body of theory – no one believes in it after twenty years of sustained attack – but it continues, for want of an alternative, as actual practice. The only way to kill off the monster is to find a substitute beast to take its place and decidedly 'Post Modern' won't do the job. We need a new way of thinking, a new paradigm based on broad theory, which enjoys a large consensus. No such consensus exists at the moment and it is in the nature of the case that such things take a long time to develop – perhaps another twenty years. What we have instead is a series of fragmented alternatives all claiming primary place . . . (p3)

Counterattack: the Pluralist City
There are many historical movements countering the trend toward an abstract and supposedly universal architecture. Each one is relatively minor, but taken as a whole they amount to a strong movement awaiting formulation as a new paradigm. It would be premature to name this paradigm; perhaps because of its inherent pluralism it can never be named or reduced to a synthesis . . . The eight alternatives:
1 *Social realism* . . . 2 *Advocacy planning and the anti-scheme* . . . 3 *Rehabilitation and preservation* . . . 4 *Adhocism and collision city* . . . 5 *Ersatz and artificial cities* . . . 6 *Semiotics and radical eclecticism* . . .7 *Radical traditionalism and piecemeal tinkering* . . . 8 *Political reorganization* . . . (pp6-14)

If there is a summary to a list of recipes and palliatives, it must be on a very general level. The disillusion of modern architects and dissatisfaction of the public with the architecture they produce have now become commonplace . . . If a lasting change is to be made, it will probably have to be the whole system of architectural production and this implies a revolution within society. Nonetheless, architects, as a critical group within society, can make an impact on the situation.

If they were trained as anthropologists, to understand the various codes which are used by different groups, then they could at least design buildings which communicated as they intended. Beyond this, they might get closer to their actual clients and buildings in a specific way – move into a locale, move on to the building site, move out of their large teams of co-ordinated experts. Then they might gain a respect for forces which they have too long overlooked. To ensure this, however, an anti-scheme should be started along with their proposal, an anti-scheme which was formulated and developed by anti-architects (real people). The resultant schizophrenia would be charming to see and a lot less costly than the one-sided efforts produced now. Alternatively, one could always build every building twice; once for the architect and once for the user, but then there'd be so much more to tear down in the future. (p14)

Extracts. Source: *Architectural Association Quarterly*, (London), vol 7; no 4, October/December 1975. © Architectural Association.

Charles Jencks, Garagia Rotunda, Cape Cod Garage Transformed, 1975-77

1975   ROB KRIER
Urban Space

*In many ways a parallel to Rowe and Koetter's Collage City, Rob
Krier's (b 1938, Grevenmacher, Luxembourg) Urban Space was equally
influential. It issues a direct attack against Modernist urbanism as
proposed by CIAM and its realisation in bastardised form after the
Second World War in the name of reconstruction. Rob Krier, like his
younger brother Leon, turns to the traditional city as a source for
solutions to the problems of urbanism, countering the Modernist isolated form in space with streets and squares defined by buildings.*

We have lost sight of the traditional understanding of urban space. The cause of
this loss is familiar to all city dwellers who are aware of their environment and
sensitive enough to compare the town planning achievements of the present and
the past and who have the strength of character to pronounce sentence on the way
things have gone . . .

Definition of the Concept 'Urban Space'
If we wish to clarify the concept of urban space without imposing aesthetic criteria, we are compelled to designate all types of space between buildings in towns
and other localities as urban space.

This space is geometrically bounded by a variety of elevations. It is only the
clear legibility of its geometrical characteristics and aesthetic qualities which
allows us consciously to perceive external space as urban space. (p15)

The two basic elements are the street and the square. In the category of 'interior space' we would be talking about the corridor and the room. The geometrical
characteristics of both spatial forms are the same. They are differentiated only by
the dimensions of the walls which bound them and by the patterns of function and
circulation which characterise them. (p16)

Typology of Urban Space
In formulating a typology of urban space, spatial forms and their derivatives
may be divided into three main groups, according to the geometrical pattern of
their ground plan: these groups derive from the square, circle or the triangle.
(p22)

I have designed streets and squares for the pedestrian, harmonised as closely as possible with the existing structure and showing the utmost consideration for the legacy of the past.

ANY PLANNING INNOVATIONS IN A CITY MUST BE GOVERNED BY THE LOGIC OF THE WHOLE AND IN DESIGN TERMS MUST OFFER A FORMAL RESPONSE TO RE-EXISTING SPATIAL CONDITIONS. (p89)

Postscript for Architects

(1) Architects . . . It is more useful to imitate something 'old' but proven, rather than to turn out something new which risks causing people suffering. The logical and attractive building types and spatial structures left to us by anonymous architects have been improved upon by countless succeeding generations. They have matured into masterpieces even in the absence of a single creator of genius, because they were based on a perfectly refined awareness of building requirements using simple means; the result of an accurate understanding of tradition as the vehicle for passing on technical and artistic knowledge. (p167)

Every new urban building must obey the overall structural logic and provide a formal answer in its design to pre-existing spatial conditions! (p169)

Knowledge gained over the course of centuries carries a certain conviction which we cannot allow to go unnoticed . . . There are almost no further discoveries to be made in architecture. In our century the problems have merely changed their dimension. This is often so dramatic that one cannot warn too emphatically against hasty, untested solutions. As long as man needs two arms and two legs, the scale of his body must be the measure of size for all building. That concerns not only staircases and ceiling height, but also the design of public space in the urban context. (p62)

Extracts. Source: Rob Krier, *Urban Space*, trans Christine Czechowski and George Black, Academy Editions (London), 1979. © Academy Editions. First published in German as *Stadtraum*, 1975.

1975 COLIN ROWE AND FRED KOETTER
Collage City

Despite and because of the rhetoric of Modernist tabula rasa urbanism, historic cities such as Rome continued to exercise a fascination over architects. By the 1960s and 70s, that fascination was helping to fill the theoretical vacuum left by the all too evident failures of Modernist planning. Colin Rowe helped to codify the view, taking Rome as a paradigm for a new urbanism, both political and physical. Rowe had already thrown Modernism into historical perspective in the 1950s with his essays such as 'The Mathematics of the Ideal Villa'. With Collage City he and Koetter used history as a cure for the ills of 20th-century urbanism – by way of the essentially 20th-century idea of collage.

Collision City and the Politics of 'Bricolage'

If we are willing to recognize the methods of science and 'bricolage' as concomitant propensities, if we are willing to recognize that they are – both of them – modes of address to problems, if we are willing (and it may be hard) to concede equality between the 'civilized' mind (with its presumptions of logical seriality) and the 'savage' mind (with its analogical leaps), then, in re-establishing 'bricolage' alongside science, it might even be possible to suppose that the way for a truly useful future dialectic could be prepared.

A truly useful dialectic? The idea is simply the conflict of contending powers, the almost fundamental conflict of interest sharply stipulated, the legitimate suspicion of others' interests, from which the democratic process – such as it is – proceeds; and then the corollary to this idea is no more than banal: if such is the case, if democracy is compounded of libertarian enthusiasm and legalistic doubt, and if it is, inherently, a collision of points of view and acceptable as such, then why not allow a theory of contending powers (all of them visible) as likely to establish a more ideally comprehensive city of the mind than any which has, *as yet*, been invented.

And there is no more to it than this. In place of an ideal of universal management based upon what are presented as scientific certainties there is also a private, and a public, emancipatory interest (which, incidentally, includes emancipation from management); and, if this is the situation and, if the only outcome is to be sought in collision of interest, in a permanently maintained debate of opposites, then why should this dialectical predicament be not just as much accepted in theory as it is in practice? The reference is again to Popper and to the ideal of keeping the game straight; and it is because, from such a criticist point of view, collision of interest is to be welcomed, not in terms of cheap ecumenicism which is only too abundantly available, but in terms of clarification (because, in the battlefield engendered by mutual suspicion, it is just possible that – as has been usual – the flowers of freedom may be forced from the blood of conflict) that, if such a condition of collisive motives is recognizable and should be endorsable, we are disposed to say, why not try?

The proposition leads us (like Pavlov's dogs) automatically to the condition of seventeenth-century Rome, to that collision of palaces, *piazze* and villas, to that inextricable fusion of imposition and accommodation, that highly successful and resilient traffic jam of intentions, an anthology of closed compositions and *ad hoc* stuff in between, which is simultaneously a dialectic of ideal types plus a dialectic of ideal types with empirical context; and the consideration of seventeenth-century Rome (the complete city with the assertive identity of subdivisions: Trastevere, Sant'Eustachio, Borgo, Campo Marzio, Campitelli . . .) leads to the equivalent interpretation of its predecessor where forum and thermae pieces lie around in a condition of inter-dependence, independence and multiple interpretability. And imperial Rome is, of course, far the more dramatic statement. For, certainly with its more abrupt collisions, more acute disjunctions, its more expansive set pieces, its inhibition, imperial Rome, far more than the city of the High Baroque, illustrates something of the 'bricolage' mentality at its most lavish – an obelisk from here, a column from there, a range of statues from somewhere else, even at the level of detail the mentality is fully exposed; and, in this context, it is amusing to recollect how the influence of a whole school of historians (Positivists, no doubt!) was, at one time, strenuously dedicated to presenting the ancient Romans as inherently nineteenth-century engineers, precursors of Gustave Eiffel, who had somehow, and unfortunately, lost their way. (pp105-107)

Collage City and the Reconquest of Time

. . . We think of Picasso's bicycle seat (Bull's Head) of 1944:

> Your remember that bull's head I exhibited recently? Out of handlebars and the bicycle seat I made a bull's head which everybody recognized as a bull's head. Thus a metamorphosis was completed; and now I would like to see another metamorphosis take place in the opposite direction. Suppose my

bull's head is thrown on the scrap heap. Perhaps some day a fellow will come along and say: 'Why there's something that would come in handy for the handlebars of my bicycle . . . ' and so a double metamorphosis would have been achieved.

Remembrance of former function and value (bicycles and minotaurs); shifting context; an attitude which encourages the composite; an exploitation and recycling of meaning (has there ever been enough to go around?); desuetude of function with corresponding agglomeration of reference; memory; anticipation; the connectedness of memory and wit; the integrity of wit; this is the laundry list of reactions to Picasso's proposition; and, since it is a proposition evidently addressed to people, it is in terms such as these, in terms of pleasures remembered and desired, of a dialectic between past and future, of an impacting of iconographic content, of a temporal as well as a spatial collision, that resuming an earlier argument, one might proceed to specify an ideal city of the mind.

With Picasso's image one asks: what is false and what is true, what is antique and what is 'of today'; and it is because of an inability to make a half way adequate reply to this pleasing difficulty that one, finally, is obliged to identify the problem of composite presence in terms of *collage*.

Collage and the architect's conscience, collage as technique and collage as state of mind: Lévi-Strauss tells us that 'the intermittent fashion for "collages", originating when craftsmanship was dying, could not . . . be anything but the transposition of "bricolage" into the realms of contemplation' and, if the twentieth-century architect has been the reverse of willing to think of himself as a 'bricoleur' it is in this context that one must also place his frigidity in relation to major twentieth-century discovery. Collage has seemed to be lacking in sincerity, to represent a corruption of moral principles, an adulteration. (pp138-139)

It is suggested that a collage approach, an approach in which objects are conscripted or seduced from out of their context, is – at the present day – the only way of dealing with the ultimate problems of, either or both, utopia and tradition; and the provenance of the architectural objects introduced into the social collage need not be of great consequence. It relates to taste and conviction. The objects can be aristocratic or they can be 'folkish', academic or popular. Whether they originate in Pergamum or Dahomey, in Detroit or Dubrovnik, whether their implications are of the twentieth or the fifteenth century, is no great matter. Societies and persons assemble themselves according to their own interpretations of absolute reference and traditional value; and, up to a point, collage accommodates both hybrid display and the requirements of self-determination.

But up to a point: for if the city of collage may be more hospitable than the city of modern architecture, it cannot more than any human institution pretend to be *completely* hospitable. The ideally open city, like the ideally open society, is just as much a figment of the imagination as its opposite. (pp144-145)

Because collage is a method deriving its virtue from its irony, because it seems to be a technique for using things and simultaneously disbelieving in them, it is also a strategy which can allow utopia to be dealt with as image, to be dealt with in *fragments* without our having to accept it *in toto*, which is further to suggest that collage could even be a strategy which, by supporting the utopian illusion of changelessness and finality, might even fuel a reality of change, motion, action and history. (p149)

Extracts. Source: Colin Rowe and Fred Koetter, *Collage City*, MIT Press (Cambridge, Mass), 1978. © 1978 by The Massachusetts Institute of Technology. A shorter version of the text first appeared in *Architectural Review*, vol CLVIII; no 942, (London), August 1975.

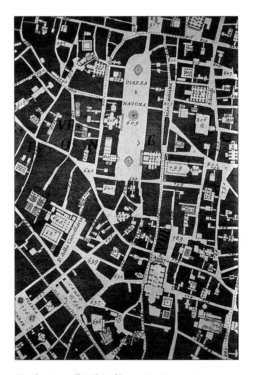

Giambattista Nolli's Plan of Rome, 1748

1975   JOSEPH RYKWERT
Ornament is no Crime

Joseph Rykwert (b 1926) studied under the Modern architectural histo-rian Sigfried Giedion. He, like his former teacher and friend, is a critic and historian with a wide view of what is relevant to architecture. His essays and books have defined key issues on the importance of myth to building, the ways the Classical Orders carry meaning, and the idea of the town (the title of one of his books). Despite having dis-claimed early use of the term Post-Modernism, Rykwert, in this essay and others, has been a force in renewing an intelligent defense of ornament, signification and style.

We must all acknowledge that, in a negative way at any rate, Loos was right: ornament, as the nineteenth-century architects and critics understood it, is wholly dead, beyond any hope of resurrection. We cannot rely on any kind of convention: the world of tangible form has to be learnt anew. Architects never think of build-ings as tangible objects, except at the one direct point of contact, the door-handle. And yet buildings are not only enclosure; they are also extensions of ourselves, like clothing. But being more stable, more permanent, more important in fact, they are subject to the importuning demand that they should enhance, enrich, improve with our handling of them. This, it is increasingly clear, will not be done as long as there is a general social assumption that reasonable returns is all we require of products. On the contrary, they must engage our imagination. And they will not do so until architects and designers have really begun to learn the lessons which the painters and sculptors have to teach; and, moreover, have learnt to work together with them, make use of their work not only as analogue, but as adorn-ment. But such a development will only be valid if it is seen to be necessary, not gratuitous: as long as it will be seen not as a problem of ornament or not orna-ment, but as a problem of meaning. (p101)

Extract. Source: Joseph Rykwert, *The Necessity of Artifice*, Academy Editions (London), 1982. © Joseph Rykwert. First published in *Studio International*, September/October 1975.

1976 ALDO ROSSI
An Analogical Architecture

By the 1980s Rossi attained the position of international cult figure, due in large part to his evocative drawings and writings such as The Architecture of the City *(1966) and* A Scientific Autobiography *(1971). The melancholic ambivalence towards Modernism and the historic city so characteristic of those earlier writings is sustained in this essay. Quoting Walter Benjamin, he declares: 'I am unquestionably deformed by relationships with everything that surrounds me.'*

Although in my architecture things are seen in a fixed way, I realize that in recent projects certain characteristics, memories, and above all associations have proliferated or become clearer, often yielding unforeseen results . . .

Each of these designs has been due increasingly to that concept of the 'analogical city' about which I wrote sometime ago; meanwhile that concept has developed in the spirit of the analogy.

Writing on that subject, I stated that it was mainly a matter of a logical-formal operation that could be translated as a design method.

In order to illustrate this concept, I cited the example of the view of Venice by Canaletto in the Parma Museum, in which Palladio's concept for the Rialto Bridge, the Basilica and the Palazzo Chiericati are arranged and depicted as if the painter had reproduced an actual townscape. The three monuments, of which one is only a project, constitute an analogue of the real Venice composed of definite elements related to both the history of architecture and that of the city itself. The geographical transposition of the two existing monuments to the site of the intended bridge forms a city recognizably constructed as a locus of purely architectonic values.

This concept of the analogical city has been further elaborated in the spirit of analogy toward the conception of an analogical architecture.

In the correspondence between Freud and Jung, the latter defines the concept of analogy in the following way:

I have explained that 'logical' thought is what is expressed in words directed to the outside world in the form of discourse. 'Analogical' thought is sensed yet unreal, imagined yet silent; it is not a discourse but rather a meditation on themes of the past, an interior monologue. Logical thought is 'thinking in words'. Analogical thought is archaic, unexpressed, and practically inexpressible in words. I believe I have found in this definition a different sense of history conceived of not simply as fact, but rather as a series of things, of affective objects to be used by the memory or in a design . . .

The quotation from Walter Benjamin: 'I am unquestionably deformed by relationships with everything that surrounds me,' might be said to contain the thought underlying this essay. It also accompanies my architecture today.

There is continuity in this, even though in the most recent projects general and personal tensions emerge with greater clarity, and in various drawings the uneasiness of different parts and elements can be felt to have superimposed itself on the geometrical order of the composition.

The deformation of the relationships between those elements surrounding, as it were, the main theme, draws me toward an increasing rarefaction of parts in favour of more complex compositional methods. This deformation affects the materials themselves and destroys their static image, stressing instead their elementality and superimposed quality. The question of things themselves, whether as compositions or components – drawings, building, models, or descriptions – appears to me increasingly more suggestive and convincing. But this is not to be interpreted in the sense of '*vers une architecture*' nor as a new architecture. I am referring rather to familiar objects, whose form and position are already fixed, but whose meanings may be changed. Barns, stables, workshops, etc. Archetypal objects whose common emotional appeal reveals timeless concerns.

Such objects are situated between inventory and memory. Regarding the question of memory, architecture is also transformed into autobiographical experience; places and things change with the superimposition of new meanings. Rationality seems almost reduced to objective logic, the operation of a reductive process which in time produces characteristic features. (pp74-76)

Extract. Source: *Architecture and Urbanism* 56, translated by David Stewart. © A + U Publishing Co Ltd.

1977 KISHO KUROKAWA
Metabolism in Architecture

Kisho Kurokawa (b 1934, Nagoya) was one of the founding members of the Metabolist Group along with Kiyonori Kikutake, Fumihiko Maki, Masato Otaka and Kiyoshi Awazu. Initially formed in 1958 as a working party to prepare for the 1960 World Design Conference in Tokyo, the Group worked together only sporadically after the conference. Kurokawa was the most active in further developing the ideas of Metabolism, producing a series of articles and books on the subject through the 1970s.

The Philosophy of Metabolism

War helped me discover Japanese culture. As I stood amidst the ruins of Nagoya, the third largest city in Japan, there was nothing but scorched earth for as far as the eye could see. In contrast to the desolate surroundings, the blue of the mountain range on the horizon was dazzling to the eyes . . . I remember that my father's library contained works on classical Greek and Roman architecture and many volumes by writers such as John Ruskin and William Morris. Reading books of this kind formed in my mind an image of architecture and of cities as entities which are eternal and do not lose their quality even if they are destroyed. (p23)

The Metabolic movement . . . came into being through the preparations for the World Design Conference. These preparations lasted for two years, beginning in 1958; and during the conference the Metabolist group made its first declaration: *Metabolism 1960 – A Proposal for a New Urbanism.* The people who collaborated on this book were architects Kiyonori Kikutake, Fumihiko Maki, Masato Otaka, and myself, and graphic designer Kiyoshi Awazu.

A key passage in this declaration reads: 'We regard human society as a vital process, a continuous development from atom to nebula. The reason why we use the biological word *metabolism* is that we believe design and technology should denote human vitality. We do not believe that metabolism indicates only acceptance of a natural, historical process, but we are trying to encourage the active metabolic development of our society through our proposals.' This is an important element in our declaration for two reasons. First, it reflects our feelings that human society must be regarded as one part of a continuous natural entity that includes all animals and plants. Secondly, it expresses our belief that technology is an extension of humanity. This belief contrasts with the Western belief that modernization is a repetition of a conflict between technology and humanity. (p27)

Obviously growth of the population and change in the age structure of the population greatly influence the nature of cities, types of residence and nature of architectural spaces. Furthermore, the speed of population growth has made it impossible to satisfy housing demand through the ordinary construction methods of the past ... As long as these conditions persist the architect must not accept them passively, as the inevitable results of technological progress. Instead he must help people to master technology and strive to produce a system whereby changes occur as the result of human judgement. The architect's job is not to propose ideal models for society, but to devise spatial equipment that the citizens themselves can operate ... (p28)

Le Corbusier said that cities consist of living spaces, working spaces, and recreational spaces connected by methods of transport. Methods of transport should be re-examined as parts of the space in which we live. Here, the important feature is not the road, which has the sole function of providing a place for vehicles to pass, but the street, which is part of daily-life space and has many functions. (p30)

At the same time that the rapid economic development of Japan began, in 1960, the Metabolist group advocated the creation of a new relationship between humanity and technology. Thinking that the time would come when technology would develop autonomously to the point where it ruled human life, the group aimed at producing a system whereby man would maintain control over technology.

Rapid economic growth in an industrial nation such as Japan promotes the development of technology of a kind more dynamic than anything previously known ...

In this no thought is given to the social significance of spaces or to value judgements about providing people with pleasing symbols. The sole consideration is economic efficiency and profit. We advocated the application of metabolic cycle theory as a way of avoiding these conditions. This theory proposed a reorganization which divides architectural and urban spaces into levels extending from the major to the subordinate and which makes it easy for human beings to control their own environments.

By distinguishing between the parts that do not change and the parts that must be preserved, it is possible to ascertain the parts that must periodically be replaced. In our plan for a prefabricated apartment building project, we devised a way of assembling a number of basic elements so as to create such major spaces as bedrooms and living rooms. Capsule units, attached from the outside, were used for subordinate spaces like those of the kitchen and service units. This kind of breakdown and recomposition of architecture enables individual expression and the production of character for the individual rooms and their contents; it establishes a kind of identity by means of things that, in the case of buildings in the modern architecture style, were buried within box-like forms . . . (p31)

The relation between society and nature is an open one. Beauty is not created solely by the artist; it is completed by the citizens, the users and the spectators, who by so doing contribute to its creation. I employ industrialization, prefabrication, and capsulization as ways of evoking this kind of participation . . .

I believe that what I call media space (or *en*-space, a term using the Japanese word *en*, which means connection or relationship) and in-between space are important in making the relationship between architecture, and society and nature an open one . . . (p33)

The principle that architecture should change with time, the principle of replaceability and interchangeability, and the principle of the metabolic cycle, as well as the belief that architecture, cities and humanity itself are ephemeral, are all in accord with the [Buddhist] doctrines of *samsara* and *laksana-Alaksanatas*.

The thought of Metabolism is theoretical and philosophical. We do not intend to create forms of styles, because these are only the provisional manifestation of thoughts. Forms and styles occur in consequence of historical, temporal, spatial, material, geographical, social, and sometimes purely personal conditions . . . (p35)

I intended my capsule spaces to be a declaration of war in support of the restoration of the oriental individuum, which has been lost in the process of modernization (*Capsule Declaration*, 1969). It is once again necessary to reject the mystification implanted in such ideas as abstracted universal space. By examining spaces for individuals we must seek new relations between the individual and society. The capsule space, which is a representation of the oriental individuum, is not a part of the piece of architecture to which it is attached. The capsule and the building exist in contradiction yet mutually include each other. Architecture that is a representation of the oriental individuum would not be a part of the city. Such architecture and cities would exist in contradiction but would mutually include another. The same kind of relation should exist between architecture and nature and between human beings and technology. The philosophy of in-between spaces and *en*-spaces should help make possible a change of direction towards attaining such relations . . . (p36)

Extracts. Source: Kisho Kurokawa, *Metabolism in Architecture*, Studio Vista (London), 1977. © Kisho Kurokawa.

1977 KENT C BLOOMER AND CHARLES W MOORE

Body, Memory and Architecture

Taking exception to the moralistic pretensions of Modernism, Charles Moore (b 1925, Benton Harbor, Michigan, d 1993) responded with wit, learning and sensitivity to place. This essentially Post-Modern combination is demonstrated in both his writing and his buildings, the latter including the Faculty Club at University of California, Santa Barbara (1968), various houses at Sea Ranch, California (1969), Kresge College, University of California, Santa Cruz (1973) and the Piazza d'Italia, (with Perez Associates and UIG) (1979).

Place, Path, Pattern and Edge

The landscape of the human inner world of landmarks, coordinates, hierarchies, and especially boundaries serves, we believe, as the only humane starting point for the organization of the space around us, which, more than being perceived, is inhabited by us. We propose here to look again at the architectural building blocks in the existential space that surrounds us, to pursue them from the boundary of the individual body to the first shared boundary (the house), and beyond that to boundaries shared by larger and larger communities, seeing how they can be a means of extending inner order outward, of making a world that is a sympathetic extension of our sense of ourselves.

The building blocks that mankind long ago invested with meaning were described in chapter one: columns, walls, and the roofs between them; porches and arcades; towers to which they stretch up; rooms and hearths which the walls enclose; and doors and windows which relate an inside to the rest of the world. These forms have been important to humankind because they accommodated the initial human act of constructing a dwelling, the first tangible boundary beyond the body, they accommodated the act of inhabiting, and they called attention to the sources of human energy and to our place between heaven and earth.

Beyond that first boundary, the inventory of pieces available to build the world does not really lengthen; the variations are changes not of form, but of position. Though the structures remain the same, the choreography of the trip to them can intensify their importance to us . . .

We start with the house (or palace or cathedral) staked out in close homage to the human (or the divine) body and note how the choreography of arrival at the house (the *path* to it) can send out messages and induce experiences which heighten its importance as a place. Far beyond the boundaries of the house lie the edges of cites and beyond them the outer boundaries of whole societies. Within those larger boundaries are places to live and to work which range from private to shared and which include highly symbolical public realms as well as unclaimed no-places. Monuments marking places of more than private importance will be found most often at either the borders or the heart. And some pattern of connections will be laid upon the earth within those boundaries, generally producing a set of inner edges upon which our comprehension of the place depends.

The inhabited world within boundaries then, can usefully be ascribed a syntax of *place*, *path*, *pattern* and *edge*. Within each of these four, architectural ordering arrangements can be considered which are made to respond to the natural landscape as well as to human bodies and memories . . . (pp77-79)

Human Identity in Memorable Places

If architecture, the making of Places, is as we propose a matter of extending the inner landscape of human being into the world in ways that are comprehensible, experiential, and inhabitable, and if the architectural world is rich in instances of this success, what then is so dramatically wrong with the way we build today? Why do people not like their houses and apartments? And why have we been guilty of desecrating or obliterating the landscape perfected by the hand of man? Why, that is, have the *insides* of our world, the places we make for our own inhabitation, which are defensible and free from the chaos or dangers outside, in our century become for many the hostile zone, while 'in wilderness is the hope of the earth.' And why is the only chance for the world thought to be for man to keep his hands off the pieces he has not yet destroyed?

What is missing from our dwellings today are the potential transactions between body, imagination, and environment. It is absurdly easy to build, and appallingly easy to build badly. Comfort is confused with the absence of sensation. The norm has become rooms maintained at a constant temperature without any verticality or outlook or sunshine or breeze or discernible source of heat or center or, alas, meaning. These homogeneous environments require little of us, and they give little in return besides the shelter of a cubical cocoon.

Buildings, we are certain, given enough *care*, are capable of repaying that care (an environmental instance of bread cast upon the waters coming back club sandwiches). We will care increasingly for our buildings if there is some meaningful order in them; if there are definite boundaries to contain our concerns; if we can actually *inhabit* them, their spaces, taking them as our own in satisfying ways; if we can establish connections in them with what we know and believe and think; if we can share our occupancy with others, our family, our group, or our city; and, importantly, if there is some sense of human drama, of transport, of tension, or of collision of forces, so that the involvement endures.

The special, immaculate collision, in which building or landscape pieces come sharply up against one another without loss of their individual identities or spirit, is especially important in the making of memorable places. A classic example is the gridiron plan of San Francisco, which collides with steep hills in a balance which has not surrendered the identity of the hills, but indeed has strengthened their image in the welter of detailed switchbacks which make the grid functional and more memorable than ever.

Architectural design becomes, in such an instance, a choreography of collision, which, like dance choreography, does not impair the inner vitality of its parts in the process of expressing a collective statement through them. Choreography, we believe, is a more useful term than composition, because of its much clearer implication of the human body and body's inhabitation and experience of place. In another simpler time, perspective drawings taken from a single station-point could describe the visual intentions of the designer, and his other intentions were understood. It seems significant in this connection, however, that the architectural works of Michelangelo, clearly meant to be experienced with all the body, were never all drawn in perspective in advance. Really, they couldn't have been. The experience of being in a place occurs in time, is far more than visual, and is generally as complex as the image of it which stays in our memory. To at least some extent every real place can be remembered, partly because it is unique, but partly because it has affected our bodies and generated enough associations to hold it in our personal worlds. And, of course, the real experience of it, from which the memory is carried away, lasts much longer than the camera's 1/125th of a second: perhaps the light plays upon it, and the shadows move; breezes blow or the air is still; or perhaps the snow is falling, blurring the edges like memory blurs time itself. The designer of every successful place both wittingly and unwittingly was choreographing all of this. In addition he may have choreographed a collision between his desires and the constraints of budget, rules, and an unpredictable client, as well as the sun, rain, and perhaps the occasional shaking of the earth.

The real places on the earth, that is to say, are susceptible to continuous readings, which is to say many readings, which is almost certainly to say complex and ambiguous ones. It seems to be a characteristic of them, too, that they have extraordinary changeability, sometimes of use, almost certainly of size (as in the notion of the city as house, and the house as city): each can be seen as a potential toy, capable of being pocketed in the memory and carried away, or taken out to fill for a while the whole of one's conscious attention . . . (pp105-107)

Extracts. Source: Kent C Bloomer and Charles W Moore, *Body, Memory and Architecture*, Yale University Press (New Haven and London), 1977. © Yale University.

Charles W Moore Associates, Xanadune, St Simon Island Condominium, Georgia, 1972

1978   LEON KRIER

Rational Architecture:
The Reconstruction of the City

Polemicist, and compelling draughtsman, Leon Krier (b 1946, Luxem-
bourg) worked with James Stirling and JP Kleihues in the late 1960s
and early 70s before setting up his own office. The primary target of
his invective has been Modernist urbanism and in 1975 he organised
the exhibition Rational Architecture *in London, bringing together the*
work of Italian, French, Belgian and German architects with a shared
concern for the traditional city. These excerpts are from the book of
the same title, an extended catalogue of the exhibition.

We want to state very clearly that Rational Architecture is not concerned with the
revival of the Rationalism of the 1920s. It is, as Massimo Scolari explains, primarily
to do with the revival of Architecture 'tout court'. If its theoretical basis is to be found
in the philosophical Rationalism of the Enlightenment its primary concern should
now lie with the re-creation of the public realm . . .

The problem of Rational Architecture can therefore not be one of choreography. It
cannot find its motivation in a 'state of mind', in the fictions of artistic or technical
progress but in the reflection on the city and its history, on its social use and content.
The revolutionary element of this new Architecture does not lie in its form but in the
model of its social use, in its coherency, in the reconstruction of the public realm . . .

Technical Progress and Industrialisation of Building
Modern building technology is still at the level of experiment and an ephemeral
progress leaves us today with a building technology which in many ways is more
primitive than at any moment in Western civilization. The recuperation of a dignified mode of production, the reconstruction of an artisan building culture will
be the basis of any new collective language.

I suppose that the restriction to a few building materials and the elaboration of
an urban building typology will create a new architectural discipline of simple
nobility and monumentality . . .

History of Architecture – History of Types
Against the anti-historicism of the modern movement we repropose the study of

the history of the city. The narrow rationalism of modern architecture is expanded to understand the city in all its typological components. The history of architecture and urban culture is seen as the history of types. Types of settlement, types of spaces (public and private), types of building, types of construction . . .

The City Within the City: Urban Life and the Quartier

If we repropose as a political choice the dynamism of urban culture as against the conservatism of suburbia, this has to be seen as an integral part of a democratic vision of society. The traffic problems which have been created by centralisation on regional and national scale can initially only be resolved on a political level through the new definition of the city with a rational organisation of the territory and finally through the reorganisation of the city into units of complex and integrated functions: quartiers, districts, homogeneous areas (Bologna), functional communities (E Saarinen). Here work, leisure and culture are integrated into compact urban districts. The size of these districts is both a physical and a social one. It can only be checked on the historical model . . . (pp38-42)

The street and the square are the only and necessary model for the reconstruction of a *public realm*. In this context, we also stress the necessary dialectical relationship between *building typology* and *morphology of urban space* and inside that dialectic, *the correct relationship of monuments* (public buildings) *and the more anonymous urban fabric* (buildings for private use) . . . (p58)

Extracts. Source: *Rational Architecture Rationelle: The Reconstruction of the European City*, Editions Archives d'Architecture Moderne (Brussels), 1978. © Leon Krier.

1978 ANTHONY VIDLER
The Third Typology

Also contained in the extended exhibition catalogue, Rational Architecture, *this essay by Anthony Vidler provides what is perhaps the most incisive account of the ideas behind the 'typo-morphological' approach to architecture as practised primarily by the Italians such as Aldo Rossi and Carlo Aymonino. A graduate of Cambridge University School of Architecture, Vidler has taught at the Architectural Association in London, the Institute of Architecture in Venice, Princeton University and now teaches at Cornell University.*

. . . In the third typology, as exemplified in the work of the new Rationalists, there is no attempt at validation. Columns, houses, and urban spaces, while linked in an unbreakable chain of continuity, refer only to their own nature as architectural elements, and their geometries are neither naturalistic nor technical but essentially architectural. It is clear that the nature referred to in these recent designs is no more nor less than the nature of the city itself, emptied of specific social content from any particular time and allowed to speak simply of its own formal condition . . .

The city is considered as a whole, its past and present revealed in its physical structure. It is in itself and of itself a new typology. This typology is not built up out of separate elements, nor assembled out of objects classified according to use, social ideology, or technical characteristics: it stands complete and ready to be decomposed into fragments. These fragments do not reinvent institutional type-forms nor repeat past typological forms: they are selected and reassembled according to criteria derived from three levels of meaning – the first, inherited from the ascribed means of the past existence of the forms; the second, derived from the specific fragment and its boundaries, and often crossing between previous types; the third, proposed by a recomposition of these fragments in a new context.

Such 'ontology of the city' is in the face of the modernist utopia, indeed radical. It denies all the social utopian and progressively positivist definitions of architecture for the last two hundred years. No longer is architecture a realm that has to relate to a hypothesized 'society' in order to be conceived and understood, no longer does 'architecture write history' in the sense of particularizing a specific

Post-Modern *77*

social condition in a specific time or place. The need to speak of [the] nature of function, of social mores – of anything, that is, beyond the nature of architectural form itself – is removed . . .

The principal conditions for the invention of object[s] and environments do not necessarily have to include a unitary statement of fit between form and use. Here it is that the adoption of the *city* as the site for the identification of the architectural typology has been seen as crucial. In the accumulated experience of the city, its public spaces and institutional forms, a typology can be understood that defies a one-to-one reading of function, but which at the same time ensures a relation at another level to a continuing tradition of city life. The distinguishing characteristic of the new ontology beyond its specifically formal aspect is that the city polis, as opposed to the single column, the hut-house, or the useful machine, is and always has been political in its essence. The fragmentation and recomposition of its spatial and institutional forms thereby can never be separated from their received and newly constituted political implications.

When typical forms are selected from the past of a city, they do not come, however dismembered, deprived of their original political and social meaning. The original sense of the form, the layers of accrued implication deposited by time and human experience cannot be lightly brushed away and certainly it is not the intention of the new Rationalists to disinfect their types. Rather, the carried meanings of these types may be used to provide a key to their newly invested meanings. The technique or rather the fundamental compositional method suggested by the Rationalists is the transformation of selected types – partial or whole – into entirely new entities that draw their communicative power and potential criteria from the understanding of this transformation . . .

The heroes of this new typology are not among the nostalgic, anti-city utopians of the nineteenth century nor even among the critics of industrial and technological progress of the twentieth, but rather among those who, as the professional servants of urban life, have directed their design skills to solving the questions of avenue, arcade, street and square, park and house, institution and equipment in a continuous typology of elements that together coheres with past fabric and present intervention to make one comprehensible experience of the city. For this typology, there is no clear set of rules for the transformations and their objects, nor any polemically defined set of historical precedents. Nor, perhaps, should there be; the continued vitality of this architectural practice rests in its essential engagement with the precise demands of the present and not in any holistic mythicization of the past. It refuses any 'nostalgia' in its evocations of history, except to give its restorations sharper focus; it refuses all unitary descriptions of the social meaning of form, recognizing the specious quality of any single ascription of social order to an architectural order; it finally refuses all eclecticism, resolutely filtering its 'quotations' through the lens of a modernist aesthetic. (pp30-32)

Extracts. Source: *Rational Architecture Rationelle: The Reconstruction of the European City*, Editions Archives d'Architecture Moderne (Brussels), 1978. © 1977 Anthony Vidler.

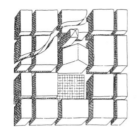
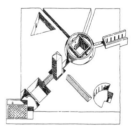

THE URBAN BLOCKS ARE THE RESULT OF A PATTERN OF STREETS AND SQUARES. THE PATTERN IS TYPOLOGI-CALLY CLASSIFIABLE.

THE PATTERN OF STREETS AND SQUARES IS THE RESULT OF THE POSITION OF THE BLOCKS. THE BLOCKS ARE TYPOLOGICALLY CLASSIFIABLE.

THE STREETS AND SQUARES ARE PRECISE FORMAL TYPES. THESE PUBLIC ROOMS ARE TYPOLOGICALLY CLASSIFIABLE.

Leon Krier, The Three Models to Conceive Urban Spaces, 1972 – the blocks are the result of a street and square pattern, the streets and squares represent the result of the position of the blocks, the streets and squares are precise spatial types

1979 CHRISTOPHER ALEXANDER
The Timeless Way of Building

Alexander's pursuit of unselfconscious architecture resulted in a series of books including The Oregon Experiment, A Pattern Language, The Timeless Way of Building *and* The Linz Cafe. *The Timeless Way is the most direct expression of the philosophy behind Alexander's later views on method and at the same time the most forceful repudiation of the reductive rationalism he had advocated in* Notes on the Synthesis of Form. *Alexander has produced only a relatively small corpus of buildings, reaching a wider audience through his writing and research. He has been associated with the School of Architecture at the University of California, Berkeley, for the past three decades, carrying out research through the Center for Environmental Structure.*

The Timeless Way
A building or a town will only be alive to the extent that it is governed by the timeless way.

1 It is a process which brings order out of nothing but ourselves; it cannot be attained, but it will happen of its own accord, if we will only let it.

The Quality
To seek the timeless way we must first know the quality without a name.

2 There is a central quality which is the root criterion of life and spirit in man, a town, a building, or a wilderness. This quality is objective and precise, but it cannot be named.

3 The search which we make for this quality, in our own lives, is the central search of any person, and the crux of any individual person's story. It is the search for those moments and situations when we are most alive.

4 In order to define this quality in buildings and in towns, we must begin by understanding that every place is given its character by certain patterns of events that keep happening there.

5 These patterns of events are always interlocked with certain geometric patterns in the space. Indeed, as we shall see, each building and each town is ultimately made out of these patterns in the space, and out of nothing else: they are the atoms and the molecules from which a building or a town is made.

6 The specific patterns out of which a building or a town is made may be alive or dead. To the extent they are alive, they let our inner forces loose, and set us free; but when they are dead, they keep us locked in inner conflict.

7 The more living patterns there are in a place – a room, a building, or a town – the more it comes to life as an entirety, the more it glows, the more it has that self-maintaining fire which is the quality without a name.

8 And when a building has this fire, then it becomes a part of nature. Like ocean waves, or blades of grass, its parts are governed by the endless play of repetition and variety created in the presence of the fact that all things pass. This is the quality itself.

The Gate

To reach the quality without a name we must then build a living pattern language as a gate.

9 This quality in buildings and in towns cannot be made but only generated, indirectly, by the ordinary actions of the people, just as a flower cannot be made, but only generated from the seed.

10 The people can shape buildings for themselves, and have done it for centuries, by using languages which I call pattern languages. A pattern language gives each person who uses it the power to create an infinite variety of new and unique buildings, just as his ordinary language gives him the power to create an infinite variety of sentences.

11 These pattern languages are not confined to villages and farm society. All acts of building are governed by a pattern language of some sort, and the patterns in the world are there, entirely because they are created by the pattern languages which people use.

12 And, beyond that, it is not just the shape of towns and buildings which comes from pattern languages – it is their quality as well. Even the life and beauty of the most awe-inspiring great religious buildings came from the languages their buildings used.

13 But in our time the languages have broken down. Since they are no longer shared, the processes which keep them deep have broken down; and it is therefore virtually impossible for anybody, in our time, to make a building live.

14 To work our way towards a shared and living language once again, we must first learn to discover patterns which are deep, and capable of generating life.

15 We may then gradually improve these patterns which we share, by testing them against experience: we can determine, very simply, whether these patterns make

our surroundings live, or not, by recognizing how they make us feel.

16 Once we have understood how to discover individual patterns which are alive, we may then make a language for ourselves from any building task we face. The structure of the language is created by the network of connections among individual patterns: and the language lives, or not, as a totality, to the degree these patterns form a whole.

17 Then finally, from separate languages for different building tasks, we can create a larger structure still, a structure of structures, evolving constantly, which is the common language for a town. This is the gate.

The Way

Once we have built the gate, we can pass through it to the practice of the timeless way.

18 Now we shall begin to see in detail how the rich and complex order of a town can grow from thousands of creative acts. For once we have a common pattern language in our town, we shall all have the power to make our streets and buildings live, through our most ordinary acts. The language, like a seed, is the genetic system which gives our millions of small acts the power to form a whole.

19 Within this process, every individual act of building is a process in which space gets differentiated. It is not a process of addition, in which preformed parts are combined to create a whole, but a process of unfolding, like the evolution of an embryo, in which the whole precedes the parts, and actually gives birth to them, by splitting.

20 The process of unfolding goes step by step, one pattern at a time. Each step brings just one pattern to life; and the intensity of the result depends on the intensity of each one of these individual steps.

21 From a sequence of these individual patterns, whole buildings with the character of nature will form themselves within your thoughts, as easily as sentences.

22 In the same way, groups of people can conceive their larger public buildings, on the ground, by following a common pattern language, almost as if they had a single mind.

23 Once the buildings are conceived like this, they can be built, directly, from a few simple marks made in the ground – again within a common language, but directly, and without the use of drawings.

24 Next several acts of building, each one done to repair and magnify the product of the previous acts, will slowly generate a larger and more complex whole than any single act can generate.

25 Finally, within the framework of a common language, millions of individual acts of building will together generate a town which is alive, and whole, and unpredictable, without control. This is the slow emergence of the quality without a name, as if from nothing.

26 And as the whole emerges, we shall see it take that ageless character which gives the timeless way its name. This character is a specific, morphological character, sharp, precise, which must come into being any time a building or a town becomes alive: it is the physical embodiment, in buildings of the quality without a name.

The Kernel of the Way

And yet the timeless way is not complete, and will not fully generate the quality without a name, until we leave the gate behind.

27 Indeed this ageless character has nothing, in the end, to do with languages. The language, and the processes which stem from it, merely release the fundamental order which is native to us. They do not teach us, they only remind us of what we know already, and of what we shall discover time and time again, when we give up our ideas and opinions, and do exactly what emerges from ourselves. (ppix-xv)

The excerpted text is the detailed Table of Contents from Christopher Alexander, *The Timeless Way of Building*, Oxford University Press (New York), 1979. © Christopher Alexander.

Christopher Alexander, Eishen Gakuen High School, Pattern of Great Hall, 1985-87

1980 DOLORES HAYDEN

What Would a Non-Sexist City Be Like?
Speculations on Housing, Urban Design,
and Human Work

A professor of architecture, urbanism and American studies at Yale
University, Dolores Hayden has focused her research and writing on
feminist and gender issues in architecture and urban design. Hayden's
is one of the most significant and persuasive voices taking the femi-
nist perspective, offering both theoretical positions and practical solu-
tions for a more egalitarian built environment.

A program to achieve economic and environmental justice for women requires, by definition, a solution that overcomes the traditional divisions between the household and the market economy, the private dwelling and the workplace. One must transform the economic situation of the traditional homemaker, whose skilled labor has been unpaid but economically and socially necessary to society; one must also transform the domestic situation of the employed woman. If architects and urban designers were to recognize all employed women and their families as a constituency for new approaches to planning and design and were to reject all previous assumptions about a 'woman's place' in the home, what could we do? Is it possible to build non-sexist neighborhoods and design non-sexist cities? What would they be like? . . .

The task of reorganizing both home and work can only be accomplished by organizations of homemakers, women and men dedicated to making changes in the ways that Americans deal with private life and public responsibilities. They must be small, participatory organizations with members who can work together effectively. I propose calling such groups HOMES (Homemakers Organization for a More Egalitarian Society) . . .

A program broad enough to transform housework, housing and residential neighborhoods must: (1) involve both men and women in the unpaid labor associated with housekeeping and child care on an equal basis; (2) involve both men and women in the paid labor force on an equal basis; (3) eliminate residential segregation by class, race, and age; (4) eliminate all federal, state, and local programs and laws that offer implicit or explicit reinforcement of the unpaid role of the female homemaker; (5) minimize unpaid domestic labor and wasteful energy consumption; (6) maximize real choices for households concerning recreation and sociability . . .

Suppose forty households in a US metropolitan area formed a HOMES group . . . There would need to be forty private dwelling units, ranging in size from efficiency to three bedrooms, all with private, fenced outdoor space. In addition to the private housing the group would provide the following collective activities: (1) a day-care center with landscaped outdoor space . . . (2) a laundromat providing laundry service; (3) a kitchen providing lunches for the day-care center, take-out evening meals, and 'meals on wheels' for elderly people in the neighborhood; (4) a grocery depot, connected to a local food cooperative; (5) a garage with two vans providing dial-a-ride service and meals-on-wheels; (6) a garden (or allotments) where some food can be grown; (7) a home help office providing helpers for the elderly, the sick and employed parents whose children are sick. The use of all these collective services should be voluntary; they would exist in addition to private dwelling units and private gardens . . .

I believe that attacking the conventional division between public and private space should become a socialist and feminist priority in the 1980s. Women must transform the sexual division of domestic labor, the privatized economic basis of domestic work, and the spatial separation of homes and workplaces in the built environment if they are to be equal members of society . . .

When all homemakers recognize that they are struggling against both gender stereotypes and wage discrimination, when they see that social, economic, and environmental changes are necessary to overcome these conditions, they will no longer tolerate housing and cities, designed around the principles of another era, that proclaim that 'a woman's place is in the home'.

Extracts. Source: Catherine Stimpson, Elsa Dixler, Martha J Nelson and Kathryn B Yatrakis (eds), *Women and the American City*, University of Chicago Press (Chicago), 1981. © 1980 University of Chicago Press. Originally published as a supplement to *Signs*, vol 5, 1980.

1980   CHARLES JENCKS
Towards a Radical Eclecticism

This essay was included in the catalogue of the First International Exhibition of Architecture held at the 1980 Venice Biennale, entitled The Presence of the Past. The exhibition, organised by Paolo Portoghesi, was one of the defining events of the Post-Modern movement. In the same way that the International Style exhibition of 1932 at the New York Museum of Modern Art helped crystallise the different strands of Modernism into a recognised style, The Presence of the Past focused the concerns of Post-Modernism for a wider audience.

What is Architecture to be About?

This is the question facing architects in a consumer society. The basic problems are social, political and metaphysical, not formal and technical. Our society is quite adept at reaching formal and technical standards of excellence, at least in Japan and America, but it has not brought forth either very exciting building tasks or metaphysical mandates. Hence the Surrationalist fantasies (Bofill, OMA, Koolhaas), trying to fill a vacuum; hence the syndicalist utopias or modest attempts at participation (the Kriers, Erskine, Kroll); hence the great American attempt at revivalism and significant cultural form. All these Post-Modern tendencies are trying to give birth to a new architecture before consumer society has given it a mandate; it is the sound, as the saying goes, of one hand clapping. It may be, however, the only sound a consumer society is willing to allow, immersed as it is in the joys of private life. This culture is essentially passive, waiting for the directions from its self-appointed elites. What messages it receives today are extraordinary in their plurality and breadth. To discriminate among these messages, as well as send them, has also fallen to an elite, that is the 'communications industry'. So we are at a most curious juncture in history that isn't in fact a turning point at all. Rather we are in for 'more of the same', much more, in fact a recapitulation of all historical architecture including that of the recent past. We are, as you will guess, in a Radically Eclectic age, an age that makes the 1870s with its relative paucity of fifteen styles look like an integrated culture. We have more styles and ideologies than they did and they probably mean less; have less conviction and semantic meaning. Gothic Revival is now a-religious and doesn't carry Pugin's moralistic fervour; Stirling at one time had Gothic arcades for his Stuttgart Museum before they were changed into Romanesque. In our *musée imaginaire*, in our museum city that has recapitulated world history, styles have lost their overall meaning and become, instead, genres – classifiers of mood and theme. This is a major point of Radical Eclecticism; it substitutes a time-bound semiotic view of architectural form for the monolithic view of the past, the Modern and Neo Gothic view. Its approach to style and meaning is relativistic, related to the context of the culture being designed for, and this entails changing those styles and meanings perhaps after they have swung too far one way, or, by contrast, need support or confirmation. The two ideas behind this are plenitude and pluralism, the idea that, given the choice, people would rather have a variety of experiences and that, as history proceeds, a plenitude of values, a richness is created on which it is possible to draw. These architectural loans must, to repeat a point, be repaid with interest, that is reinvention. In short the content of our buildings is not the Space Age or the Energy Problem, not the Machine Age or High Technology, but the variety of cultural experience, the plurality of psychic, social and metaphysical states possible to people. For the museum we have the museum city, for a single meaning of history we have all of history, for a single political view we have the res publica and for architecture we hope for an eclecticism that is radical. A Radical Eclecticism should be founded on requirements of function, hints of the place and the desires of symbolism; it should respond to the tastes of the users while, if it is radical, extending and challenging them with new meaning.

Extracts. Source: *The Presence of the Past*, catalogue to the First International Exhibition of Architecture. La Biennale di Venezia, The Corderia of the Arsenale, Architectural Section, Edizioni La Biennale di Venezia, Electa Editrice (Milan), 1980. © Edizioni 'La Biennale di Venezia' Venice.

Arata Isozaki, Disney Building, Florida, 1989-91 – from different systems, each eclected for a special function

1980   PAOLO PORTOGHESI
The End of Prohibitionism

Another of the essays included in the catalogue of the exhibition The
Presence of the Past *at the 1980 Venice Biennale, Paolo Portoghesi's
(b 1931, Rome) contribution is a clear development of his activities
as architect and architectural historian, a combination not atypical in
Italy. While the Italians have produced some of the most striking
and convincing Modernist architecture (Sant'Elia, Terragni), they have,
more than others, lived with history. The result is an ambivalence well
expressed in Portoghesi's essay.*

The re-proposed 'presence of the past' is neither simply ironic, nor, least of all,
purely unnecessary and consumerist. It contains a lot of truth because it realizes
its impotence in elaborating a real psychological conflict. The possibility of confronting and resolving the problem of replanning the city depends on overcoming
this conflict. This is seen in the unresolved contradiction between historic centers
and periphery, between the space of meaning and quality (that of the ancient city)
and the space of quantity and the absence of meaning (that of the periphery).
Closed in the ghetto of the ancient city, memory has become inoperative, a factor
of separation and privilege. Circulating once again in the present city beyond the
fences erected to defend its alleged purity, memory can help us leave our impotence behind, and exchange the magical act that once deluded us into exorcizing
the past and building a new world without roots, for the lucid and rational act of
the reappropriation of the forbidden fruit . . .

The past whose presence we claim is not a golden age to be recuperated. It is not
Greece as the 'childhood of the world' which Marx talked about, ascertaining the
universality, duration and exemplariness of certain aspects of European tradition. The
past with its 'presence' that can today contribute to making us children of our time is
the past of the world. In our field, it is the whole system of architecture with its finite
but inexhaustible sum of experiences connected or connectable by a society which
has refused a monocentric culture, a main tradition with no competition.

Nineteenth-century eclecticism had already recognized this curvilinear horizon that makes us embrace a visual field of 360° and denies us the privilege of a
fixed orientation with respect to which everything is measured. But the eclecticism of that time, like old imperialism, proceeded from a sort of natural history of

civilization, from a systematic cataloguing of closed repertories or from their naïve mixture directed towards the realization of characteristic beauty or towards assigning styles a value of illusionistic contents in the great history of urban typologies.

The relationship with the history of architecture which the 'post-modern' condition makes possible doesn't need the eclectic method any more, because it can count on a form of 'disenchantment', on a much greater psychological detachment. The civilization of the quantified image, the civilization of sacred images that knows the barbarities of the new imperialism and its progressive shattering can use the past without being more involved in illusory revivals or in naïve philological operations. History is the 'material' of logical and constructive operations whose only purpose is that of joining the real and imaginary through communication mechanisms whose effectiveness can be verified; it is material utilizable for the socialization of aesthetic experience, since it presents sign systems of great conventional value which make it possible to think and make others think through architecture.

In this sense, architecture can once again be returned to the places and regions of the earth without a return to a racial or religious metaphysic. It can be the means of removal of the old Eurocentric system based on the myth of classicism. It can also be the recognition of the relative and partial validity of all conventional systems provided that one accepts belonging to a polycentric network of experiences, all deserving to be heard. (pp10-12)

Extracts. Source: *The Presence of the Past*, catalogue to the First International Exhibition of Architecture, The Corderia of the Arsenale, La Biennale di Venezia, Architectural Section, Edizioni La Biennale di Venezia, Electal Editrice (Milan), 1980. © Edizioni 'La Biennale di Venezia' Venice.

1980   SITE

Notes on the Philosophy of SITE

> A multi-disciplinary group based in New York concerned with archi-
> tecture and environmental art, SITE (originally Sculpture in the Envi-
> ronment) came to define their work as 'de-architecture'. The idea was
> set out by SITE principal James Wines (b 1932, Oak Park, Illinois) in
> several articles in Architecture + Urbanism over 1974 and 1975.
> The group, whose other members include Emilio Sousa, Alison Sky
> and Michelle Stone, are perhaps best known for the series of Best
> Products showrooms using tilted or disintegrating facades.

The basic purpose of De-architecture, in both its theoretical and built form, is to
explore new possibilities for changing professional and popular response to the
sociological, psychological, and aesthetic significance of architecture and public
space. With these objectives in mind, the following statements are intended as a
summary of SITE's particular applications of the concept.

Rather than treat art as a decorative accessory to architecture, SITE's work is
a hybrid fusion of both disciplines, with the purpose of eliminating the conventional distinctions between art and architecture as separate entities.

For SITE, architecture is the *subject matter* or *raw material* of art, and not the
objective of a design process. A building is usually treated as a given quantity, as a
paradigm or typology, with all of its intrinsic sociological significance conditioned
by habitual use and reflex identification. To completely re-create an architectural
type – whether in the form of a house, civic center, or a market place – would, in
SITE's view, destroy its more important associative content. Therefore, rather than
impose a totally new design, SITE endeavors to expand or invert the already
inherent meaning of a building by changing the structure very little on a physical
level, but a great deal on a psychological level.

SITE's work rejects Modern design's traditional preoccupation with architecture as form and space, in favor of architecture as information and thought; a shift
in priority from physical to mental . . .

It is SITE's opinion that architecture is the only intrinsic public art – all others,
like painting, sculpture, and crafts, being only incidentally or by conscious choice
a part of the public domain. Assuming that this public status implies communication to the largest number of people under the least exclusive circumstances, SITE

has chosen to work primarily in the most populated and commonplace of urban/suburban situations.

Traditional architectural iconography has been based on specific symbols which, by continuous repetition, reinforce the institutions they signify. SITE's imagery is a complete inversion of this legacy – reversing the appearance of institutional security and replacing it with a message of ambiguity and equivocation.

SITE's work often uses such phenomenological concepts as indeterminacy, entropy, fragmentation, and disorder as sources for architectural imagery. These concerns parallel, from an aesthetic standpoint, the scientific principles, of relativity, dematerialization, and infinity. As an alternative to architecture's familiar celebrations of rational order, certain of SITE's structures suggest that a building is conclusive (and most intriguing) at that moment of its greatest indecision.

From all indications, a distrust of technological, economic, and political establishments appears to be one of the few consolidating forces uniting contemporary American society. A responsive architectural imagery, in SITE's view, should be a reflection of this disenchantment and a critical monitor of these declining institutions.

The term 'De-architecture' has been criticized as sounding negative; however, in a world where contraction and short supply will define the industrialized civilizations' options for the future, negation has become the philosophical equivalent of a new optimism.

In summary, SITE's philosophy is based on a commitment to the sociological and psychological content of architecture. Without forfeiting the practical needs of shelter, it is the objective of SITE to increase the communicative level of buildings and public spaces by drawing upon sources outside of architecture's formal, functional, and symbolic conventions.

In a world of disparity, indeterminacy, and change, it has become meaningless for architecture to persist as a celebration of inflexible services or extraneous institutions – and, even worse, as a celebration of itself. We presently lack the cultural estate and unifying ideals necessary to sustain those early 20th-century principles with any degree of urgency or confidence. As an alternative SITE proposes that, if architecture is to regain its status as a meaningful public art, it should be questioned in most of its prevailing definitions in order to become responsive to the diversity, complexity, and subconscious motivations of our pluralist society. (pp15-17)

Extracts. Source: SITE, with contributions by Pierre Restany and Bruno Zevi, *SITE: Architecture as Art*, Academy Editions (London), 1980. © SITE.

1982   MICHAEL GRAVES

A Case for Figurative Architecture

One of the New York Five along with Peter Eisenman, Charles Gwathmey, John Hejduk and Richard Meier, Michael Graves (b 1934, Indianapolis) was included for his 'White', rationalist purism. Yet of the five, Graves was the most allusive and over the 1970s grew increasingly concerned with symbol, representation, history and myth. He became a leading figure of Post-Modernism both through his teaching and with buildings such as the Plocek House, New Jersey (1977), the Portland Public Services Building, Portland, Oregon (1982), the Humana Medical Corporation, Louisville, Kentucky (1984) and later work for Walt Disney World in Florida.

While any architectural language, to be built, will always exist within the technical realm, it is important to keep the technical expression parallel to an equal and complementary expression of ritual and symbol. It could be argued that the Modern Movement did this, that as well as its internal language, it expressed the symbol of the machine and therefore practised cultural symbolism. But in this case, the machine is retroactive, for the machine itself is a utility. So this symbol is not an external allusion but rather a second, internalized reading. A significant architecture must incorporate both internal and external expressions. The external language, which engages inventions of culture at large, is rooted in a figurative, associational, and anthropomorphic attitude.

We assume that in any construct, architectural or otherwise, technique, the art of making something, will always play a role. However, it should also be said that the components of architecture have not only derived from pragmatic necessity but also evolved from symbolic sources ... Architectural elements require this distinction, one from another, in much the same way as language requires syntax; without variations among architectural elements, we will lose the anthropomorphic or figurative meaning. The elements of any enclosure include wall, floor, ceiling, column, door, and window. It might be wondered why these elements, given their geometric similarity in some cases (for example, floor and ceiling) must be understood differently. It is essential in any symbolic construction to identify the thematic differences between various parts of the whole. If the floor as ground is regarded as distinct from the soffit as sky, then the material, textural, chromatic, and decorative inferences are dramatically different. Yet in a formal sense, these are both horizontal planes.

We as architects must be aware of the difficulties and strengths of thematic and figural aspects of the work. If the external aspects of the composition, that part of our language which extends beyond internal technical requirements, can be thought of as the resonance of man and nature, we quickly sense an historical pattern of external language. All architecture before the Modern Movement sought to elaborate the themes of man and landscape. Understanding the building involves both association with natural phenomena (for example, the ground is like the floor), and anthropomorphic allusions (for example, a column is like a man). These two attitudes within the symbolic nature of building were probably originally in part ways of justifying the elements of architecture in a prescientific society. However, even today, the same metaphors are required for access to our own myths and ritual within the building narrative . . .

In making a case for figurative architecture, we assume that the thematic character of the work is grounded in nature and is simultaneously read in a totemic or anthropomorphic manner . . .

In this discussion . . . an argument is made for the figural necessity of each particular element and, by extension, of architecture as a whole. While certain monuments of the Modern Movement have introduced new spatial configurations, the cumulative effect of nonfigurative architecture is the dismemberment of our former cultural language of architecture. This not so much an historical problem as it is one of a cultural continuum. It may be glib to suggest that the Modern Movement be seen not so much as an historical break but as an appendage to the basic and continuing figurative mode of expression. However, it is nevertheless crucial that we re-establish the thematic associations invented by our culture in order to fully allow the culture of architecture to represent the mythic and ritual aspirations of society. (pp11-13)

Extracts. Source: Karen Vogel Wheeler, Peter Arnell and Ted Bickford (eds), *Michael Graves: Buildings and Projects 1966-1981*, Rizzoli (New York), 1982. © 1982 Michael Graves.

1982 OSWALD MATHIAS UNGERS
Architecture as Theme

In his manifesto of 1960 with Reinhard Gieselmann, Oswald Mathias Ungers (b 1926, Kaisersesch) declared, 'Form is the expression of spiritual content,' and called for a move away from functionalism and the use of technology for its own sake. While he equally repudiated following a tradition for its own sake, Ungers has been particularly sensitive to place and promoted a contextualist approach. In Architecture as Theme, he sets out a series of specific tropes that serve to reveal the temporal as well as the spatial quality of architecture.

The Theme of Transformation or the Morphology of the Gestalt

Formation is inconceivable without transformation and inversely there is no transformation that does not produce new formation in its turn. In this connection the phenomenon of transformation may be seen as a process that exerts a determining influence on creative thought, since not only does it inform thought as far as contrasts and alternatives are concerned, but above all with respect to complex interdependencies and correlations . . . (p13)

This concept can be clarified by referring to . . . a supporting element: this can be a pole, beam, pillar, bar, strut, post, pier or column, according to the situation in which it is found and according to the concept that the architect wishes to express by it. So, architecture can be liberated from a reduction to purely functional thought by the adoption of morphological transformation as an instrument of design . . . (pp13-14)

When architecture is seen as a continuous process, in which theses and antitheses are dialectically integrated, or as a process, in which history is as closely involved as anticipation of history, in which the past has the same weight as looking forward to the future, then the process of transformation is not only the instrument of design, but is the very object of design . . . (p15)

Trajan's shrine on the island of Philae in Egypt and KF Schinkel's project for the Acropolis constitute the best examples of dialectical architecture, founded on the principle of transformation . . . (p17)

The Theme of Assemblage or the Coincidence of Opposites

The criteria by which one makes an evaluation of architecture usually aim at a homogeneous, definitive and complete situation, while contradictions are seen as something that [have] to be eliminated. The complete form stands in the middle and provides simultaneously both measure and limit. All value judgements would be overturned if what is incomplete, or in other words the unresolved contradiction, was placed at the centre of the conception and of the plan and hence of architectural studies . . . (p31)

The building as a fragment, as discontinuous object, composed of different unrelated parts, is not, if looked at historically, unusual . . . The concept of fragmentary does, in this context, not at all mean the same thing as the concept of romantic. Rather it unfailingly contains a stratification, a degree of complexity not met with in an architectural work or urban structure that is conceived as a unity . . . (pp31-33)

Here we have a principle that brings together, in a higher conception based on the unresolved contradiction, both creative contradiction and continuity, spontaneity and plan, chance as much as the established order . . .

Persius overcame the constriction of the unitary style when he designed the Teufelsbrücke in the Schlosspark of Glienicke by combining different fragments. He made use of the archaic, natural element as well as the technical, refined one, original elements along with the most sophisticated ones; the complete work is an abridgement of the whole spectrum between natural and artistic. (p33)

The Theme of Incorporation or the 'Doll within the Doll'

The theme of the doll inside the doll or – to put it another way – of the Russian Easter egg . . . describes a sequence which could theoretically carry on indefinitely, a continual process that is no longer intelligible in logical terms . . .

This is recognizable in the historical development of buildings or even of towns. Starting from a simple cell, rich and complex spatial structures are often built up . . .

The Church of St Severinus in Cologne may be seen as the prototype of growth of this kind. Here five different layouts of five churches that were built one on top of the other in succession are superimposed, and elements of each are still in existence and can be distinguished. Here the theme of the doll inside a doll or of the house within a house has operated over the course of time, and therefore more or less by chance. But it can be consciously introduced into architecture as a principle of design, a principle that makes differentiation and variety possible in very diverse tasks. (p57)

The Theme of Assimilation or the Adap[ta]tion to the 'Genius Loci'

Architecture only stays alive when it is in a constant dialogue with the genius loci for which it is created. It takes its theme from the environment in which it is set and develops the form, the language, the formal repertory, or the vocabulary, out of this context. When it has no relationship with the spatial and conceptual conditions architecture becomes an empty gesture, devoid of meaning. The theme of adaptation to the genius loci is at the same time the thematization of architecture as a dialogue with tradition, with historically formed values and with their enhancement in order to form a new artistic expression. (p77)

The Theme of Imagination or 'The World as Idea'
. . . There is a strong need in every man to create himself a reality that corresponds to his capacity for perception. A reality in which objects are significant not because they are verifiable and measurable, but as a result of the image that they communicate.

. . . If . . . the process of design starts out with a conceptual image that forms the basic principle around which the whole is organized, then it is possible to develop, within this image, the full range of fantasy. Designing with conceptual images makes it possible to move from pragmatic to creative thought, from the metric space of number to the visionary space of coherent systems. This is a thought process that is based on qualitative rather than quantitative values and which concentrates more on synthesis than on analysis. (p107)

Extracts. Source: Oswald Mathius Ungers, *Architettura con tema/Architecture as Theme*, Lotus Documents, Electa (Milan), 1982. © Gruppo Editoriale Electa Milano.

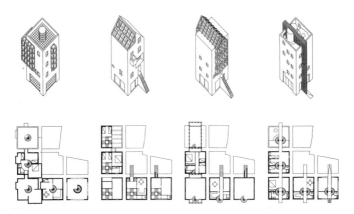

Oswald Mathius Ungers, Typology of Detached Houses Showing a Different Conception Based on a Constant Underlying Grid, 1982

1983 KENNETH FRAMPTON

Towards a Critical Regionalism: Six Points for an Architecture of Resistance

Kenneth Frampton (b 1930) a Professor of architecture at Columbia University, is an historian and critic of Modern architecture. A version of this essay was first published in Perspecta *in 1982 and a year later in Hal Foster's collection* The Anti-Aesthetic: Essays on Postmodern Culture. *Including pieces by Jurgen Habermas and Conrad Jameson, the book illustrated the increasing importance of critical theory in the development of the Post-Modernist debate. Frampton's contribution attempts to drive a middle course between the extremes of Enlightenment idealism and New Historicist materialism.*

3 Critical Regionalism and World Culture

Architecture can only be sustained today as a critical practice if it assumes an *arrière-garde* position, that is to say, one which distances itself equally from the Enlightenment myth of progress and from a reactionary, unrealistic impulse to return to the architectonic forms of the preindustrial past. A critical *arrière-garde* has to remove itself from both the optimization of advanced technology and the ever-present tendency to regress into nostalgic historicism or the glibly decorative. It is my contention that only an *arrière-garde* has the capacity to cultivate a resistant, identity-giving culture while at the same time having discreet recourse to universal technique.

It is necessary to qualify the term *arrière-garde* so as to diminish its critical scope from such conservative policies as Populism or sentimental Regionalism with which it has often been associated. In order to ground *arrière-gardism* in a rooted yet critical strategy, it is helpful to appropriate the term Critical Regionalism as coined by Alex Tzonis and Liane Lefaivre in 'The Grid and the Pathway' (1981) . . .

The fundamental strategy of Critical Regionalism is to mediate the impact of universal civilization with elements derived *indirectly* from the peculiarities of a particular place. It is clear from the above that Critical Regionalism depends on maintaining a high level of critical self-consciousness. It may find its governing inspiration in such things as the range and quality of the local light, or in a *tectonic* derived from a particular structural mode, or in the topography of a given site . . .

The case can be made that Critical Regionalism as a cultural strategy is as much a bearer of *world culture* as it is a vehicle of *universal civilization*. And while it is obviously misleading to conceive of our inheriting world culture to the same degree as we are all heirs to universal civilization, it is nonetheless evident that since we are, in principle, subject to the impact of both, we have no choice but to take cognizance today of their interaction. In this regard the practice of Critical Regionalism is contingent upon a process of double mediation. In the first place, it has to 'deconstruct' the overall spectrum of world culture which it inevitably inherits; in the second place, it has to achieve, through synthetic contradiction, a manifest critique of universal civilization (pp20-21) . . .

4 The Resistance of the Place-Form

While we may remain sceptical as to the merit of grounding critical practice in a concept so hermetically metaphysical as Being, we are, when confronted with the ubiquitous placelessness of our modern environment, nonetheless brought to posit, after Heidegger, the absolute precondition of a bounded domain in order to create an architecture of resistance. Only such a defined boundary will permit the built form to stand against – and hence literally to withstand in an institutional sense – the endless processal flux of the Megalopolis.

The bounded place-form, in its public mode, is also essential to what Hannah Arendt has termed 'the space of human appearance', since the evolution of legitimate power has always been predicated upon the existence of the 'polis' and upon comparable units of institutional and physical form. While the political life of the Greek polis did not stem directly from the physical presence and representation of the city-state, it displayed in contrast to the Megalopolis the cantonal attributes of urban density . . .

While the strategy of Critical Regionalism as outlined above addresses itself mainly to the maintenance of an *expressive density and resonance* in an architecture of resistance (a cultural density which under today's conditions could be said to be potentially liberative in and of itself since it opens the user to manifold *experiences*), the provision of a place-form is equally essential to critical practice, inasmuch as a resistant architecture, in an institutional sense, is necessarily dependant on a clearly defined domain. Perhaps the most generic example of such an urban form is the perimeter block although other related, introspective types may be evoked, such as the galleria, the atrium, the forecourt and the labyrinth. (pp24-25)

5 Culture vs Nature: Topography, Context, Climate, Light and Tectonic Form

Critical Regionalism necessarily involves a more directly dialectical relation with nature than the more abstract, formal traditions of modern avant-garde architecture allow . . .

The bulldozing of an irregular topography into a flat site is clearly a technocratic gesture which aspires to a condition of absolute *placelessness*, whereas the terracing of the same site to receive the stepped form of a building is an engagement in the act of 'cultivating' the site.

Clearly such a mode of beholding and acting brings one close once again to Heidegger's etymology; at the same time it evokes the method alluded to by the Swiss architect Mario Botta as 'building the site'. It is possible to argue that in this last instance the specific culture of the region – that is to say, its history in both a geological and an agricultural sense – becomes inscribed into the form and realization of the work. This inscription, which arises out of 'in-laying' the building into the site, has many levels of significance, for it has a capacity to embody, in built form, the prehistory of the place, its archeological past and its subsequent cultivation and transformation across time. Through this layering into the site the idiosyncrasies of place find their expression without falling into sentimentality . . .

A constant 'regional inflection' of the form arises directly from the fact that in certain climates the glazed aperture is advanced, while in others it is recessed behind the masonry facade (or, alternatively, shielded by adjustable sun breakers).

The way in which such openings provide appropriate ventilation also constitutes an unsentimental element reflecting the nature of local culture . . .

Despite the critical importance of topography and light, the primary principle of architectural autonomy resides in the *tectonic* rather than the *scenographic*: that is to say, this autonomy is embodied in the revealed ligaments of the construction and in the way in which the syntactical form of the structure explicitly resists the action of gravity. It is obvious that this form of discourse of the load borne (the beam) and the load-bearing (the column) cannot be brought into being where the structure is masked or otherwise concealed . . .

The tectonic remains to us today as a potential means for distilling play between material, craftwork and gravity, so as to yield a component which is in fact a condensation of the entire structure. We may speak here of the presentation of a structural poetic rather than the re-presentation of a facade.

6 The Visual vs the Tactile

The tactile resilience of the place-form and the capacity of the body to read the environment in terms other than those of sight alone suggest a potential strategy for resisting the domination of universal technology . . .

One has in mind a whole range of complementary sensory perceptions which are registered by the labile body: the intensity of light, darkness, heat and cold; the feeling of humidity; the aroma of material; the almost palpable presence of masonry as the body senses its own confinement; the momentum of an induced gait and the relative inertia of the body as it traverses the floor; the echoing resonance of our own footfall . . .

Critical Regionalism seeks to complement our normative visual experience by readdressing the tactile range of human perceptions. In so doing, it endeavors to balance the priority accorded to the image and to counter the Western tendency to interpret the environment in exclusively perspectival terms . . .

The tactile opposes itself to the scenographic and the drawing of veils over the surface of reality. Its capacity to arouse the impulse to touch returns the architect to the poetics of construction and to the erection of works in which the tectonic value of each component depends upon the density of its objecthood. The tectonic and the tactile jointly have the capacity to transcend the mere appearance of the technical in much the same way as the place-form has the potential to withstand the relentless onslaught of global modernization. (pp26-29)

Extracts. Source: Hal Foster (ed), *The Anti-Aesthetic: Essays on Postmodern Culture*, Bay Press, Port Townsend (Washington), 1983. © Bay Press. A version of this essay was first published in *Perspecta*, 20, 1982.

1983   LUCIEN KROLL
The Architecture of Complexity

Architect and urbanist, Lucien Kroll (b 1927, Brussels) has been noted for his apparently anarchistic methods and aesthetic of 'organic disorder'. He was an early advocate of participatory design, an approach that produced one of his most well-known buildings, the Paramedical Faculty Buildings Complex, Catholic University of Louvain (1970-77). In The Architecture of Complexity *he examines the ways of achieving his aims within the constraints of an industrialized building process.*

Diversity

Diversity encourages creativity, while repetition anaesthetises it. Often architecture is too homogeneous, sometimes because of a self-centred desire to see buildings apart from their context, sometimes because of an exaggerated aesthetic commitment which tends to a precious 'architects' architecture'. But whatever the cause, such homogeneity makes it difficult for the users to add anything of their own, and we lose that rich resource of popular creativity which can transform a space into a place and give it life . . .

If we were able to obtain the space and the means to allow the inhabitants to organise their own buildings, they would by their own efforts generate both the diversity and the close relation to the fabric which is lacking: that has always been the case. However, with the limited and prescribed conditions under which we work today it is very difficult to achieve such ends . . .

How could one combine the advantages of organisation and spontaneity? Through real or simulated participation by inhabitants, and through our efforts to exploit the variety suggested by the place and time, we are able to produce a diversity which we push as far as the circumstances will permit . . . (pp29-30)

Our Approach to Industry

Our approach to industrial construction has been irrational and, moreover, moral: yes to industry if it produces an acceptable architecture, no if it proposes an image incompatible with or destroys the social and cultural context . . .

We have always opposed the alarming spread of heavy prefabricated concrete systems and their tendency autistically to dominate areas swept clean of all historical reference, but we have persisted in our belief nonetheless that industrial know-how could one day provide the means for an organic architecture . . . (p31)

Our Sly Engineering

How is mass housing usually conceived? First the dwelling types are worked out in detail, then they are lined up and piled up around stairs and service stacks. There is no reason to avoid serial repetition, left–right handing and simple accumulation, since all elements are identical. Thus, ever obedient to the dictates of its digestive systems, arises a 'sewer architecture'.

The same kind of thinking applies also at a large scale: the blocks are set up according to rules governing roads, sewers and other services, always with a tree-like hierarchical organisation rather than a network . . .

To avoid the 'sewer' approach, one can start by interspersing single houses amongst the blocks of flats. If these are based on town-house types they can facilitate the transition between the two. This achieved, we then design the flats, but we vary them according to size, position and connections in ways that appeal to us. We do produce handed versions, but with a differing orientation we vary both layout and fenestration. We avoid dominant central staircases, preferring to set the dwellings side by side or one above the other in less rigid ways, sometimes creating maisonettes, sometimes clusters, always through empathy and not by sheer calculation. The approaches to the dwellings remain dispersed and independent: no mechanical ordering, and little centralised management . . . (pp77-78)

Industrial Components

Before they become a means of construction, components involve a redistribution of power and of roles, reversing the significance of what is built. If we fail to realise this we shall remain at the mercy of manufacturers of prefabricated systems who, knowing their products to be out-dated, yet reintroduce them – renamed overnight – as components, taking advantage of the confusion . . . (p83)

Power of the Tool Over the Product

The computer has a built-in and cunning tendency to dominate, to reorganise things in its own image (but who made it so?). It only accepts such material as it can digest, lending it in the process an absolute precision, often at a stage where a softer, vaguer approach would be more appropriate. It is logical certainly, but what if tacit, approximate, irrational aspects were the most vital? . . .

How does one resist? First one must remember that the over-precise results are only provisional hypotheses despite their final appearance and one must be determined to disbelieve them. This is only possible through making modification of data as easy as its introduction. One must also dismantle some of the automation, reduce the tendency to run on regardless, and preserve the widest possible choice of menu. This will of course both complicate the program and require more commitment from the architect-operator . . . (p106)

In current circumstances it would be illogical to favour one more super-system of construction which might turn out to be just as limited as those that have gone before: far better to make a 'giant concrete block' in all sizes with holes in any position, very cheap and available to all small firms. It should not be assembled by the manufacturer: firms are less 'industrial' when they want to take over the whole process of construction.

The geometry of components should be based on a finer modular system to determine lengths, widths, thicknesses, densities, positions of holes, connections with identical elements, with components of a different kind, and with the work of craftsmen. The tools should be adapted to ensure diversity yet take due account of economic constraints. This diversity could easily be achieved with computers: CAD could lead in turn to CAM (Manufacture) and computerised controls of orders, or CAAs (Assembly) which will automatically produce working drawings, specifications and estimates . . .

We propose claddings of a more industrial, more economic kind. Their relative crudeness can be relieved with some architectural games. Also there can be 'vegetable cladding': climbing plants add insulation, weather protection and a natural presence.

Preliminary participative consultation and later contacts prepare the inhabitants to put down roots more easily, to get to know each other and to discover how to act together upon their environment. In view of this we take the trouble to leave space for future extensions and to organise the rules of the architecture (both constructionally and culturally) to encourage such initiative. It is as much the readiness to believe as the readiness to get involved which allows a neighbourhood to regenerate itself by itself, and to develop quickly into a vital urban organ. (pp115-123)

Extracts. Source: Lucien Kroll, *The Architecture of Complexity*, BT Batsford (London),1986, translation and foreword by Peter Blundell Jones. © (translation and forward) Peter Blundell Jones. First published as *Composants – faut-il industrialiser l'architecture*, éditions SOCOREMA (Brussels), 1983. © éditions SOCOREMA.

1984 MEMPHIS

The Memphis Idea

The work of Memphis draws a taut connection between sensuality and dissent. Based in Milan, the group began to coalesce around 1980, driven primarily by the efforts and energy of Ettore Sottsass Jr (b 1917, Innsbruck, of Italian parents). Memphis produced furniture and object designs intended to provide an antidote to the tasteful banality of contemporary furniture and interiors. The result was what many would consider quintessential Post-Modern objects.

A precise Memphis idea, in the sense of a manifesto, statute, or declaration of intent, doesn't exist. It doesn't exist because to spell things out has never seemed necessary; it doesn't exist because until now actions have seemed more important than words, the ideas, decisions, and points of view having surfaced, settled and taken shape through experience; it doesn't exist because the roots, thrust and acceleration of Memphis are eminently anti-ideological.

Memphis is anti-ideological because it seeks possibilities not solutions. It is concerned above all with breaking ground, extending the field of action, broadening awareness, shaking things up, discussing conditions, and setting up fresh opportunities. This doesn't mean that the various designers, both individually and as a group, are without opinions, points of view, or stylistic propensities. The fact is that all decisions, initiatives, and inventions are treated as provisional – as tentative approaches or chance variants, not as certainties.

One might object that even this is an ideology, and maybe it is. But even so, it is an ideology whose outlines are deliberately blurred and flexible – a sort of superideology that one prefers to call an attitude. This attitude assimilates, or at least acknowledges, anthropological, sociological, and linguistic inquiry, from Levi-Strauss to Barthes to Baudrillard; and it recognizes the impact of quantum and particle physics on the theories of knowledge.

Memphis does not propose utopias. It does not set itself up, as the radical avant-gardes did, in a critical position toward design; it does not practise design as an ideological metaphor to say or demonstrate something else. Rather, it proposes design as a vehicle for direct communication, and it attempts to improve the potential of its semantic dynamics as well as to update its contents. Memphis has abandoned the myths of progress and a program of cultural regeneration capable of changing the world according to a rational design. Having also abandoned the utopias of the sixties and seventies, it has taken the first step toward the recomposition of an open and flexible design culture that is aware of history, conscious of consumption as a search for social identity and of the object as a sign through which a message is conveyed. This culture is actively engaged, as Branzi says, in the reconstruction of a system of expressive and emotional relations between man and the objects of his domestic habitat, reaching out from design to architecture and to the city . . .

Sottsass: By dint of walking among the areas of the uncertain (due to a certain mistrust), by dint of conversing with metaphor and utopia (to understand something more) and by keeping out of the way (certainly due to an innate calmness), we now find we have gained some experience; we have become good explorers. Maybe we can navigate wide, dangerous rivers, and advance into jungles where no one has ever set foot.

There is absolutely no need for concern.

Now at last we can go ahead with a light tread. The worst is over. We can sit down without too much danger and let even poisonous snakes or obscure spiders crawl over us; we can avoid mosquitos too, and eat crocodile meat with the greatest of ease, which doesn't mean excluding chocolate and cream and crêpes-suzettes au Grand Marnier. We can do – nearly – anything because, dear friends, as we were saying, we are old and skilled navigators on wide open seas.

The fact is that we aren't afraid any more, I mean, to represent or not represent things or persons, be they élite or derelicts, traditions or boorish.

Our fear of the past is gone, and so is our still more aggressive fear of the future.

Extracts. Source: Barbara Radice, *Memphis*, Rizzoli (New York), 1984. © Gruppo Editoriale Electa Milano and Thames and Hudson. Memphis as of September 1981 included: Ettore Sottsass, Architect and Designer; Renzo Brugola, Furniture Maker; Mario and Brunella Godani, Furniture Retailers; Ernesto Gismondi, President; Barbara Radice, Art Director and Coordinator; Aldo Cibic, Micheli De Lucchi, Marco Zanini, Martine Bedin, Nathalie du Pasquier, George Sowden, Matteo Thun, Architects and Designers.

1987 KISHO KUROKAWA
The Philosophy of Symbiosis

A further development of Metabolism, Kurokawa's philosophy of symbiosis draws on Buddhism, biology and a characteristically Japanese view of technology as natural. The latter perhaps helps to explain the visually rectilinear character of Kurokawa's designs, in apparent contrast to the biological concepts. Kurokawa's buildings include the Nakagin Capsule Tower, Tokyo (1972), the Sony Tower, Osaka (1973), Fukuoko Bank Headquarters, Fukuoka (1975), National Bunraku Theatre (1981), and Hiroshima City Museum of Contemporary Art (1986).

The Architecture of the Age of Life

The intercultural architecture that I advocate . . . is a hybrid architecture, in which elements of different cultures exist in symbiosis, an architecture that exists in symbiosis with the environment through the symbiosis of tradition and the most advanced technology . . .

If the architecture of the age of the machine expressed function, the architecture of the age of life expresses meaning. The plurality of life is the plurality of genes. Differences are precisely the proof of life's existence; and it is these differences which create meaning . . .

Just as the plurality of life is created by heredity, architecture acquires plurality through the inheritance of its historical tradition. This inheritance takes place on many levels, and there is no single common method by which it occurs. The Japanese style of architecture called *Sukiya* employs a method in which historical forms are followed but new techniques and materials are introduced to produce gradual change . . .

A second method of inheriting tradition is to dissect fragments of historical forms and place them freely throughout works of contemporary architecture, the method of recombining. Following this method, the meaning that the historical forms one had is lost, and in their recombination they acquire a new, multivalent signification. This method is fundamentally different from that of recreating historical architecture.

Yet another method of inheriting the architectural past is to express the invisible ideas, aesthetics, lifestyles and historical mind-sets that lay behind historical symbols and forms. Following this method, the visible historical symbols and forms are manipulated intellectually, creating a mode of expression characterised by abstraction, irony, wit, twists, gaps, sophistication and metaphor . . .

One important point of focus in the transformation from the age of the machine to the age of life is the conversion from standpoints of Eurocentrism and Logocentrism to the symbiosis of different cultures and to ecology . . .

The architecture of the age of life will be an architecture open to regional contexts, urban contexts, and nature and the environment. It will move towards a symbiosis of nature and human beings, of the environment and architecture.

In the age of life, the movement will be from dualism to the philosophy of symbiosis. Symbiosis is essentially different from harmony, compromise, amalgamation, or eclecticism. Symbiosis is made possible by recognising reverence for the sacred zone between different cultures, opposing factors, different elements, between extremes of dualistic opposition. The sacred zone of another's individuality, or a region's cultural tradition is an unknown region, though we respect that sacred zone . . .

The belief that all aspects of a particular people's lives are an inviolable sacred zone, an exclusive type of nationalism or closed regionalism, is not conducive to achieving symbiosis.

The second condition necessary to achieve symbiosis is the presence of intermediary space. Intermediary space is important because it allows the two opposing elements of a dualism to abide by common rules, to reach a common understanding. I call this a tentative understanding. Intermediary space does not exist as a definite thing. It is extremely tentative and dynamic. The presence of intermediate space makes possible a vibrant symbiosis that incorporates opposition.

As mutual penetration and mutual understanding of two opposing elements proceeds, the bounds of the intermediate space are always in motion. This process, because of the presence of intermediate space reveals the life principle itself, in all its ambivalence, multivalence and vagueness. Tolerance, the lack of clear cut boundaries, and the interpenetration of interior and exterior are special features of Japanese art, culture and architecture . . .

The Buddhist thought that runs through the base of all Japanese culture is also a philosophy of symbiosis, with the result that there is a strong natural connection between the architecture of the age of life and Japanese culture.

Intermediate space can occasionally act as a stimulus for metamorphosis. Metamorphosis is one of the special features of the life process. A larva is transformed into a butterfly, an egg into a bird, or a fish. There is no life principle more sudden or extreme. Architecturally speaking, gates, atriums, large-scale and other extraordinary spaces move people because they make them perceive some sort of leap into the extraordinary, a sudden drama that cannot be explained by the function of the space alone. Such intermediary spaces as street space, plazas, parks, waterfronts, street scenes, city walls, city gates, rivers, landmark towers and the urban infrastructures of highways and freeways play a role as stimuli that make possible the existence of individual buildings . . .

As opposed to the high-tech architecture of the age of the machine, created as a metaphor for the machine, the high-tech architecture of the age of life will be faced with the extremely difficult problem of expressing invisible technologies. The autonomy of the facades will allow for the birth of a new symbolic architecture. The expression of technology will proceed on a parallel course with the autonomy of the facade in architecture of the age of life, while the spirit of the invisible technologies of the age of life will be abstractly or symbolically expressed.

My own architecture will continue to pursue the architecture of the age of life, based on the three key concepts of metabolism, metamorphosis and symbiosis.(pp25-32)

Extracts. Source: Kisho Kurokawa, *The Philosophy of Symbiosis*, Academy Editions (London), 1994. © Academy Group Ltd and Kisho Kurokawa. The Japanese version of this text was first published in 1987 and a revised English version was published as *Intercultural Architecture: The Philosophy of Symbiosis* in 1991. A further revised edition was published in 1994.

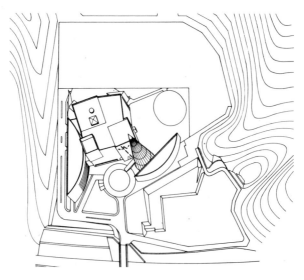

Kisho Kurokawa, Ehime Prefectural Museum of
General Science, Ehime, Japan, 1991-95

1989   STEVEN HOLL
Anchoring

'Architecture does not so much intrude on a landscape as it serves to explain it.' Steven Holl is concerned with both the metaphysical and phenomenological connection between architecture and its location. He has worked out of New York City since 1976 having studied at the University of Washington, in Rome and at the Architectural Association in London.

Anchoring

Architecture is bound to situation. Unlike music, painting, sculpture, film and literature, a construction (non-mobile) is intertwined with the experience of place. The site of a building is more than a mere ingredient in its conception. It is its physical and metaphysical foundation.

The resolution of the functional aspects of site and building, the vistas, sun angles, circulation, and access, are the 'physics' that demand the 'metaphysics' of architecture . . .

Building transcends physical and functional requirements by fusing with a place, by gathering the meaning of a situation. Architecture does not so much intrude on a landscape as it serves to explain it. Illumination of a site is not a simplistic replication of its 'context'; to reveal an aspect of place may not confirm its 'appearance'. Hence the habitual ways of seeing may well be interrupted.

Architecture and site should have an experiential connection, a metaphysical link, a poetic link.

When a work of architecture successfully fuses a building and situation, a third condition emerges. In this third entity, denotation and connotation merge; expression is linked to idea which is joined to site. The suggestive and implicit are manifold aspects of an intention . . .

Idea and Phenomena

The essence of a work of architecture is an organic link between concept and form. Pieces cannot be subtracted or added without upsetting fundamental properties. A concept, whether a rationally explicit statement or a subjective demonstration, establishes an order, a field of inquiry, a limited principle.

Within the phenomena of experience in a built construction, the organizing idea is a hidden thread connecting disparate parts with exact intention . . .

The intertwining of idea and phenomena occurs when a building is realized. Before beginning, architecture's metaphysical skeleton of time, light, space, and matter remain unordered. Modes of composition are open: line, plan, volume, and proportion await activation. When site, culture, and program are given, an order, an idea may be formed. Yet the idea is only conception . . .

An architecture of matter and tactility aims for a 'poetics of revealing' (Martin Heidegger), which requires an inspiration of joinery. Detail, this poetics of revealing, interplays intimate scaled dissonance with large scale consonance . . .

Architectural thought is the working through of phenomena initiated by idea. By 'making' we realize idea is only a seed for extension in phenomena. Sensations of experience become a kind of reasoning distinct to the making of architecture. Whether reflecting on the unity of concept and sensation or the intertwining of idea and phenomena, the hope is to unite intellect and feeling, precision with soul.

Proto-Elements of Architecture (an Open Language)

The open vocabulary of modern architecture may be extended by any compositional element, form, method, or geometry. A situation immediately sets limits. A chosen ordering concept and chosen materials begin the effort to extract the nature of the work. Prior to site, even prior to culture, a tangible vocabulary of elements of architecture remains open. Here is a beautiful potential: proto-elements of architecture.

Proto-elements: possible combinations of lines, planes, and volumes in space remain disconnected, trans-historical, and trans-cultural. They float about in a zero-ground of form without gravity but are precursors of a concrete architectonic form. There are elements that are transcultural and transtemporal, common to the ancient architecture of Kyoto and Rome. These elements are fundamental geometric precepts common to ancient Egypt and high Gothic, to twentieth-century rationalism and expressionism . . . (pp9-12)

The aspects of things that are most important for us are hidden because of their simplicity and familiarity. (L Wittgenstein)

Extracts. Source: Steven Holl, *Anchoring*, Princeton Architectural Press (New York), 1989. © Princeton Architectural Press and Steven Holl.

1991   FRANK O GEHRY
On his own House

Seldom committing his ideas to writing, Frank O Gehry (b 1929, Toronto) has carried out a polemic directly through his designs. Beginning in the 70s, he started to explore the strength and vitality of unfinished construction, using 'cheap' materials in unconventional ways, notably in his own house (Santa Monica, 1978). The results have contributed to the development of a regional style in Los Angeles, where Gehry has worked since 1962.

Throughout my life I have, by economic reality, been associated with that great mass of humanity called the middle class and have lived to this day in the neighborhoods of Canada and the US designated for people of that class. Those neighborhoods have certain common visual characteristics although there are many themes, variations on themes, and notable exceptions. I became interested in the local characteristics of the middle class neighborhood in which I chose to live around 1978. My wife picked the house and became my client for extensive re-modelling. I proceeded in the conventional process to understand the context and deal with the program.

The existing house we bought was a two-story gambrel-roof bungalow, sixty years old . . .

As I became acquainted with my future neighbors, I discovered a high incidence of camper vehicles, trailers with boats, and front lawns with automobiles on blocks ready for weekend mechanics. There was a lot of chain-link fencing, concrete-block fencing, picket fencing. Other than that, the materials of the buildings were modest . . .

Now comes to this scene yours truly, by nature a bit legalistic. Like, if you do this it means that. If you use chain link and park camper trucks in your garden, you must have chosen to do so and you must like that or feel comfortable with that. That I understand.

I walked right into the cannon. I agonized about the symbols of the middle class to which I belonged and to the particular symbols of my future neighbors. I searched my soul for an interpretation of what I found that could suit my family, myself. I dug deep into my own history and education for cues and clues and then followed my intuitions . . .

I wanted to preserve the iconic quality of the existing house and I became obsessed with having it appear that the existing structure remained intact, captured inside the new structure and interacting with it. It was my idea that the old and new could read as distinct strong self-sufficient statements which could gain from each other without compromising themselves.

The idea that buildings under construction have more energy intrigued me. My artist friends, Ed Moses and Larry Bell, had built windows, in their studios, over 2-by-4 framing. I decided to explore that idea further as I cut open the old house and built new sections. The toughness, the rawness, the immediacy of that language appealed to me, not only visually but sociologically. There was the terrible irony of our times wherein we could muster forward with incredible technological feats while struggling in our home-building with a primitive craft in serious decline. I exposed the fallacy by using the lack of craft as a visual strength, like the song: if you aren't with the craft you love, then you love the craft you are with. That led to exposed pipes for plumbing and exposed conduit for electrical.

Contrary to popular myths about my house, most of the work was carefully planned and detailed . . .

Living in one's own stew for ten years has had its mixed blessings. We have enjoyed the natural light as it has played with the building from season to season and year to year. The building is warm and friendly, comfortable and forgiving. The tough part, for me, has been trying to change things around to accommodate new needs. I find it most difficult to deal with my past self. My work has changed with time. New areas interest me. My 1978 model is a tough adversary in 1991. I was recently lamenting this fact to a reporter who innocently asked if maybe another architect could do today's needed remodelling and if so who? To which, without thinking, I replied Robert Venturi. Hey Bob, do you need some work?(pp38-39)

Extracts. Source: *GA Architect 10*, ADA. EDITA (Tokyo), 1993. © ADA EDITA.

1991   ITSUKO HASEGAWA
Architecture as Another Nature

After working in the offices of Kiyonori Kikutake, one of the founding members of the Metabolist group, and Kazuo Shinohara over the 1960s and 70s, Itsuko Hasegawa (b 1941) formed her own practice in Tokyo in 1979. She took with her the essentially Japanese and Metabolist view that sees human activity and technology as a part of nature. Her works, such as the Shonandai Cultural Centre (1990) make use of crystalline and organic forms, often using her trademark perforated metal, to create a diverse landscape of the human environment.

One of my aims is to reconsider architecture of the past, which was adapted to the climate and the land and permitted human coexistence with nature, and to see human beings and architecture as part of the earth's ecosystem. This includes a challenge to propose new design connected with new science and technology. We also ought to think seriously about restoring architecture to the people in society who use the architecture. It has long been my wish to explore ways of allowing users to participate in a true dialogue with the architect . . .

A building that is used by many people, whatever its scale, ought to be designed not as an isolated work, but as a part of something larger. In other words it must have a quality of urbanity. The city is a changing, multifaceted entity that encompasses even things that are in opposition to it. My second major aim has been to try to eliminate the gap between the community and architecture by taking such an approach to public architecture and to give architecture a new social character.

I believe any new building must make up for the topography and space that is altered because of its introduction and help create a new nature in the place of the one that used to be there. I feel any new building ought to commemorate the nature that had to be destroyed because of it and serve as a means of communicating with nature. The theme of my work is 'architecture as another nature'. We must stop thinking of architecture as something constructed according to reason and distinct from other forms of matter. In creating spaces we must recognise that human beings are a part of nature. Architecture must be responsive to the ecosystem as all of human existence is ultimately encompassed by nature.

To put it another way, architecture ought to be such that it allows us to hear the mysterious music of the universe and the rich, yet by no means transparent, world of emotions that have been disregarded by modern rationalism. We need to harness both the spirit of rationalism and the spirit of irrationalism, pay heed to both what is international and what is local, and recognise the nature of contemporary science and technology in trying to create an architecture of the society of the coming era . . .

I have consistently taken an ad hoc approach to architecture rather than an exclusionary stance. Having completed the Shonandai Cultural Centre I realise quite clearly now that I want to create an inclusive architecture that accepts a multiplicity of things rather than an architecture arrived at through reflection and elimination. The idea is to make architecture more realistic through what might be called a 'pop' reasoning that allows for diversity as opposed to a logical system of reasoning that demands extreme concentration. Such an approach represents a shift to a feminist paradigm, in the sense that an attempt is made to raise the consciousness of as many people as possible.

Human beings were born to live in a relationship of interdependence with nature. We are adaptable to change and are physically and spiritually rugged enough to live practically anywhere. I believe this 'feminine' tolerance and consciousness can help to dissolve the system in which we are presently locked and bring about a regeneration.

To sum up, buildings as well as human beings are born of nature, receive their images from nature, and return to a more profound form of life through death and destruction. Another nature will come into being when ideas of the global environment, traditional modes of thought and the 'feminine' concept are married to today's technology. The idea of 'architecture as another nature' is one I will continue to espouse until the arrival of the meta-industrial society and the creation of spaces that are both natural and comfortable to human beings. (pp14-15)

Extracts. Source: Andreas Papadakis (ed), *Architectural Design*, Profile 90, Academy Group (London), 1991. © Academy Group Ltd.

1991 ERIC OWEN MOSS
Which Truth Do You Want To Tell

'Does the bank define what's real, or are you prepared to contest that?' This is the kind of question central to the work of Eric Owen Moss (b 1943, Los Angeles). Dismissive of the linear rationality implicit in Modernism yet equally uninterested in architectural history and quotation, Moss rather seeks to puncture architectural preconceptions and extend the realms of the possible. His buildings include the Petal House, Los Angeles (1982), 8522 National Boulevard, Los Angeles (1988), Central Housing Office Building, Irvine (1989), Cineon Kodak at Samitaur (1996) and Pittard Sullivan (1997).

These buildings don't uncover a single truth, so which truth do you want to tell.

Inevitably there are experiences that affect or 'infect' the work. You can see a shift in the projects, over a period of years, from an attitude that is more extroverted (responding to the world as external stimuli), to one that is more introverted (trying to understand the world based on one's internal perceptions). And yet you can't get rid of the external quality entirely.

Architecture has the ability to expand that internal boundary. It can punch a hole in your sky. You have one frame of reference, someone else has another; we all have a certain way of understanding the world. You start to think that it's enclosed, that it has limits, but it really doesn't. You think it has those limits, even if you claim you don't.

And then somebody kicks out the lid. It's theological; it's a revelation. I borrowed the line 'hole in the sky' from a peyote user and saxophone player whom I knew a long time ago in Berkeley. He used that expression to describe LSD (which, at the time, had an alleged esoteric association). So this is the *hole in the sky theory*, which has to do with the impact of a building on people who experience it, and see that it reveals possibilities that stretch their understanding. That revelation could be social or political or something else. If they refer back to themselves, it might open up something which was not previously available.

It's not so much that there is a right and a wrong understanding; it's more that there seem to be a number of rights and wrongs overlapping. There are a number of possibilities, but not an infinite number. This is not the 'everything's relative; pick a card' theory. Buildings make specific things available . . .

There seems to be a need to find an analytical side or a causal explanation for everything. We need to be able to give things a sequence, a method, a logic. Simultaneity is a different reality, which you can't explain that way. There are possible linkages; it's not that logic doesn't exist, but that it's plural . . .

There is a good argument for the end of the modern movement in architecture. It's the end of a kind of adolescent confidence in linear scientific thinking. Science is good and it's bad and it understands and it misunderstands and all of that. But it's a one-sided view.

You can't avoid the inclinations that produced the preeminence of science in the world because you're walking around with a head. You're always trying to understand what's going on and what things mean. And even when somebody has a rule that doesn't work, it doesn't mean there are no rules; it means that you try to modify or adjust.

Working on buildings for me, is like re-writing a text. It's an attempt to contest the conventions and un-conventions in architecture and the way people experience their lives . . .

The beauty of the railroad car, which has become the *railroad car theory*, is not a kind of idolatry. It has to do with adding to the lexicon of beauty, in terms of the erogenous qualities of machinery. It also indicates a sympathy for the ability to dissect and understand things rationally. And a belief that, as one understands the world and develops technique (and techniques is manifest in equipment and machines), a philosophical point of view is translated – a way of understanding the world in a scientific sense. So, the belief in science and in the ability to make the world amenable, to rational analysis, has this 'child' in the machine, and the rational world adopts that child and says, this correlates.

But the machine moved beyond that simple correlation. It started to have the appeal of image and style beyond its role as one stage in the long history of ideas. It started to make the pages of *Vogue* magazine – it was shiny, it was precise and it always worked. And although the machine was not pretty in a conventional sense, it become associated with a certain kind of beauty – a *stylistic* beauty. That's not the kind of association I'm interested in.

The railroad car in this discussion has grease on the wheels, and sometimes goes off the tracks. It's like the helicopters Jimmy Carter sent to Iran that didn't work because they got sand caught in the propellers. It's that kind of machine . . .

But you see all the time how the obligations of the world become the reason for not doing things . . .

Does the bank define what's real, or are you prepared to contest that? When you contest it, you're attacked, as though you're oblivious, or simple-minded, or some sort of knucklehead – as though you don't really know how the world works. *And how does the world really work?* That changes too. I'm prepared to say I can alter that perception, even if it's an exception. It can be done. Not only in your head but out there. And people will recognize it. I think that's objective.

It's funny –

when you do this, you're always denying connections . . .

and then you suddenly start seeing all the connections.

You can boil it all down to one building, and quit lying.

(pp10-17)

Extracts. Source: Brad Collins and Diane Kasprowicz (eds), *Eric Owen Moss: Buildings and Projects*, Rizzoli (New York), 1991. © Rizzoli International Publications Inc.

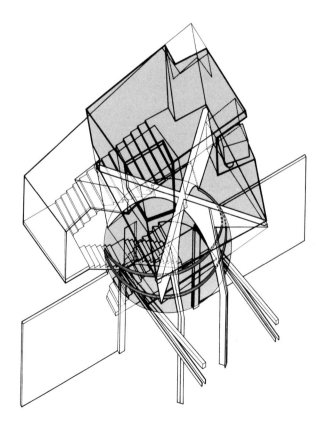

Eric Owen Moss Architects, The Box, Culver City, California, 1994

1993   FRANK O GEHRY

On The American Center, Paris
An Interview

While he is sometimes credited with helping to initiate the deconstructivist movement, Gehry firmly refuses to be categorised. On the one hand, 'when somebody calls and says, "You're an artist" I say, "no, I'm an architect,"' but on the other, he takes painting and contemporary culture as some of the sources for his architecture. His more recent works have become increasingly sculptural and expressive, including the Law School Building at Loyola University, Los Angeles (1981), the California Aerospace Museum, Los Angeles (1982), the Walt Disney Concert Hall, Los Angeles (1988-), the Vitra Design Museum, Weil-am Rhein (1992) and the American Center, Paris (1993).

Q: You've often been quoted as saying that your architecture is informed by painting and sculpture, causing some to think of you more as an artist than an architect.
FOG: I am an architect. I do think that art and architecture come from the same source. They involve some of the same struggles. My first work, when I started to do my own stuff, was encouraged by artists, not by other architects. Actually, other architects were suspicious of my work. Ed Ruscha, Ed Moses, the Los Angeles artists have always been very, very supportive. They became my support system and they are still my support system today. I am a product of the sixties. People like Ruscha, Richard Serra, Claes Oldenburg, Carl Andre – they came out of the same time, the same mentality. I have always been interested in their work. I always related to their thinking and to the expression of that time – Minimalism, Pop Art. I relate to these guys. In a lot of ways we are very similar, but I'm an architect.

Q: Where are the similarities?
FOG: I came to architecture through the fine arts and painting is still a fascination for me. Paintings are a way of training the eye. You see how people compose a canvas. The way Bruegel composes a canvas versus the way Caravaggio composes a canvas or Jasper Johns. I learned about composition from their canvases. I picked up all those visual connections and ideas. And I find myself using them sometimes ...

Piet Mondrian has inspired the window and wall elevations of many buildings from Gropius to Corbusier. I have been fortunate to have had support from living painters and sculptors. I have never felt that what artists are doing and architects are doing is very different. I've always felt there is a moment of truth when you decide what color, what size, what composition. How you get to that moment of truth is different and the end result is different . . .

The moment of truth is when you have to face yourself and put down the first line or the first brush stroke if you're an artist. There is a point where I have to make a decision, take a direction. There are a lot of them in a building. It's essentially what makes a building look like it does, like the American Center building, which is the aggregate of all those moments of truth and my selection. It's what the shape of a building will be, which comes from inside your own values, unless you copy other stuff . . .

Q: How much of a problem is the development of Bercy [site of the American Center] for you? How do you deal with a site where, eventually, thirteen other projects will surround you? Do you try to stand out? How do you make an original statement and still not be overpowering or out of scale.

FOG: . . . My perception has always been to deal with the world the way it is and to deal with it optimistically. I don't try to change it because I know I can't, so I try to fit in and mess with [it] at the same time. Working in the city requires more than a passive interaction.

Q: And how about technical problems? What place do they have in the artistry of architecture?

FOG: Solving all the functional problems is an intellectual exercise. This is a different part of my brain. It's not less important, it's just different. And I make a value out of solving all those problems, dealing with the context and the client and finding my moment of truth after I understand the problem. If you look at our process, the firm's process, you see models that show the pragmatic solution to the building without architecture. Then you see the study models that go through leading to the final scheme. We start with shapes, sculptural forms. Then we work into the technical stuff . . .

Q: It seems as though many architects have been trying to make their buildings seem more important, more substantial, by appropriating a lot of forms and details from the past, by turning to Neoclassicism.

FOG: You know, I got very angry when other architects started making buildings that look like Greek temples. I thought it was a denial of the present. It's a rotten thing to do to our children. It's as if we're telling them there's no reason to be optimistic about the future. So I got angry. That's really when I started drawing the fish, because the fish has been around for thousands and thousands of years. It's nature's creature, very fluid. It's a continuous form and it survives. And it's not contrived. To tell the truth, I didn't intend it to become a central form when it first occurred to me. It was an instinctive thing . . .

Q: . . . Pluralism seems to dominate architecture today. Does this make for incoherence, or do you think it just reflects the incoherence of the world today?

FOG: . . . As far as architecture is concerned, I think pluralism reflects the times in America . . .

I think pluralism is wonderful. That is the American way. Individual expression. It hasn't hurt us in painting and sculpture. It hasn't hurt us in literature. And it won't hurt us in architecture. (pp172-178)

Extracts. Source: *GA Architect 10*, ADA EDITA (Tokyo), 1993. © ADA EDITA.

Frank Gehry, American Centre, Paris, 1994

1993   JEFFREY KIPNIS
Towards a New Architecture: Folding

This polemic on folding and the following one by Greg Lynn developed out of Peter Eisenman's work on the subject. Both could be classified either as New- or Post-Modern. Although the emphasis is on the new it is also, for Kipnis (b 1951) on heterogeneity of the ideas rooted in the larger paradigm of Complexity Theory – hence its inclusion in this section. His books include In the Manner of Nietzsche, *1990 and, as co-editor,* Strategies in Architectural Thinking *(1991).*

'A new architecture'. Today one whispers this phrase with trepidation and embarrassment, perhaps for good reason . . . (p41)

In Post-Modernism's most virulent practices, those that use reiteration and recombination to insinuate themselves into and undermine received systems of power, a relationship to the New is maintained that is optimistic and even progressive, albeit not teleologically directed. In such post-modern practices as deconstruction, the project of the new is rejected. New intellectual, aesthetic and institutional forms, as well as new forms of social arrangements, are generated not by proposition but by constantly destabilising existing forms. New forms result as temporary restabilisations, which are then destabilised. Accelerated evolution replaces revolution, the mechanisms of empowerment are disseminated, heterogeneous spaces that do not support established categorical hierarchies are sought, a respect for diversity and difference is encouraged. Far from being nihilistic, Post-Modernism in this conception is broadly affirmative . . . (pp41-42)

Frankly, I cannot believe that in the short span of our history we have experimented with and exhausted the possibilities of form. It seems to me that every indication today is to the contrary; whether one considers the political transformations in Eastern Europe or the technological transformations that characterise today's society. The building of the catalogue of available forms, aesthetic forms, institutional forms and of forms of social arrangement has only just begun.

I have already indicated some of the broader criteria for a New Architecture. If it is not to repeat the mistakes of Modernism, it must continue to avoid the logic of erasure and replacement by participating in recombinations. As far as possible, it must seek to engender a heterogeneity that resists settling into fixed hierarchies. Furthermore, it must be an architecture, ie. a proposal of principles (though not prescriptions) for design. Finally, it must experiment with and project new forms . . . (p42)

Indicative of that detachment is the degree to which some New Architecture theorists, notably Sanford Kwinter and Greg Lynn, have shifted their attention from post-structural semiotics to a consideration of recent developments in geometry, science and the transformations of political space, a shift that is often marked as a move from a Derridian towards a Deleuzian discourse.[3]

In these writings, the Deleuzian cast is reinforced with references to Catastrophe Theory – the geometry of event-space transformations – and to the new Biology. Not only are geometry and science traditional sources *par excellence* of principles and form for architecture, but, more importantly, the paramount concern of each of these areas of study is morphogenesis, the generation of new form. However provocative and invaluable as resources these studies in philosophy or science are, it must be said that neither provide the impetus for a New Architecture, nor the particulars of its terms and conditions. Rather, these have grown entirely out of architectural projects and developments within the discipline of architecture itself.

One contributing factor to the search for a New Architecture is the exhaustion of collage as the prevailing paradigm of architectural heterogeneity. In order to oppose Modernism's destituting proclivity for erasure and replacement, Post-Modernism emphasised grafting as the recombinatorial instrument of choice. The constellations of collage, in all its variations,[4] offered the most effective model of grafting strategies. From Rowe to Venturi to Eisenman,[5] from PoMo to the deconstructivists, collage has served as the dominant mode of the architectural graft . . . (p42)

According to Ungers, such an architecture must be vast and blank, it must point and be incongruous and incoherent.[9] It is not clear from the lecture how Unger intended his criteria to be interpreted but I was struck by the degree to which, with one exception, they lent themselves to a discourse on grafting alternative to collage. Particularly interesting to me was how well these criteria read as generalisations of the spacial/formal project of Modernism outlined in Le Corbusier's points . . . (pp42-3)

(i) Vastness – negotiates a middle-ground between the homogeneity of infinite or universal space and the fixed hierarchies of closely articulated spaces . . . (p43)

(ii) Blankness – extrapolates the Modernist project of formal abstraction understood as the suppression of quotation or reference through the erasure of decoration and ornament to include canonic form and type. By avoiding formal or figural reference, architecture can engage in unexpected formal and semiotic affiliations . . . (p43)

(iii) Pointing – architecture must be projective, ie, it must point to the emergence of new social arrangements and to the construction of new institutional forms . . . (p43)

(iv) Incongruity – a requirement to maintain yet subvert received data, including, for example, the existing site as a given condition and/or the programme brief. Maintenance and subversion are equally important either alone leads inexorably to spatial hypostatisation. Design implication: a repeal of the architectural postulates of harmony and proportion, structural perspicuity and system co-ordination (eg, among plan, section and facade, or between detail and formal organisation).

(v) Intensive Coherence – in fact, Unger stresses the necessity for incoherence, understood as a repeal of the architectural postulate of unity or wholeness. However, because incoherence is the hallmark of post-modern collage, I suggest as an alternative, a coherence forged out of incongruity. Intensive coherence implies that the properties of certain monolithic arrangements enable the architecture to enter into multiple and even contradictory relationships. It should not be confused with Venturi's notion of the 'difficult whole', in which a collage of multiplicity is then unified compositionally . . . (p43)

DeFormation, the subject of this volume, seeks to engender shifting affiliations that nevertheless resist entering into stable alignments. It does so by grafting abstract topologies that cannot be decomposed into simple, planar components nor analysed by the received language of architectural formalism.

Rejecting the deconstructivist themes of fragments, signs, assemblages and accreted space, Shirdel pursued a new, abstract monolithicity that would broach neither reference nor resemblance. Shirdel was interested in generating disciplined architectural forms that were not easily decomposable into the dynamics of point/line/plane/volume of modern formalism. We will come to refer to these forms in terms of anexact geometries and non-developable surfaces, but Shirdel's black-stuff set the stage for the Deformationist principle of non-referential, monolithic abstraction we have already discussed. The Alexandria Library competition, a design that evolved from a disciplined relaxation of a painting of folded cloth by Michelangelo. In that figure of the fold, Shirdel found precisely the formal qualities he sought. Although the final form shows no obvious traces of the original painting, relationships among surface, form and space are captured in the architecture . . . (p45)

Neither pure figure nor pure organisation, folds link the two; they are monolithic and often non-representational, replete with interstitial and residual spaces, and intrinsic to non-developable surfaces. As a process exercised in a matrix such as urban site, folding holds out the possibility of generating field organisations that negotiate between the infinite homogeneity of the grid and the hierarchical heterogeneity of finite geometric patterns, an effect which Peter Eisenman employs in his housing and office park in Rebstock, Germany.[22] Finally, when exercised as a process on two or more organisations simultaneously, folding is a potential smoothing strategy . . .(p47)

Notes

3 Other post-structural architectural theorists, notably Jennifer Bloomer and Robert Somoi, have appealed to the writings of Deleuze and Guattari, though to different ends.

4 'Collage' is used here as a convenient, if coarse, umbrella term for an entire constellation of practices, eg bricolage, assemblage and a history of collage with many important distinctions and developments. This argument is strengthened by a study of the architectural translations of the various models of collage and its associated practices. As we proceed further into the discussion of affiliative effects below, one might be inclined to argue that surrealist collage, with its emphasis on smoothing the seams of the graft, might provide an apt model. Though there is merit in this position, it seems to me that so-called seamlessness of surrealist collage, like all collages, acts actually to emphasise by irony the distinct nature of the elements of the collage and therefore the incoherent disjunctions at work. A better model might be Jasper John's cross-hatch paintings, prints and drawings. Though these works certainly employ many techniques associated with collage, their effect is quite different. In them non-ideal, grid-like organisations are materialised by grafting elements whose form is disjointed from the overall organisation. Moreover, in some of these works, other cloud-like shapes entirely outside of the dominant formal/tonal language are built up of the medium itself and camouflaged within the work. For me, these paintings are good examples of a cohesive heterogeneity engendered out of an intensive coherence in the elements themselves.

5 For example the Wexner Center for the Visual Arts and his 'scaling' projects eg, 'Romeo and Juliet.'

9 See Unger, 'The Better Futures of Architecture', in Anyone Davidson (ed), Rizzoli, 1991.

22 For more on the Rebstock project see R Somol, 'Accidents Will Happen', *A+U*, September 1991 and John Rajchman, 'Perplications', the catalogue essay for the Unfolding Frankfurt exhibition, Aedes Gallery, Ernst & Sohn, Verlag, 1991. For Eisenman on folding see 'Visions Unfolding', *Incorporations*, Crary and Kwinter, eds, UrZone Books, 1992. An earlier version is in *Domus*, June 1992.

Extracts. Source: 'Folding in Architecture', *Architectural Design*, Vol 63, nos 3-4/1993.
© Academy Group Ltd.

1993   GREG LYNN

Architectural Curvilinearity:
The Folded, the Pliant and the Supple

Because of this article, the argument for an inclusive architecture based on smoothness and folding in difference – like a food blender mixes in different ingredients – became part of La Scuola di Eisenmano in New York. Lynn (b 1964) modifies Gilles Deleuze's influential book Le Pli *and ideas of a supple, pliant paradigm from Husserl, D'Arcy Thompson and the software which facilitates a curvilinear, 'blob' architecture.*

In response to architecture's discovery of complex, disparate, differentiated and heterogeneous cultural and formal contexts, two options have been dominant: either conflict and contradiction or unity and reconstruction. Presently, an alternative smoothness is being formulated that may escape these dialectically opposed strategies. Common to the diverse sources of this post-contradictory work – topological geometry, morphology, morphogenesis, Catastrophe Theory or the computer technology of both the defence and Hollywood film industries – are characteristics of smooth transformation involving the intensive integration of differences within a continuous yet heterogeneous system. Smooth mixtures are made up of disparate elements which maintain their integrity while being blended with a continuous field of other free elements.

Smoothing does not eradicate differences but incorporates[3] free intensities through fluid tactics of mixing and blending. Smooth mixtures are not homogeneous and therefore cannot be reduced. Deleuze describes smoothness as 'the continuous variation' and the 'continuous development of form'[4] . . . (p8)

Both pliancy and smoothness provide an escape from the two camps which would either have architecture break under the stress of difference or stand firm. Pliancy allows architecture to become involved in complexity through flexibility. It may be possible to neither repress the complex relations of differences with fixed points of resolution nor arrest them in contradictions, but sustain them through flexible, unpredicted, local connections. To arrest differences in conflicting forms often precludes many of the more complex possible connections of the forms of architecture to larger cultural fields. A more pliant architectural sensibility values alliances, rather than conflicts, between elements. Pliancy implies first an internal flexibility and second a dependence on external forces for self-definition.

If there is a single effect produced in architecture by folding, it will be the ability to integrate unrelated elements with a new continuous mixture. Culinary theory has developed both a practical and precise definition for at least three types of mixtures. The first involves the manipulation of homogeneous elements; beating, whisking and whipping change the volume but not the nature of a liquid through agitation. The second method of incorporation mixes two or more disparate elements; chopping, dicing, grinding, grating, slicing, shredding and mincing eviscerate elements into fragments. The first method agitates a single uniform ingredient, the second eviscerates disparate ingredients. Folding, creaming and blending mix smoothly multiple ingredients 'through repeated gentle overturnings without stirring or beating' in such a way that their individual characteristics are maintained.[6] For instance, an egg and chocolate are folded together so that each is a distinct layer within a continuous mixture.

Folding employs neither agitation nor evisceration but a supple layering. Likewise, folding in geology involves the sedimentation of mineral elements or deposits which become slowly bent and compacted into plateaus of strata. These strata are compressed, by external forces, into more or less continuous layers within which heterogeneous deposits are still intact in varying degrees of intensity.

A folded mixture is neither homogeneous, like whipped cream, nor fragmented, like chopped nuts, but smooth and heterogeneous . . . (pp8-9)

Viscous Mixtures

Unlike an architecture of contradictions, superpositions and accidental collisions, pliant systems are capable of engendering unpredicted connections with contextual, cultural, programmatic, structural and economic contingencies by vicissitude. Vicissitude is often equated with vacillation, weakness[8] and indecisiveness but . . . these characteristics are frequently in the service of a tactical cunning[9] . . .

This recent work may be described as being compliant; in a state of being plied by forces beyond control. The projects are formally folded, pliant and supple in order to incorporate their contexts with minimal resistance. Again, this characterisation should not imply flaccidity but a cunning submissiveness that is capable of bending rather than breaking . . . (pp9-10)

The Supple Curvilinear

At an urban scale, many of these projects seem to be between contextualism and expressionism. Their supple forms are neither geometrically exact nor arbitrarily figural. The curvilinear figures of Shoei Yoh's roof structures are anything but decorative but also resist being reduced to a pure geometric figure . . . (p10)

Folding and Other Catastrophes for Architecture

Thom's nets were developed to describe catastrophic events. What is common to these events is an inability to define exactly the moment at which a catastrophe occurs. This loss of exactitude is replaced by a geometry of multiple probable relations. With relative precision, the diagrams define potential catastrophes through cusps rather than fixed co-ordinates . . . (p13)

Despite the differences between these practices, they share a sensibility that resists cracking or breaking in response to external pressures. These tactics and strategies are all com*pli*ant to, com*pli*cated by, and com*pli*cit with external forces in manners which are: submissive, suppliant, adaptable, contingent, responsive, fluent, and yielding through involvement and incorporation. The attitude which runs throughout this collection of projects and essays is the shared attempt to place seemingly disparate forces into relation through strategies which are externally plied. Perhaps, in this regard only, there are many opportunities for architecture to be effected by Gilles Deleuze's book *Le Pli*. The formal characteristics of pliancy – anexact forms and topological geometries primarily – can be more viscous and fluid in response to exigencies. They maintain formal integrity through deformations which do not internally cleave or shear but through which they connect, incorporate and affiliate productively. Cunning and viscous systems such as these gain strength through flexible connections that occur by vicissitude . . . (p14)

What is being asked...is: How can architecture be configured as a complex system into which external particularities are already found to be plied? . . . (p15)

Notes

3 See Sanford Kwinter and Jonathan Crary, 'Forward', *Zone 6: Incorporations*, Urzone Books (New York), 1992, pp12 -15.

4 Deleuze, Gilles, *A Thousand Plateaus: Capitalism and Schizophrenia*, University of Minnesota Press (Minneapolis), 1987, p478.

6 Cunningham, Marion, *The Fannie Farmer Cookbook*, 13th edition, Alfred A Knopf (New York) 1990, pp41-47.

8 An application of vicissitude to Kipnis' logic of undecidability and weak form might engender a cunning logic of non-linear affiliations. This seems apt give the reference to both undecidability and weakness in the definition of vicissitudes.

9 Ann Bergren's discussion of the *metis* is an example of cunning manipulations of form. For an alternative reading of these tactics in Greek art also see Jean-Pierre Vernant.

Extracts. Source: 'Folding in Architecture', *Architectural Design*, Vol 63, nos 3-4/1993.
© Academy Group Ltd

1996 ARATA ISOZAKI
The Island Nation Aesthetic

Arata Isozaki (b 1931, Oita City) worked with Kenzo Tange from 1954 to 1963 and made significant contributions to Metabolism, though never as a member of the Metabolist Group. He remained critical of what he considered their reductive view of Modernism and in his own work made increasing use of eclectic architectural quotation both from Japanese and Western sources.

I have written an essay on the Katsura Imperial Villa, where I claim that the architecture which is now deemed legendary is in fact a text which allows multivalent interpretations, and that the style of the building consists of interpretation, selection and quotation from various early texts of Japan, China and even the West (*nanban*). I sought to read into this textual manœuvre a correspondence with my own manner of design for contemporary society (which I call *maniera*); and in the life of Sir John Soane, which was full of personal setbacks, and in his work, which always fluctuated between a rigorous system and complex images, I thought I saw an image similar to that I saw at Katsura.

One day I noticed two books on these subjects sitting side by side on a bookshelf, and realised it is possible that two types of architecture from two different places (*spatiality*) and times (*temporality*) can be equidistant from my position, not to mention similar to my methodological preferences. One architecture was built in London one-and-a-half centuries ago and the other built in Kyoto three-and-a-half centuries ago, but they are both, nevertheless, the same distance from me . . . Having gone beyond the process of modernisation, we see Japan from a viewpoint similar to that of Westerners. It follows that the latter view of England incorporates the same mechanism of distancing as our view of England . . . The Ise shrine, the stone gardens of Ryoan-ji Temple, Stonehenge, the works of Edwin Lutyens . . . We all see these architectures as fictive constructs.

For this reason, in order to design I determined to adopt an ambiguous stance by taking reality as an accumulated inheritance and reading it as fictive text. By a technique induced from a reading of text, the programme as given is disassembled and recomposed; this is the process I mentioned earlier as my manner (*maniera*) . . . (pp7-9)

Following the crisis that I began experiencing in 1968, I resolved to initiate a thorough process of return to the compositional elements espoused by Modernism in its earliest phase. I decided to adhere to fundamental geometrical forms and to allow architectural configurations to emerge automatically from them. In this way I would be able to suppress the aesthetic appreciation cultivated in me as a result of a Modernist background, while at the time escaping from the patched functionalist compositional system. By means of a fundamental process of reduction, I intended to delve into the basis of the Modernist vocabulary, and by doing so, bring about its dissolution. This is the meaning of *maniera* . . .

From the time *maniera* was defined as an automatic stylistic movement, it depended on the characteristic, broader historical syntax of 'architecture'. It should be possible to abstract the stylistic nature of historical, regional and local items of architectural vocabulary just as readily as it is to abstract those from Modernist vocabulary. A kind of atavism born of manipulating pure forms led me to revert to the distinctive vocabulary of 'architecture' . . .

When the Fujimi Country Club was completed I became aware that the cut-cylinder section in its facade was a negative version of the entrance porch of Palladio's Villa Poiana. Suddenly, a building that was supposed to have been the outcome of the manipulation of pure geometric forms evoked an historical architectural example.

To discover the sources of this phenomenon, I analysed examples of classical style architecture and learned that without exception they all employed Platonic solid figures. Furthermore, I discovered that those eighteenth-century master architects with whom I had felt the greatest affinity since my student days, most vigorously exposed geometry in their exterior designs. Modern architects such as Le Corbusier are no exception . . .

Discovering the Platonic solid within the classical compositional principles forced me to put myself outside the game. In other words, in order to get outside Modernist architectural vocabulary, I once again had to articulate the Platonic solids within classical architectural vocabulary. Behind the assembly of classical architecture is the mega-vocabulary called 'Architecture' with a capital 'A' . . .

Even after stimulating the independent movement of the *maniera* system, I saw that I could not escape from the mega-vocabulary framework of Architecture with a capital 'A'. When this happened, in addition to pure geometrical figures, quotations become conspicuous in my work. I quoted systems, formerly complete in themselves, as metaphors functioning as references to generate different meanings . . . (pp40-45)

I . . . believe that new buildings should stimulate the creation of new contexts in their surroundings. This is why my buildings assume either an aggressive or a defensive posture in relation to their settings . . .

In other words, my doctrine of *maniera* is anti-contextualist. From the outset, my buildings are expected to generate discord with their settings . . .

The *maniera* method achieves transformations because once the struggle with the location is over, direct confrontation with the broader culture behind it becomes possible. (p47)

In the case of the design for the Museum of Contemporary Art in Los Angeles . . .

The architectural forms projecting above ground are based on Platonic solids but at the same time allude to such historical precedents as the pyramids, Palladio, the palazzo, and so on. Juxtaposing the abstract and the concrete, the modern and the classical, and hard and smooth materials results in ambivalence. Nothing is clearly quoted as a reference source, nor did I intend to revive any single style. Instead, my aim was to dismantle apparently integrated architectural styles and to fragment them so that, at the moment when they seem to be in ruins, a schizophrenic state of suspension is created. The fragments lose their birthplaces and points of origin. Dispersed as forms, shapes, elements and pieces devoid of meaning in the space called contemporary time, they flash on and off through the operation of metaphor. The effective method in this case is assembling fragments, as in a collage or a patchwork quilt.

It is necessary to point out that under such circumstances all architectural style is reduced to ruins. The only things available for architectural design are the fragments scattered about in the ruins. Should reconstruction be accomplished, the results would no doubt still resemble ruins. This is the reason why architecture must become schizophrenic and eclectic. The art of assembling fragments in a given place to intersect with the local context is political in nature. Consequently, architecture may well have to be reinterpreted on the basis of political significance. When this happens, architecture will find itself under a new programme of discourse. (pp49-52)

Extracts. Source: Arata Isozaki, The *Island Nation Aesthetic*, Academy Editions (London), 1996. © Academy Group Ltd.

1996   CHARLES JENCKS

13 Propositions of Post-Modern Architecture

This summary of the Post-Modern movement, made for architectural students at UCLA, collects together in a concise way the major ideas of thirty years.

General Values

1 Multivalence is preferred to univalence, imagination to fancy.

2 'Complexity and contradiction'are preferred to over-simplicity and 'Minimalism'.

3 Complexity and Chaos theories are considered more basic in explaining nature than linear dynamics; that is, 'more of nature' is nonlinear in behaviour than linear.

4 Memory and history are inevitable in DNA, language, style and the city and are positive catalysts for invention.

Linguistic and Aesthetic

5 All architecture is invented and perceived through codes, hence the languages of architecture and symbolic architecture, hence the double-coding of architecture within the codes of both the professional and populace.

6 All codes are influenced by a semiotic community and various taste cultures, hence the need in a pluralist culture for a design based on Radical Eclecticism.

7 Architecture is a public language, hence the need for a Post-Modern Classicism which is partly based on architectural universals and a changing technology.

8 Architecture necessitates ornament (or patterns) which should be symbolic and symphonic, hence the relevance of information theory.

9 Architecture necessitates metaphor and this should relate us to natural and cultural concerns, hence the explosion of zoomorphic imagery, face houses and scientific iconography instead of 'machines for living'.

Urban, Political, Ecological

10 Architecture must form the city, hence Contextualism, Collage City, Neo-Rationalism, small-block planning, and mixed uses and ages of buildings.

11 Architecture must crystallise social reality and in the global city today, the Heteropolis, that very much means the pluralism of ethnic groups; hence participatory design and adhocism.

12 Architecture must confront the ecological reality and that means sustainable development, Green architecture and cosmic symbolism.

13 We live in a surprising, creative, self-organising universe which still gets locked-into various solutions; hence the need for a cosmogenic architecture which celebrates criticism, process and humour.

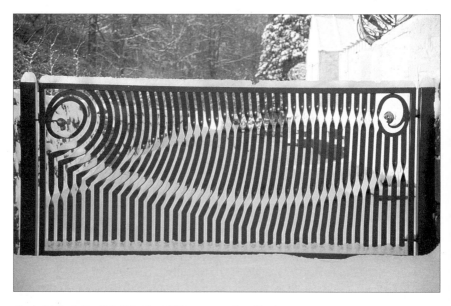

Charles Jencks, Soliton Gate III, Scotland, 1995 – cosmogenic architecture

POST-MODERN ECOLOGY

Kenneth Yeang, Menara Mesiniaga, Selangor, Malaysia, 1992 – the bioclimatic skyscraper

1969   IAN McHARG
Design with Nature

*Ian McHarg (b 1920, Clydebank, Scotland) studied landscape archi-
tecture at Harvard and has taught at the University of Pennsylvania
since 1954. His principal work,* Design with Nature, *was published
at the height of the period of environmental activism in the late 1960s.
The book was an instant success and one of the few works to combine a cogent set of general principles derived from the discipline of
ecology with practical methods of design.*

Prospect

Does the process of creation involve the employment of energy and matter in
raising levels of order? Matter is not destroyed but order can be reduced; is then
destruction better termed reduction-anticreation? Is it accurate and useful to
consider the earth as a single superorganism, the oceans and the atmosphere as
organic? Do the processes of creation and reduction each exhibit characteristics
and can these be subsumed under negentropy and entropy? Are fitness and fitting
measures of creation in ecosystems? If form and process are merely aspects of the
single phenomenon of being, can there be a conception of intrinsic form? And
finally, are health and pathology the most synoptic criteria for creation and reduction, fitting and unfitting? If so, we have a model. Moreover, we have criteria.
The first is negentropy, the increase in levels of order. The second is apperception, the capacity to transmute energy into information and thence to meaning –
and to respond to this. The third is symbiosis, the cooperative arrangement that
permits increase in levels of order and requires apperception. The fourth is fitness and fitting – the selection of a fit environment and the adaptation of that
environment, and of the organism, to accomplish a better fitting. The final criterion is the presence of health or pathology – the evidence of creative fitting,
requiring negentropy, apperception and symbiosis.

This model contains the possibility of an inventory of all ecosystems to determine their relative creativity in the biosphere. This same conception can be applied
to human processes . . .

This suggests an ecological value system in which the currency is energy.
There is an inventory of matter, life forms' apperceptive powers, roles, fitness,
adaptations, symbioses and genetic potential. Consumption optimally involves

the employment of energy in the raising of levels of matter. Matter is not consumed but merely cycled . . .

The application of this model requires elaborate ecological inventories. Happily, recent technological advances facilitate these. Earth satellites with remote scanning devices with high-level identification can provide rich data and time series information on the dynamism of many natural processes. When such inventories are completed they can be constituted into a value system . . .

Certainly the most valuable application of such inventories is to determine locations for land uses and most particularly for urbanization . . .

The benefits of the ecological view seem patent to me, but equally clear are the profound changes which espousal of this view will effect. The Judeo-Christian creation story must be seen as an allegory; dominion and subjugation must be expunged as the biblical injunction of man's relation to nature. In values it is a great advance from 'I-it' to 'I-Thou', but 'we' seems a more appropriate description for ecological relationships. The economic value system must be expanded into a relative system encompassing all biophysical processes and human aspirations. Law must reflect that death or injury through flood, drought, avalanche, mudslide or earthquake can result from human negligence or malice and thus should fall within the jurisdiction of the courts. Medicine must be more concerned with creating the environment of health than with therapy alone. Industry and commerce must expand their accounting to include all costs and benefits. But it is in education that the greatest benefits lie. Here separatism rules, yet integration is the quest. This ecology offers: the science of the relations of organisms and the environment, integrative of the sciences, humanities and the arts – a context for studies of man and the environment.

In the quest for survival, success and fulfillment, the ecological view offers an invaluable insight. It shows the way for the man who would be the enzyme of the biosphere – its steward, enhancing the creative fit of man-environment, realizing man's design with nature. (pp196-197)

Extracts. Source: Ian McHarg, *Design with Nature*, John Wiley & Sons Inc (New York), 1992. © 1992 Reprinted by permission of John Wiley & Sons Inc. First published in 1969 by the Natural History Press.

1979 SIM VAN DER RYN AND STERLING BUNNELL

Integral Design

Sim van der Ryn served as State Architect to the state of California and teaches at the University of California, Berkeley. He was involved with the Farallones Institute in setting up the integral urban house in west Berkeley, an experimental house intended to be as self-sufficient as possible in terms of energy, food and waste. The project was described in The Integral Urban House, *from which this extract is taken.*

Integral design applies lessons from the biology of natural systems to the design of environments for people. This emerging integration of architecture and ecology – some have dubbed it bioarchitecture or ecotecture – is in its infancy although we can identify principles and patterns that earlier cultures have known and applied. This discussion is necessarily more speculative and philosophical than the 'how-to' chapters in the book, yet it is at the center of what this book is all about.

An obvious question is, 'Why emulate natural design; what is there about the behaviour of natural systems that we should pay attention to in designing our cities, towns, and houses?' The answer is framed by the most basic observed fact on earth: that the source of all life energy is the sun. But the earth is only habitable through the action of autotrophs – green plants (from the lowly algae to the towering redwoods) that capture a small percentage (about 1 percent) of solar energy and transform and fix it into useful forms of energy for other forms of life. Without complex natural systems to fix and transform energy, all solar energy would be lost as waste heat and life would not be sustained. We call this process entropy, the tendency of all energy to degrade into unusable waste heat, radiated back into space. Negentropy – the sum total of all life processes that capture and transform energy into usable forms – is the basis for life and civilization.

Evolution is the process by which natural systems become increasingly diverse, complex, and differentiated in order to counteract entropy. Evolution through negentropy may be seen as nature's slow but certain strategy to achieve stability in the face of the inevitable entropic degradation and eventual death of the planet.

Human beings cannot hope to improve on the efficiency of natural negentropic processes. However, a goal can be to design habitat and culture in such a way that natural systems and the information contained in them are not degraded and destroyed . . . (pp16-17)

We can contrast the properties of the integral system with what we call the *linear* system – the 'early-succession ecology' or monoculture that seems to characterize most human support systems:

integral system	linear system
* Energy flows through loops	* Energy flows along straight lines
* Parts fit overlapping functions	* Parts are specialized modular components
* Low entropy/high information	* High entropy/low information
* Open system/closed loops	* Closed system/no loops
* Memory stored diffusely	* Memory stored in centralized components
* High rate of material recovery	* High rate of material loss
* Multiple alternate channels	* Single channels
* Little waste	* High waste
* Self-regulating	* Imbalance passed along
* Multipurpose	* Single purpose
* Steady flow of energy	* Surging flow of energy
* Diversity, complexity, stability	* Uniformity, simplicity, instability
* High number of species	* Low number of species
* Biomorphic aesthetic	* Linear aesthetic

These properties exist on a continuum. The important thing is to get a feeling for when the design of a particular system approaches the integral and when it approaches the linear.

The closed integral loop is fundamental to the nature of living systems. Many benefits are realized from the intentional application of this concept to the design of the built environment . . .

Webbing implies multiple channels and loops. Webbing allows the meaningful transfer of energy, materials, and information, and constitutes the connections that comprise living systems, whether they are called cells, organisms or ecosystems. If energy and nutrients flow along webs or pathways, they can be retained longer within living boundaries, and thus an internal steady state environment for life systems is established. Multiple parallel pathways allow compensating flow to take place when a channel is impaired. Loops allow both cycling and self-regulation . . .

Negative feedback loops are found in biochemical pathways of cellular metabolism and the population swings of ecosystems, in which the expansion of particular species is limited by predators, or where stresses related to crowding inhibit reproduction. Healthy steady-state recycling is maintained by the linkage of complementary systems so that the wastes of one system are the necessary inputs of the other . . . (pp19-20)

Another principle contributing to homeostasis is that in natural systems energy is most efficiently used by organisms when released in small increments . . .

A part of our concern here is the boundaries between systems. In integral systems, boundaries are permeable and systems mesh together with such intricacy that transactions across the boundaries of systems flow without waste or upheaval. By contrast, our modern urban systems are monocultural crazy quilts stitched loosely together with waste . . .

In the continued cycling of energy and materials through time, information is stored as genetic evolution and culture. Information is precious and needs to be conserved. While species have continuously appeared and disappeared throughout earth's history, every major information advance has been retained. *The real harvest of the ecological fabric evolving through time is information,* including human culture . . .

Too much energy flow is detrimental to ecological systems. An overload or surge of energy flowing through a system can be destructive to the information content that is embodied in its structure and form. This is true of natural as well as man-made systems . . . (p21)

The task, then, of integral design at the household level is to begin to recreate the opportunities for people to derive meaning and satisfaction from their experience of natural cycles as these occur in the household. This assumes that the occupant becomes an active and intelligent participant in managing, maintaining, and adapting the dwelling. The 'hot rod' is one example of an aesthetic that grows out of the young American male's attempt to find meaning in everyday industrial culture. Maybe the day is not too far off when millions of Americans will be 'hot rodding' their new denatured houses into finely tuned, multichanneled, closed-looped, organic instruments for processing nature's flow. (p35)

Extracts. Source: Helga Olkowski, Bill Olkowski, Tom Javits and the Farallones Institute Staff, *The Integral Urban House,* Sierra Club Books (San Francisco), 1979. © Sierra Club Books.

1984 ANNE WHISTON SPIRN
The Granite Garden

In one sense, Anne Whiston Spirn (b 1947) moves Le Corbusier's notion of the 'tower in the park' from the realms of the rhetorical and aesthetic to the scientific. For all his adulation of engineering and its basis in scientific analysis, Le Corbusier never faced up to the realities of sustaining vegetation in the urban environment. Spirn faces and explores them in order to provide a basis for improving the quality of life in the city – not by erasing and replacing but complementing it.

Cities must resist the habit of fragmenting nature, a habit reinforced by the organization of government bureaucracies and the boundaries of professions and academic disciplines. While some specialization is necessary, the absence of a single coordinating agency prevents the effective management of resources and hazards and discourages the resolution of multiple problems with one solution. Only by viewing the entire urban natural environment as one interacting system can the value of nature in the city be fully appreciated. Only when the social values of natural processes are recognized can priorities be set, and conflicting and complementary values be resolved or married. Only then can urban form fully reflect the values inherent in nature as well as other social values.

An understanding of the urban natural environment should underlie all aspects of the physical design of the city: the location of specific land uses; the shape, size, and landscaping of urban parks and plazas; the alignment and width of streets and highways; and the overall pattern of the city's transportation network and places of work, residence, and play. In particular, the integration of all urban open land into a unified plan promises to extend the traditionally accepted aesthetic and recreational value of open space to a crucial role in health, safety, and welfare. Parks and plazas, water bodies and streams, floodplains and marshy lowlands, steep hillsides and rocky outcrops, and even parking lots and highway corridors could be included in a cohesive open space system to improve air quality and climate, to reduce flooding and improve water quality, to limit the impact of geological hazards, such as earthquakes, subsidence, and landslides, to provide a diverse community of plants and animals within the city, to conserve energy, water, and mineral resources, and to enhance the safe assimilation of the city's wastes . . .

The nineteenth-century achievement in sanitary reform was awesome and inspiring, but fell short in the twentieth century. Today's problems require a new effort. Modern technology is equal to the task; most existing institutions are not, though effective models do exist. Each city should consider which existing institutions or what new ones could coordinate the assembly and dissemination of information. First and foremost, each city must appreciate the social values inherent in natural processes and understand that urban form and human purposes can evolve in concert with nature . . . (pp201-202)

Extracts. Source: Anne Whiston Spirn, *The Granite Garden: Urban Nature and Human Design*, Basic Books, (New York) 1984. © 1984 by Anne Whiston Spirn. Reprinted by permission of BasicBooks, a division of HarperCollins Publishers Inc.

1984 NANCY JACK TODD AND JOHN TODD

Bioshelters, Ocean Arks and City Farming: Ecology as the Basis of Design

Nancy Jack Todd and John Todd founded the New Alchemy Institute with William O. McLarney in 1969, moving from California to Cape Cod Massachusetts in 1971. All three worked at Woods Hole Oceanographic Institute but sought through New Alchemy to apply their knowledge of biology and ecology to issues less favoured by established research institutions. Drawing on the work of Buckminster Fuller and Gregory Bateson, they have begun to establish both basic principles and specific technologies for ecological design.

Emerging Precepts of Biological Design

The formulation of these early precepts as they are applied and tested will contribute, in time, to the creation of a science of applied biotechnology which will serve in turn as a foundation for future design.

Precept One: *The living world is the matrix of all design*
Although the myriad life forms, processes and natural cycles of the Earth have been thoroughly studied and documented, the question of a pattern of patterns, or a metapattern, that would make the entirety of life comprehensible continues to elude us. The most far-reaching, yet credible theory to date, to our way of thinking, comes from the brilliant research of Drs Lynn Margulis of Boston University and James Lovelock of England. Called the Gaia hypothesis . . .

The importance of the Gaia hypothesis to a science of design lies not as a precise tool, or blueprint, but as a profound multidimensional paradigm for the designs, a meta-model, a basis for thinking about how the world works within which to frame more concrete questions about design . . .

Precept Two: *Design should follow, not oppose, the laws of life*
Our second precept of design is therefore that biology is the model for design . . .

Precept Three: *Biological equity must determine design*
If enough future design took the welfare of not the poorest third of humanity but

only a small fraction of that, as integral from the outset, slowly the fate of the poorest third might become less desperate.

Precept Four: *Design must reflect bioregionality*
For most of humanity's evolution bioregionalism has been unselfconsciously and effortlessly a part of design – from the yurts of Central Asia to the magnificent Pueblo dwellings of the American southwest, to the tents of wandering bands of nomads – culture and identity, geography, topography, climate, and indigenous resource all have been for millennia silently but eloquently expressed in a manner appropriate to the bioregion

Precept Five: *Projects should be based on renewable energy sources . . .*

Precept Six: *Design Should Be Sustainable Through the Integration of Living Systems . . .*

Precept Seven: *Design should be coevolutionary with the natural world*
With the age of computers well upon us, the coefficient that marks our time as so different from all preceding periods is the fathomless wealth of information that is available to us. Drawing on this resource we would designate a precept that, when possible, hardware and fossil-fuel-powered machines be replaced by either information or organisms or, in a surprising number of cases, a combination of both . . .

Precept Eight: *Building and design should help heal the planet*
In attempting to formulate guidelines for thinking about the kind of design that will evolve harmoniously within the natural continuum there is a factor that has been little considered now or in the past . . . We have acquired the knowledge of biology, the technology, and the potential partnership in coevolution with the organic world to begin a process of planetary healing.

Precept Nine: *Design should follow a sacred ecology*
. . . [The] interconnectedness of the human and natural worlds in an unknowable 'metapattern which connects' is what we have come to think of as sacred ecology. It is the foundation and the summation of all the preceding precepts of design. (pp19-92)

Biology and Architecture: The New Synthesis

In the evolving synthesis of biology and architecture a neigborhood could begin to function in a manner analogous to an organism. On the proposed block or neighborhood scale, parts become symbiotic to the whole and the basic social and physical functions work together. The workings are felt and understood by residents, who live with and operate the components . . .

A village or community could be created in the form of a wheel. The main spokes would be roads and the minor spokes walkway and bicycle arteries. All lead to an interior ring or hub. At the center is a lake ringed by plants and trees framed by a floral border. The village is a mixture of solid materials, transparent membranes, and mass linked to technical and biological elements. It can be thought of as a single structure with varying degrees of closure to the sky. It combines the orthodox functions of a village like housing and commerce, with a range of biological activities. The sections or wedges designated for agriculture are open to the sky in warm and hot seasons and covered by tent-like transparent envelopes during cold. Housing is compactly arranged, but each house has an individual solar courtyard that is seasonally adjustable. Waste is recycled in interconnected geodesic bioshelters . . . (p116-117)

Extracts. Source: Nancy Jack Todd and John Todd, *Bioshelters, Ocean Arks and City Farming: Ecology as the Basis of Design*, Sierra Club Books (San Francisco), 1984. © Nancy Jack Todd and John Todd.

1986 HASSAN FATHY

Natural Energy and Vernacular Architecture

The work of Hassan Fathy (b 1899, Egypt, d 1989) shows the close connection between the ecological approach, or at least a strand within it, and vernacular traditions. As described in Housing for the Poor, *Fathy made use of traditional forms and construction methods beginning in the 1940s. This work was followed by extensive research into the thermodynamics of those forms and methods. The result was a fruitful insight into the complex workings of apparently simple buildings, serving as a basis for improving thermal efficiency while maintaining a building's value within the local culture and reducing its impact on the environment.*

The techniques and equipment available to the architect today free him from nearly all material constraints. He has the run of centuries of styles and can choose his plans from every continent on earth. But he must remember that he is not building in a vacuum and placing his houses in empty space, as mere plans on a blank sheet of paper. He is introducing a new element into an environment that has existed in equilibrium for a very long time. He has responsibilities and does violence to the environment by building without reference to it, he is committing a crime against architecture and civilization . . . (p5)

. . . Before the advent of the industrial era and mechanization, man depended on natural sources of energy and available local materials in forming his habitat according to his physiological needs. Over many centuries, people everywhere appear to have learned to interact with their climate. Climate shapes the rhythm of their lives as well as their habitat and clothes. Thus, they build houses that are more or less satisfactory at providing them with the microclimate that they need.

Successful solutions to the problems of climate did not result from deliberate scientific reasoning. They grew out of countless experiments and accidents and the experience of generations of builders who continued to use what worked and rejected what did not. They were passed on in the form of traditional, rigid, and apparently arbitrary rules for selecting sites, orienting the building, and choosing the materials, building method and design . . . (p7)

Changing a single item in a traditional method will not ensure an improved response to the environment, or even an equally satisfactory one. Yet change is inevitable, and new forms and materials will be used, as has been the case throughout history. Often the convenience of modern forms and materials makes their use attractive in the short term. . .

[But] any architect who makes a solar furnace of his building and compensates for this by installing a huge cooling machine is approaching the problem inappropriately and we can measure the inappropriateness of his attempted solution by the excess number of kilocalories he uselessly introduces into the building. Furthermore, the vast majority of the inhabitants of the Tropics are industrially underdeveloped and cannot afford the luxury of high-technology building materials or energy-intensive systems for cooling. Although traditional architecture is always evolving and will continue to absorb new materials and design concepts, the effects of any substitute materials or form should be evaluated before it is adopted. Failure to do so can only result in the loss of the very concepts that made the traditional techniques appropriate.

Only a scientific approach to the evaluation of such new developments can save the architecture of the Tropics and Subtropics. The thoughtless application of modern methods in this region is seldom successful. A thorough understanding of the climatic environment and developments based thereon is essential for appropriate solutions. Although traditional architecture was evolved intuitively over long periods, it was based primarily on scientifically valid concepts. The modern academic world of architecture does not emphasize the value of investigating and applying concepts and, therefore, has no respect for vernacular architecture. Now is the time to bridge the gap between these widely different approaches.

All traditional solutions should be evaluated scientifically before they are discarded or substitutes proposed . . . (pp8-9)

Extracts. Source: Hassan Fathy, *Natural Energy and Vernacular Architecture: Principles and Examples with Reference to the Hot Arid Climates,* Walter Shearer and Abd-el-rahman Ahmed Sultan (eds), University of Chicago Press (Chicago) 1986, published for the United Nations University. © 1986 Hassan Fathy.

1987 KENNETH YEANG
Tropical Urban Regionalism

Kenneth Yeang studied at the Architectural Association in London and the University of Pennsylvania under Ian McHarg, completing a Doctorate at Cambridge University. Returning to his native Malaysia to practice, he has realised and continues to develop his ideas on bioclimatic architecture.

Regionalist Design Intentions

Regionalist architecture seeks to incorporate in its design the 'spirit' of the place in which it is located. Its intentions are for a contextual architecture which responds self-evidently to the local conditions. It should relate to the deeper sensibilities and tangible realities of the place, rather than relating primarily to international influences and trends. More specifically, *the emergent regionalist architecture seeks its architectural significance through relating its built configuration, aesthetics, organisation and technical assembly and materials to a certain place and time.*

This endeavour is both cultural and technical. A particular place would have a physical, social, economic and political status quo besides a cultural and architectural heritage, and natural history. Architecture's function in relating its attributes as a technological product to a particular place and time is as a vital connector that links *technology* with *culture*. The regionalist design approach seeks to articulate this linkage.

The design process should involve the synthesis of the selective combination of a series of functional connections together into built form. These connections include: *a direct connection* which involves the direct creative development and adaptation for contemporary uses of the existing range of built forms, devices, patterns and aesthetics that can be identified from the cultural tradition and architectural heritage of the place; *an indirect (abstract) connection* through the interpretation into form by design of those general principles and lessons derived through an analysis of the cultural tradition and architectural heritage of the place; *an inclusive contemporary connection* in design through the selective use and localisation of current technology, forms and ideas that are relevant to the programme and context; *a landscape connection* in the design that reflects, incorporates and integrates the built configuration with the physical features and natural history of the place (that must include its climate, topography and ecology); and a *forward connection* in which the design considerations include an anticipation of the likely future historical consequences of the building. (p12)

An Armature for Interpretation

Design efforts at evolving a regionally appropriate vocabulary in the urban context are often based on careful analyses of solar angles, wind movements and the thermal properties of materials, etc, and fail to produce an architecture which belongs to the region . . . What is needed is an holistic concept that can permit the building enclosure itself to be perceived systematically without a prior fixation to a particular aesthetic, so as to enable a regionalist inventory of forms particular to a place and time to emerge.

A separate position might start from our examination of the systematic functions and attributes of the building enclosure itself and relations it might have with the *climate of the place* being one of the dominant reasons for any enclosure in the first place . . . (p34)

Buildings might be regarded as enclosural *systems.* Two differing viewpoints can be held. One regards the building as being analogous to a *closed system*; the other to an *open system* . . .

The open-system analogy [is one] in which the function of the building enclosure is regarded as a perforated barrier or as an *environmental filter.* The filter acts as a sieve that enables selective exchanges between the external climate and the internal spaces that are designed to achieve the desired internal conditions . . .

In the design process, a configuration and image has to be given to the enclosural system. These then become susceptible to the regionalist design considerations of the location and the connections to be made. The proposition of the enclosure as an environmental filter therefore provides us only with a general and technical *armature* over which regionalist design interpretations take place. The designer has to synthesise these aspects into a built form . . . (pp40-57)

Consequences

We might hope that the armature would enable the wider development and understanding of regionalist architecture, one that would use the appropriate technology but which belongs and performs to the region and place. In the process of giving form to the regionalist connections, the results that emerge might appear immediately visually unfamiliar despite the intentions and sources of forms and devices. We must be prepared for this if a new architecture is to emerge. More important is if it is responsive to the local environmental, cultural context and those problems of that society; then by being responsive it works, it is authentic and it contributes to the locality.

Extracts. Source: Kenneth Yeang, *Tropical Urban Regionalism*, Minar Books, Concept Media Pte Ltd (Singapore), 1987. © Concept Media Pte Ltd.

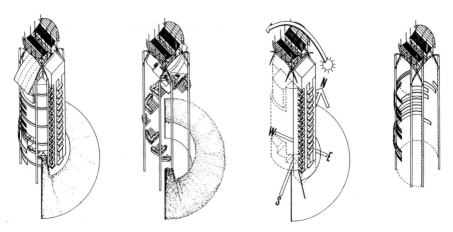

Kenneth Yeang, Menara Mesiniaga, Selangor, Malaysia, 1992 – the bioclimatic skyscraper

1990 CHRISTOPHER DAY
Places of the Soul

Trained as an architect and sculptor, Christopher Day is concerned with both the human response to buildings and the effect of buildings on the environment. His starting point for a design is the feeling elicited by a place, building around it to cultivate and reinforce it. While seeking to operate outside the polarities of current stylistic debates, Day has developed a recognizable combination of forms, avoiding straight lines and right angles, using mainly masonry and timber. Places of the Soul, from which this text has been excerpted, attempts to set out the principles giving rise to those forms.

Architecture has such profound effects on the human being, on place, on human consciousness, and ultimately on the world, that it is far too important to bother with stylistic means of appealing to fashion. It can have such powerful negative effects that we must also think, can it, if consciously worked with, have equally strong positive effects?

Anything with such powerful effects has *responsibilities* – power, if not checked by responsibility, is a dangerous thing! Architecture has responsibilities to minimize adverse biological effects on occupants, responsibilities to be sensitive to and act harmoniously in the surroundings, responsibilities to the human individualities who will come in contact with the building, responsibilities not only in the visual aesthetic sphere and through the outer senses but also to the intangible but perceptible 'spirit of place'.

These responsibilities involve energy conservation ranging from insulation, organizing buildings around a focal heat source like a heating/cooking stove, conservatory or hypercaust wall, re-use of waste heat – for instance retrieving heat from waste water or refrigeration coils – to alternate energy production such as solar heating. They involve careful selection of building materials and the ways they are put together, both with regard to occupants' and manufacturing and building workers' health, and to the environmental impact of products from primary extraction to demolished rubbish. Such wider criteria cast a new light on, for example, tropical hardwoods, the extraction of which in almost all cases entails massive ecological damage; on plastics, which commonly require some 15 or so synthesis operations, each around 50% efficient, so that the final product is only some 0.002% of the original material; and on water, new reservoirs for which are brutally destructive of upland communities.

This attitude of responsibility involves putting away stylistic or individualistically-enhancing preferences in favour of listening to what the place, the moment, and the community ask for. (pp15-16)

Architecture as Art

Architectural demands so often lead in different directions, in potential conflict – like energy conservation and biological effects, the straight and the curved, cosmic geometry and organic response to environmental circumstance – that the results will be one-sided and disastrous unless they can be brought into a conversational balance. Similarly, architectural elements need to be brought into conversation or they fight against each other.

I am not just talking about what is nice or not but about what is nourishing for the human spirit. To be nourishing, things must match what we need, just as a stoker and a meditating hermit need different diets. Our surroundings therefore must satisfy necessary material functions; they must provide the right biological climate; they must give support to our life and mood and feeling. But to carry architecture beyond the threshold of the materially useful, the biologically supportive or emotionally satisfying, we need to cultivate and bring together both the inspiration which gives moral force to our ideas and the sense of listening to environment which makes those ideas appropriate. This interweaving conversation between idea and material can only exist in the artistic sphere. (p29)

Conversation or Conflict

Harmony in our surroundings is no mere luxury. Our surroundings are the framework which subtly confine, organize and colour our daily lives. Harmonious surroundings provide a support for outer social and inner personal harmony. Harmony can be achieved by rules – but rules lack life. Or it can arise as an inevitable but life-filled consequence of listening conversation. Even between the same group of people, different times and places trigger different conversations – even more so when the people are different. This one principle can give rise to many forms – not just the way I do it! This inspiration is so much at the centre of my approach to architecture, that I could not imagine working without it. (p70)

Ensouling Buildings

Materials and light are two completely opposite poles which belong together. Thick walls with sunbeams through deep windows, dark rocks in luminously still water, trees fringed with light against the sun: these joy the heart. The[y are] unphotographable because they are alive. Light and matter is the greatest of architectural polarities – the polarity of cosmos and substance, one bringing enlivening, renewing rhythms, the other stable, enduring, rooted in place and time. This polarity is the foundation of health giving architecture, for the oneness of stability, balance and renewal underlies health.

The ancient druids worked with this polarity with rock and sun, for in the tension between them health-giving life arises. I also try to work with it in a qualitative way, and it is sensitivity to qualities that has led me in this direction rather than thinking my way. I started just by having a *feeling* for these things. I have therefore made a lot of mistakes, but the process I have gone through is similar to that with which one needs to nurture a spirit of place.

It starts with developing a feeling for what is the appropriate mood, then building a strong soul of a place with materials and experiences of appropriate sensory qualities. It starts with the feelings; architecture built up out of adjectives – architecture for the soul. (p123)

Extracts. Source: Christopher Day, *Places of the Soul*, The Aquarian Press (London), 1990. © Christopher Day. The Aquarian Press is an imprint of HarperCollins Publishers Limited.

1990   JAMES WINES
Architect's Statement

In much of the early work of Wines' firm SITE there is an incipient 'green' architecture evident in a play between artificial and natural elements. In this essay Wines makes a more explicit argument for green architecture as an antidote to the technological extremes of Modernism and the theoretical extremes of deconstruction.

The potential variations on green architecture are infinite . . . and represent a great variety of aesthetic, social, technical, and political interpretations for the future. This green objective suggests a complete reordering of priorities in design theory and the nature of what will constitute the higher levels of discourse in this era . . . Far too much of the critical and theoretical dialogue for the past ten years has revolved around a continual playing out of variations on Modernism and Constructivism. This addiction to the past has tended to limit the parameters of discourse; so that even when a progressive ideal like deconstruction is introduced to architecture, its demonstrations derive from the totally antithetical Socialist ideals and formalist aesthetic of Constructivism more than seventy-five years ago . . .

In no way does deconstruction seem to be about the positivist objectives of Constructivism, or the orderly orthodoxy of formalist design. It is a game of the mind; so, in fact, are certain aspects of the human relationship to the environment. Like the often contradictory propositions of deconstruction, assumptions about nature cannot be trusted; every conclusion is its own question, every evidence of a pattern is a misleading illusion, every attempt to impose an order encourages a higher level of disorder. There appear to be certain areas of essential cooperation with nature that can encourage its favorable response and perhaps lengthen our visit on this planet; however, in the formation of a symbolic content for a new architecture, the challenges are in the mind and the development of images that relate to a larger psychological and critical perspective.

The problem with architecture as art, and as a public monitor of the psyche, is its dependence for expression on the rather ponderous elements of construction technology. For our argument here, this handicap is all the more reason to engage the ever-changing and unpredictable ingredients of nature. Their inclusion in an architectural context is the ideal critical device to question and contradict the methodical processes of building. Landscape is also primal and universal. It strips away redundancies and constantly reveals new information. It is rich in associations. It is dialectical, evolutionary, and indeterminate. It is, finally, an iconographic force that can advance the language of architecture and, at the same time, confirm the inalienable right of people to try to salvage the earth before it is too late. (p70)

Extracts: *Architecture and Urbanism*, vol 12; no 243, 1990. © A+U Publishing Co Ltd.

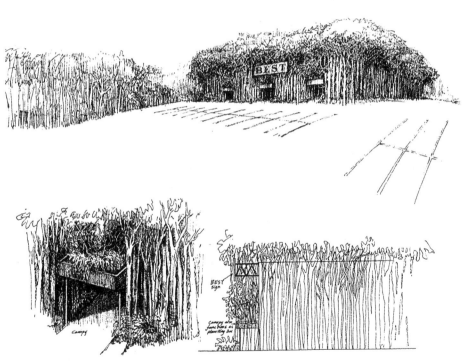

SITE, James Wines, Richmond Showroom, Best Products, 1980

1991   TEAM ZOO/ATELIER ZŌ
Principles of Design

Now a network of affiliated design groups or 'ateliers', Team Zoo began as the single group Team Zō (Elephant) in 1971, founded by Keiko Arimura, Hiroyasu Higuchi, Koichi Otake, Tsutomu Shigemura and Reiko Tomida. However diverse the present constellation of groups, they are united around a common concern for the relation between the natural and cultural features of a place and the human response to them in the form of building.

Expression of Region

It is our desire that the architecture reflects the locality where it stands. We attempt to express the identity of the area or region in what we design. We walk around the village, survey the landscape, observe how people are living and investigate the local history. In this way we eventually uncover clues or keys for expressing the locality in our designs.

What is a house?
What is a school?
What is a city hall?

We observe the basic living process of a community, school or a family, and try to find the fundamental demands for the architecture that they plan to build. Sometimes the clients or community are not fully aware of their own wants or needs. It becomes part of our work to think with them and to propose a plan for the new way of life. Our objective is to create spaces that answer the current demands of the client and community, while providing new opportunities to broaden the horizons of life.

Diversity

Architecture is an opportunity for various people to meet. Spaces affect how people make contact. Integrating spatial diversity into the structures presents a variety of environments where people can interact. By communicating diversity in form, materials and scale, we seek to develop in people using the architecture a sense of recognition and peace.

Emotional World

We design buildings to inspire an emotional response from the inhabitants. Upon entering our structures, people should experience some slight shock or stimulation of their five senses in order to alert them to the character of the space and its connection with the outside world.

The textures of materials and the forms we use within the space often represent the natural elements on the outside. Wind and water, sunlight and starlight, or a distant mountain view, are transmitted into the space in a very direct way. We utilize the organization of the space to activate the kinetic sense and impart the experience of time in a way that a soft, homogeneous environment cannot. We feel strongly that the architecturally defined space should be a sensory experience.

Enhancing and Enjoying Nature

The structure and the space it defines impose a degree of control on the climate. To enjoy the climate there should be devices to soften the severe elements of heat, cold and humidity. Deep eaves, earth covered roofs, wind passages and airwells are some of the softening devices we employ. The imperative of our design process is to search for balance between a mechanically controlled environment and nature in a building. Feeling hot or cold and being able to mark the changes of seasons within the structure is an important factor. From aeons of living with nature, our bodies have evolved an internal awareness of the march of time. We want to design spaces that enhance our sensitivity to the events of the seasons, keeping the rhythm of our internal clock.

Aimai Moko and *Jiku*

It is our aim to create harmony between architecture and the environment. For that purpose we apply *aimai moko* and *jiku*. First, *aimai moko* means that which is undefined, vague or ambiguous. An aimai moko space is by nature multi-functional and able to evoke various responses and moods. Such a space serves to stimulate the imagination with an ambiance that is boundless, free-flowing and peaceful. As one example, to erase the division of inside and outside we provide *aimai moko* spaces as areas of transition. The porch, veranda, platform, eaves, piloti, open colonnade, arbor and trellis are elements we employ to create transition spaces. These spaces generate continuity in passing from outside to inside without an abrupt change of atmosphere. The spaces also serve to control sunlight and wind, rainfall and sound, while framing the view. Through these areas the community enters the building and the function of the building radiates into the community. People can meet here in their comings and goings and are provided with greater opportunities for communication. This is the 'hand-shaking' point between the building and community.

Second we apply the traditional concept of *jiku*, which means axis. By using points of reference found in the natural landscape, the organization of the local town, celestial bodies or the changing of the seasons, we establish axes that converge on the site. From the layering of these geographical, celestial, directional, seasonal or urban axes, we select the orientation and capture the dynamic flow of the landscape and cosmos. The axes focus energy into the structure. Once we are inside the building, our imagination is propelled along the axes outward. Our purpose is to awaken people's sense of belonging to the cosmos. Finally, the greening of space with vegetation is most important. (pp112-113)

Extracts. Source: Manfred Speidel (ed), *Team Zoo: Buildings and Projects 1971-1990*, Rizzoli (New York), 1991. Translated from the German by Michael Robinson; translated from the Japanese by Manfred Speidel. © Verlag Gerd Hatje, Stuttgart.

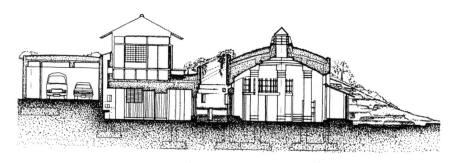

Atelier Zö, Tokuda Residence, section, Natsumidai, 1985

1991 BRENDA AND ROBERT VALE
Green Architecture

Well known for their book The Autonomous House, *Brenda and Robert Vale run an architectural practice and lecture at the University of Nottingham. In both practice and research they focus on low energy use, from the production of materials to the thermodynamics of individual buildings, promoting a holistic approach to design.*

Attitudes to Architecture
Listen to Le Corbusier in 1927: *You employ stone, wood, and concrete, and with these materials you build houses and palaces; that is construction. Ingenuity at work. But suddenly you touch my heart, and do me good, I am happy and I say: 'This is beautiful'. That is architecture. Art enters in* . . . (p7)

Architecture and the Survival of the Planet
To the ancients, all matter was composed of the four elements of earth, water, fire and air, in varying proportions. Today the composition of matter is known to be far more complex, but the four elements still provide a useful way of looking at how buildings interact with the world. For buildings are constructed of materials taken from the earth, they are serviced with water and 'fire', and they interact with the air, water, 'fire' and earth that their occupants depend upon for survival . . . (p15)

Assessing Western Patterns of Consumption – and their Alternatives
In Western society, such everyday actions as turning on the light or setting out for work are performed without thought for their consequences. If it were possible to understand the consequences of these actions in terms of their impact on the environment, it might also be possible to conceive of less harmful ways to achieve the same ends. Heating and lighting, discarding materials or even buildings, and moving between home and work, all have grave consequences. Yet even quite small changes in the way such actions are performed could be enough to bring a sustainable future . . . (p43)

Design in Action
Many buildings have some attributes which may be described as 'green'. Few in

the West are entirely benign in their effects on the environment . . . Six principles are proposed that together could build into a green architecture. (p69)

Principle 1: Conserving energy
A building should be constructed so as to minimize the need for fossil fuels to run it . . .

Principle 2: Working with climate
Buildings should be designed to work with climate and natural energy sources . . .

Principle 3: Minimizing new resources
A building should be designed so as to minimize the use of new resources and, at the end of its useful life, to form the resources for other architecture . . .

Principle 4: Respect for users
A green architecture recognizes the importance of all the people involved with it . . .

Principle 5: Respect for site
A building will 'touch-this-earth-lightly' . . .

Principle 6: Holism
All the green principles need to be embodied in a holistic approach to the built environment. (pp70-150)

Ground Rules for the Green City
A green architecture involves more than the individual building on its plot; it must encompass a sustainable form of urban environment. The city is far more than a collection of buildings; rather it can be seen as a series of interacting systems for living, working and playing – crystallized into built forms. It is by looking at systems that we can find the face of the city of tomorrow . . . (p169)

Towards a Green Aesthetic
It has been argued that it is no longer sufficient that the design satisfies the client, can be built within the budget allowed, and earns the aesthetic approval of architectural peers; the designer of a building must also realize the responsibility that resides in making any part of the built environment, however small – that design for the few affects the many . . .

It is necessary to begin by providing a common ground by which both architect and user perceive the same building. Without such a common ground, a shared judgement, the heart cannot be touched. Without the stone, wood and concrete technology, there is not architecture.

To survive on a planet with five billion people requires that a shared system of values is arrived at, so that the ramifications of any action are anticipated, both now and for the future. An architecture that would look at buildings with a similar judgement, and determine beauty through performance might not be so bad. For too long architecture has been dragged into the inaccessibility of fine art, only obtainable by the very rich or in a poor reproduction by those less wealthy. Maybe a green approach to the built environment will succeed not least because it can provide again an architecture for all. (pp181-186)

Extracts. Source: Brenda and Robert Vale, *Green Architecture: Design for a Sustainable Future*, Thames and Hudson (London), 1991. © Thames and Hudson Ltd.

Anton Alberts, NMB Bank, Amsterdam, 1984-87 – the largest ecologically sound building in Europe at that time

Post-Modern Ecology *159*

1992 WILLIAM McDONOUGH
The Hannover Principles

A central figure in the drive for sustainable development in the United States, William McDonough studied at Dartmouth College and Yale University and is now the Dean of the School of Architecture at the University of Virginia and principal of William McDonough and Partners.

1 Insist on rights of humanity and nature to co-exist in a healthy, supportive, diverse and sustainable condition.

2 Recognize interdependence. The elements of human design interact with and depend upon the natural world, with broad and diverse implications at every scale. Expand design considerations to recognize even distant effects.

3 Respect relationships between spirit and matter. Consider all aspects of human settlement including community, dwelling, industry, and trade in terms of existing and evolving connections between spiritual and material consciousness.

4 Accept responsibility for the consequences of design decisions upon human well-being, the viability of natural systems, and their right to co-exist.

5 Create safe objects of long-term value. Do not burden future generations with requirements for maintenance or vigilant administration of potential danger due to the careless creation of products, processes, or standards.

6 Eliminate the concept of waste. Evaluate and optimize the full life-cycle of products and processes, to approach the state of natural systems.

7 Rely on natural energy flows. Human designs should, like the living world, derive their creative forces from perpetual solar income. Incorporate this energy efficiently and safely for responsible use.

8 Understand the limitations of design. No human creation lasts forever and design does not solve all problems. Those who create and plan should practice humility in the face of nature. Treat nature as a model and mentor.

9 Seek constant improvement by the sharing of knowledge. Encourage direct and open communication between colleagues, patrons, manufacturers, and users to link long-term sustainable considerations with ethical responsibility, and re-establish the integral relationship between natural processes and human activity . . .

Extract. Source: William McDonough, *The Hannover Principles: Design for Sustainability*, William McDonough Architects (New York), 1992. © William McDonough Architects.

1993   PETER CALTHORPE
The Next American Metropolis

Lecturer at the University of California, Berkeley, and practising archi-tect, Peter Calthorpe (b 1949) has been involved with the environ-mental movement for many years. He has worked with Sim van der Ryn on the two co-authored Sustainable Communities, *published in 1986. In* The Pedestrian Pocket Book, Calthorpe *introduced the idea of Transit Oriented Developments, a concept developed further in* The Next American Metropolis.

Redefining the American Dream

It is time to redefine the American Dream. We must make it more accessible to our diverse population: singles, the working poor, the elderly, and the pressed middle-class families who can no longer afford the 'Ozzie and Harriet' version of the good life. Certain traditional values – diversity, community, frugality, and human scale – should be the foundation of a new direction for both the American Dream and the American Metropolis. These values are not a retreat to nostalgia or imitation, but a recognition that certain qualities of culture and community are timeless. And that these timeless imperatives must be married to the modern condition in new ways.

The alternative to sprawl is simple and timely: neighborhoods of housing, parks, and schools placed within walking distance of shops, civic services, jobs, and transit – a modern version of the traditional town. The convenience of the car and the opportunity to walk or use transit can be blended in an environment with local access for all the daily needs of a diverse community. It is a strategy which could preserve open space, support transit, reduce auto traffic, and create order in our balkanized metropolis. It could balance inner-city development with suburban investment by organizing growth around an expanding transit system and setting defensible urban limit lines and greenbelts. The increments of growth in each neighborhood would be small, but the aggregate could accommodate regional growth with minimal environmental impacts; less land consumed, less traffic gen-erated, less pollution produced.

Such neighborhoods, called Pedestrian Pockets or Transit-Oriented Develop-ments, ultimately could be more affordable for working families, environmentally responsible, and cost-effective for business and government. But such a growth strategy will mean fundamentally changing our preconceptions and local regulatory

Post-Modern Ecology 161

priorities, as well as redesigning the federal programs that shape our cities.

At the core of this alternative, philosophically and practically, is the pedestrian. Pedestrians are the catalyst which makes the essential qualities of communities meaningful. They create the place and the time for casual encounters and the practical integration of diverse places and people. Without the pedestrian, a community's common ground – its parks, sidewalks, squares, and plazas – become useless obstructions to the car. Pedestrians are the lost measure of a community, they set the scale for both center and edge of our neighborhoods. Without the pedestrian, an area's focus can be easily lost. Commerce and civic users are easily decentralized into distant chain store destinations and government centers. Homes and jobs are isolated in subdivisions and office parks . . . (pp16-17)

Definitions

Transit-Oriented Development: A Transit-Oriented Development (TOD) is a mixed-use community within an average 2,000-foot walking distance of a transit stop and core commercial area. TODs mix residential, retail, office, open space, and public uses in a walkable environment, making it convenient for residents and employees to travel by transit, bicycle, foot, or car . . .

Guiding Principles

Relationship to Transit and Circulation: The site must be located on an existing or planned trunk transit line or on a feeder bus route within 10 minutes transit time from a stop on the trunk line. Where transit may not occur for a period of time, the land use and street patterns within a TOD must function effectively in the interim . . .

Mix of Uses: All TODs must be mixed-use and contain a minimum amount of public, core commercial and residential uses. Vertical mixed-use buildings are encouraged, but are considered a bonus to the basic horizontal mixed-use requirement . . .

Residential Mix: A mix of housing densities, ownership patterns, price, and building types is desirable in a TOD. Average minimum densities should vary between 10 and 25 dwelling units/net residential acre, depending on the relationship to surrounding existing neighborhoods and location within the urban area . . .

Street and Circulation System: The local street system should be recognizable, formalized, and inter-connected, converging to transit stops, core commercial areas, schools and parks. Multiple and parallel routes must be provided between the core commercial area, residential, and employment uses so that local trips are not forced onto arterial streets. Streets must be pedestrian friendly; sidewalks, street trees, building entries, and parallel parking must shelter and enhance the walking environment . . .

General Design Criteria: Buildings should address the street and sidewalk with entries, balconies, porches, architectural features, and activities which help create safe, pleasant walking environments. Building intensities, orientation, and massing should promote more active commercial centres, support transit, and reinforce public spaces. Variation and human-scale detail in architecture is encouraged. Parking should be placed to the rear of buildings . . .

Ecology and Habitat

Open Space Resource Protection: Major creeks, riparian habitat, slopes, and other sensitive environmental features should be conserved as open space amenities and incorporated into the design of new neighborhoods. Fencing and piping of creeks should be avoided and channelization should be minimized . . .

Urban Growth Boundaries: Urban Growth Boundaries (UBG) should be established at the edge of metropolitan regions to protect significant natural resources and provide separation between existing towns and cities. Lands within the UGB should be transit accessible, contiguous to existing development, and planned for long-term urbanization . . .

Wastewater Treatment and Water Reclamation: On-site wastewater treatment facilities which use biological systems to reclaim water should be used whenever possible. The reclaimed water should be used for on-site-irrigation or for nearby farming . . .

Drainage and Wetlands: Existing drainageways and wetlands should be maintained or enhanced in a natural state. In lower-density areas, drainage systems should recharge on-site groundwater by using swales and surface systems, rather than storm drains. All urban runoff must be treated on site with biological retention and filtration areas. (pp56-75)

Extracts. Source: Peter Calthorpe, *The Next American Metropolis*, Princeton Architectural Press, (New York), 1993. © Princeton Architectural Press Inc.

1994   KENNETH YEANG
Bioclimatic Skyscrapers

Developing and adding to ideas set out in Tropical Urban Regionalism, *Yeang applies them to the problem of the high building in* Bioclimatic
Skyscrapers. *An inescapable building type, particularly in areas prone
to rapid urbanization, the skyscraper might seem the least amenable
to a bioclimatic approach. Yeang demonstrates the extent to which
this is not the case and opens an area of design with huge potential.*

The Bioclimatic Rationale

What is the justification for designing with climate? . . .

The most obvious justification must be the lowering of costs as a result of
decreasing energy consumption in the operation of the building. This can be as
much as 40 per cent of the overall life-cycle energy costs of the building since the
bulk of energy consumption happens during its operational phase . . .

Another rationale derives from the impact on the users of tall buildings. The
climatically responsive tall building can enhance its users' sense of well being while
enabling them to be aware of and to experience the external climate of the place . . .

A further justification is ecological. Designing with climate would result in a
reduction of the overall energy consumption of the building by the use of passive
(non-mechanical) structural devices . . .

There is a further justification – a regionalist one. Climate, viewed in the overall
perspective of human history and built settlements, is the single most constant
factor in our landscape, apart from its basic geographical structure. While socio-
economic and political conditions may change almost unrecognizably over a period
of, say, one hundred years, as may visual taste and aesthetic sensibility, climate
remains more or less unchanged in its cyclical course . . .

These aspects and principles should remain as guides for interpretation rather
than as dogma for form. The bioclimatic energy-conserving agenda provides us
with a set of theoretical principles for shaping buildings which must eventually
allow for a permissiveness in poetic interpretation by design.

The Design Agenda

. . . [Our] initial research and development had focused primarily on developing
a broad theoretical base for ecological design and planning of the built

environment (1971-1974). The practice that followed (TR Hamzah & Yeang Sdn Bhd 1976) began with the problem of how to integrate and better relate vegetation with buildings. The starting premise is that vegetation is an important indigenous aspect of place and should therefore be an important regionalist design factor, besides being ecologically vital. It might also be argued that vegetation (and other biotic components of the location) needs to be introduced into the built environment in far greater abundance than is currently common . . .

The problem of the abiotic/biotic synthetically designed relationship between planting and building might be described as essentially one of designing the relationship between the built systems which are primarily inorganic (as in reinforced concrete constructions, in steel or masonry, etc) and the organic materials (plants, soil, etc) . . .

Our second area of preoccupation is with the creation of variable deep air zones at the façades of buildings, either as transitional spaces, or as interstitial spaces, or as residual spaces. These can be in the form of large open-to-the-sky naturally ventilated atriums with overhead louvred-coverings, or recessed balconies, or large skycourts.

These transitional spaces are particularly successful in creating a layered building façade. They also soften the impact of the flat and hard faces of the built systems on its external environment and provide semi-enclosed and inbetween shaded areas at the upper parts of the building . . .

In tropical climatic zones, transitional spaces are already evident in much traditional architecture (for example, as verandahways and terraces); these spaces are a crucial part of the local lifestyle at ground level. Incorporation of skycourts in tall buildings enables us to recreate existing ground-level conditions in the space in the sky.

Explorations into the layering of the external wall from the inside to the outside environment, interfaced through transitional spaces, led to our concern for a variable wall design. There followed a series of studies on the external wall as a varied skin that changes its sectional profile depending on its solar orientation . . .

Current work involves exploration of ambient wind as a design influence and feature. Wind-gust velocities at the upper parts of tall buildings can be significant (nearly 50 metres per second in downtown Kuala Lumpur). The proposition here is that this ambient wind energy might be incorporated as free energy in the building's design to increase the cross-ventilation opportunities to the inner parts of the tall building. This energy might also be stored to power some of the building's M&E systems. However, besides the self-evident ecological benefits of this proposition, this environmental factor could also provide new opportunities for sculpting design features. (pp21-27)

The Bioclimatic City
The bioclimatic city reacts like the human body to changes in its environment. As the body maintains its organic stability, for example by cooling via its extremities and by its homeostatic systems, so can the tropical city employ cooling layers and use the principles of homeostasis to maintain levels of comfort.

In the bioclimatic city, the role of the architect is to identify and design new structures, devices and spaces to protect and enhance climatically the local urban environment, meeting criteria to improve existing layers of bioclimatic control . . . (p135)

Extracts. Source: Kenneth Yeang, *Bioclimatic Skyscrapers*, Artemis (London), 1994. © Kenneth Yeang.

1996 SIM VAN DER RYN AND STUART COWAN

Ecological Design

One of the longest standing advocates of ecological design, Van der Ryn here contributes with Cowan a statement of principles informed by both practice and research. It is also the fruit of a line of ecological thinking from Gregory Bateson and Ian McHarg to EF Schumacher and Ivan Illich.

If we are to create a sustainable world – one in which we are accountable to the needs of all future generations and all living creatures – we must recognize that our present forms of agriculture, architecture, engineering, and technology are deeply flawed. To create a sustainable world, we must transform these practices. We must infuse the design of products, buildings, and landscapes with a rich and detailed understanding of ecology.

Sustainability needs to be firmly grounded in the nitty-gritty details of design. Policies and pronouncements have their place, but ultimately we must address specific *design* problems: How can we design our products and manufacturing processes so that materials are completely reclaimed? How can we create wastewater treatment systems that enhance rather than damage their surrounding ecosystems? How can we design buildings that produce their own energy and recycle their own waste? How can we create agricultural systems that are not dependent on subsidies of pesticides, fertilizers, and fossil fuels?

Design problems like these bridge conventional scientific and design disciplines. They can be solved only if industrial designers talk to biochemists, sanitation engineers to wetland biologists, architects to physicists, and farmers to ecologists. In order to successfully integrate ecology and design, we must mirror nature's deep interconnections in our own epistemology of design. We are still trapped in worn-out mechanical metaphors. It is time to stop designing in the image of the machine and start designing in a way that honors the complexity of life itself . . .

First Principle: Solutions Grow from Place

Ecological design begins with the intimate knowledge of a particular place. Therefore, it is small-scale and direct, responsive to both local conditions and local people. If we are sensitive to the nuances of place, we can inhabit without destroying . . .

Second Principle: Ecological Accounting Informs Design

Trace the environmental impacts of existing or proposed designs. Use this information to determine the most ecologically sound design possibility . . .

Third Principle: Design with Nature

By working with living processes, we respect the needs of all species while meeting our own. Engaging in processes that regenerate rather than deplete, we become more alive . . .

Fourth Principle: Everyone is a Designer

Listen to every voice in the design process. No one is participant only or designer only: Everyone is a participant-designer. Honor the special knowledge that each person brings. As people work together to heal their places, they also heal themselves . . .

Fifth Principle: Make Nature Visible

De-natured environments ignore our need and our potential for learning. Making natural cycles and processes visible brings the designed environment back to life. Effective design helps inform us of our place within nature . . .

Extracts. Granted with permission from *Ecological Design* by Sim van der Ryn and Stuart Cowan, published by Island Press (Washington, DC) and Covelo, California, 1996. © 1996 Island Press.

TRADITIONAL

Leon Krier, Roma Interotta – City in the Vatican City

1969 HASSAN FATHY
Architecture for the Poor

Originally published under the title Gourna: A Tale of Two Villages, *the book from which the text is taken is an account of the planning and construction of New Gourna, a rural village near Thebes and Luxor in Egypt. As architect and coordinator for the project, Fathy turned to traditional forms and methods of construction, seeking both to accommodate the needs of the community and to 'hint at a way to begin a revived tradition of building'.*

Reestablishment of the 'Trinity': Owner, Architect, and Craftsman

One of the great advantages of using traditional building methods and bringing the craftsmen back into the team is that by so doing the architect is relieved of the work that he had unnecessarily taken over from the craftsman. In this method of construction the unit of design is the room; the masons can be trusted to supply it in standard quality and all sizes almost as if it came prefabricated from a factory. Such economy could never be obtained with concrete or other alien materials and techniques.

Ideally, if the village were to take three years to build, the designing should go on for two years and eleven months; right up to the last moment I should be learning, modifying, and improving my designs and making them fit more perfectly the families that would live in them. In spite of these good intentions, however, I found at Gourna that it was very difficult to interest the peasants in their new houses . . .

Anticipating this difficulty of getting the Gournis to take a constructive part in the planning of their houses, very early on I built some twenty houses to show them the kind of architecture we were proposing, as they couldn't understand plans. I hoped, too, to observe the families actually living in them, and thus, as it were, 'consult' them by seeing their needs in practice.

This may seem a lot of trouble to take, and the reader may wonder whether the Gournis ever did make any contribution in their role as clients. I believe, though, that the contribution the client makes to a design, however ignorant or even suspicious he may be, is something we cannot do without . . .

The intelligent participation of the client is absolutely essential to the harmonious working-out of the building process. Client, architect, and craftsman, each in his province, must make decisions, and if any one of them abdicated his responsibility, the design will suffer and the role of architecture in the cultural growth and development of the whole people will be diminished . . .

Change with Constancy

An architect is in a unique position to revive the peasant's faith in his own culture. If, as an authoritarian critic, he shows what is admirable in local forms, and even goes so far as to use them himself, then the peasants at once begin to look on their own products with pride. What was formerly ignored or even despised becomes suddenly something to boast about, and moreover, something that the villager can boast about knowingly. Thus the village craftsman is stimulated to use and develop the traditional local forms, simply because he sees them respected by a real architect, while the ordinary villager, the client, is once more in a position to understand and appreciate the craftsman's work . . .

It is not enough to copy even the very best buildings of another generation or another locality. The method of building may be used, but you must strip from this method all the substance of particular character and detail, and drive out from your mind the picture of the houses that so beautifully fulfilled your desires. You must start right from the beginning, letting your new buildings grow from the daily lives of the people who will live in them, shaping the houses to the measure of the people's songs, weaving the pattern of a village as if on the village looms, mindful of the trees and the crops that will grow there, respectful to the skyline and humble before the seasons. There must be neither fake tradition nor faked modernity, but an architecture that will be the visible and permanent expression of the character of a community. But this would mean nothing less than a whole new architecture. Change would certainly come to Gourna anyway, for change is a condition of life . . .

I hoped that Gourna might just hint at a way to begin a revived tradition of building, that others might later take up the experiment, extend it, and eventually establish a cultural barricade to stop the slide into false and meaningless architecture that was gathering speed in Egypt. The new village could show how an architecture made one with the people was possible in Egypt . . . (pp39-45)

Extracts. Source: Hassan Fathy, *Architecture for the Poor*, University of Chicago Press (Chicago), 1973. © 1973 by University of Chicago. Originally published under the title *Gourna: A Tale of Two Villages* in a limited edition, by the Ministry of Culture, Cairo.

1976 ROBERT MAGUIRE
The Value of Tradition

Described as 'romantic pragmatists', the firm of Maguire and Murray gained a reputation for church and educational buildings as well as housing. Robert Maguire (b 1931, London) was the architect of the partnership (Keith Murray trained as a silversmith) and was educated at the Architectural Association. He was the Head of the Oxford School of Architecture from 1975 to 1985. This text is a slightly edited version of a talk given at a RIBA conference in Hull in 1976, originally titled, Something out of the Ordinary?.

Where we have got to – and this is not a theory of architecture, still less a philosophy, but it is at least a satisfying structure which enables us to get on and do things – where we have got to is a kind of reversal of traditional modern-architectural attitudes by setting aside at the beginning intentions or ambitions about creating architecture as such, and just starting off with the intention of serving life through buildings (or even through no buildings, if that would serve life better). 'To serve life', that sounds a bit pretentious but I mean it at a rather simple level, in the sense of making things which help people in their lives as individuals or as communities, rather than placing burdens upon them; and I include in that emotional burdens placed at the price of physical convenience . . .

We see our job as craft rather than as a fine art and the aim of most of what we do as the achievement of a high standard of ordinariness . . .

It seems extraordinary to us now that anyone should sit down to design housing thinking 'Aha! Now I am going to create a true work of architecture, a work of art'. If ever there was a field in which an attitude of careful craft in the service of life were appropriate, it must surely be housing. I believe the difference of attitude is fundamental. It is certainly a different matter from simply updating the jargon – of referring to 'needs' rather than those 'requirements' we used to refer to five years ago. It means losing, so far as you can, those modern-architectural inhibitions . . . How?

Well, I think one has to learn all over again to invent. Constantly to ask oneself the simple, even, naive question. A simpler vocabulary helps. Why have I just done that? Am I ruling out some possibilities? Am I prepared to look at any solutions? Even a traditional one? Even a historical one? Really? And to invent, I think you also have to go around seeing all the time; looking at what things do, storing up what you observe and then being able to remember things at the point where they are needed and to develop them if appropriate for the particular case . . .

The vernacular is not a style, still less a style to be copied. To see it like that is to cease to look. It can't be copied. It dies on your drawing board; you kill the butterfly in order to mount it. The significance of the vernacular is as a learning tool.

First, the vernacular shows how to be straightforward; for example, how to put materials – any appropriate materials – together to form a structural whole which has character because it is coherent. Related to this is a properly balanced view of economy. This is not the economy of the slave-ship and the back-to-back house . . . but the economy of a living organism, an economy in the true sense of the word.

Second, the vernacular demonstrates how quite complex character – we can see it now as architectural character – emerges from this straightforwardness, as simplicity builds up into an apparent complexity by being constantly applied.

Third, it has that elusive quality, human scale. It is of course built in a very direct way by people for people. Not many drawing boards were used . . .

The pitched roof is not inevitable in our work; but (and we can back this with bitter experience as to the converse) we have observed that for getting water off a roof there is nothing quite like tilting it.

Appropriateness

One of the main tests we apply to our decisions when we are designing is that of appropriateness, and since many aspects of vernacular buildings are so timelessly appropriate to the common situations they meet, it would be surprising to me if traditional ways of doing things did not crop up frequently in our work . . .

The nice thing about inventing is that you don't have to be original. The idea is to notice as much as possible all the time, and not to reject out of hand. There are things, and ways of doing things, all about us just waiting to be connected to a differently appropriate job.

But we shall need a new freshness of outlook, a greater openness, and as I have said, I think that we need a simpler language. And some sense of humour – particularly to be able to laugh at ourselves. (pp292-295)

Extracts. Source: *The Architects' Journal*, The Architectural Press, vol 164; no 33, 18 August 1976. © Robert Maguire.

1977   DAVID WATKIN
Morality and Architecture

In an extended and closely argued critique, architectural historian David Watkin fires a polemical torpedo at both Modernist architecture and the architectural historians and theorists who supported it. Watkin draws on Sir Karl Popper's critique of historicism and traces, from AWN Pugin to Sir Nikolaus Pevsner, the essentially Whig or operative version of architectural history that provided the moral imperative underpinning Modernism. Like Popper, Watkin lays open the fallacies within such notions as the Zeitgeist *and the necessity to be true to it through constant change in architecture.*

What can it mean to imply that it is 'real' for Lord Burlington to look back to Palladio but not for [Marshall] Sisson to look back to Vanbrugh? This denuding of the artist of all cultural resonances, of all possibility of a tradition of his own, derives from a historicist and *Zeitgeist*-inspired belief that human nature has changed radically, that a new man has been born who must either learn to express himself in a radically new way which is externally dictated by economic and political conditions, or must himself be changed radically in order to conform to these new conditions. But according to an older belief, human nature does not alter from generation to generation. Moreover, artists develop traditions which are capable of interpretation and development by other artists. It is these facts which make possible the survival and development of tradition in a culture, though the forms adopted will have different meanings for different people at different times, and possibly also at the same time since individuals may differ as much from other individuals living at the same time as they do from those living at other times . . . (p7)

Historians and theorists have ignored that, whatever else it may do, architecture cannot escape involvement with image-making. Instead, they have been searching 'from an ideological base which would remove architecture once and for all from the arena of style and fashion', a base from which they could propose ruthlessly rationalistic and collectivist solutions to 'the whole question of the relationship of the total environment to community need'. Pevsner believed that the final solution of this question had been reached with the International Modern Movement and that any deviation from it would be anti-social and immoral. This quasi-religious commitment to a secular ideal acquires a particular emphasis in men who have abandoned formal religious belief themselves or who, like Pugin, have temporarily confused religions with architecture. Pugin argued that what he was defending was 'not a *style* but a *principle*', and that pathetic fallacy is echoed again and again in the nineteenth and twentieth centuries by men anxious to cling to some objectively existing truth in a godless world . . . (pp12-13)

Pevsner is insistent that every feature of every building must have a tangible material use, and he emphasizes that in attacking buildings he is 'trying . . . always to stop short, where shapes and forms of the kind I am concerned with have a functional justification'. It is the old argument for Pugin of 'convenience, construction, or propriety' and it allows its user to proceed in utter freedom; thus for Pugin it was somehow able to justify the spire but not the portico; for Pevsner it can justify the glazed spiral staircases at either end of Gropius's Administrative Office Building at the Werkbund Exhibition of 1914 . . . What, however, can be the functional justification of wrapping a glass wall around the exposed spiral staircases at the Werkbund building? The only answer is that it has an aesthetic justification. How far the result is aesthetically pleasing will naturally always be a matter for debate, and in the process of assessing Gropius's success one will naturally want to draw comparisons with the use other architects have made of spiral staircases and of glass. What is impossible is that we should feel a moral obligation to prefer Gropius's solution on the spurious argument contained in his own claim that 'the ethical necessity of the New Architecture can no longer be called in doubt' . . . (pp109-110)

Our conclusion is that an art-historical belief in the all-dominating *Zeitgeist*, combined with a historicist emphasis on progress and the necessary superiority of novelty, has come dangerously close to undermining, on the one hand, our appreciation of the imaginative genius of the individual and, on the other, the importance of artistic tradition. (p115)

Extracts. Source: David Watkin, *Morality and Architecture: The Development of a Theme in Architectural History and Theory in the Gothic Revival to the Modern Movement*, Clarendon Press (Oxford), 1977, by permission. © Oxford University Press.

1978 THE BRUSSELS DECLARATION
Reconstruction of the European City

While publishing a few texts on early 20th century Modernist archi-
tecture, the Archives d'Architecture Moderne (AAM) became most
well known over the 1970s for promoting more or less anti-Modernist
architecture and urbanism based on historical and typological analy-
sis. The figures most closely associated with the AAM were Maurice
Culot and Leon Krier, whose work often featured in its publications.
These two were instrumental in drawing together participants from
across Europe for a colloquium on the city of Brussels at which the
following statement was made.

The participants of the International Colloquium held in Brussels from the 15th to
the 17th of November under the aegis of the *Commission Française de la Culture
and the Agglomeration de Bruxelles* have decided, under the terms of their activities, to formulate the following declaration:

– they highlight the value of the combined actions initiated by the residents'
groups of Brussels in the effort to defend and restore their city, directly affected
by brutal and aberrant transformations to its structure; they condemn in particular the irresponsible politics of the EEC whose destructive activities in
siting its own buildings have affected, all equally seriously, cities such as Luxembourg, Strasbourg and Brussels; they demand the formation, within the European Institutions, of a Commission that will at last take into account the objectives
of the Reconstruction of the European City required by its inhabitants;

– they ask all the schools of architecture to focus their teaching and research on
the task of repairing European cities;

– they ask that the technical and professional training of the building trades be
directed toward the same ends;

– they mean by repairing the European city, the integration of history in urban
practice: the building heritage must be protected not just in the so-called historic
centres.

All intervention in the European city must focus on what the city has always
been, that is: streets, squares, avenues, blocks, gardens . . . and 'quarters'.
All intervention in the European city must, on the other hand, banish urban
clearways and motorways, mono-functional zones and residual green space.

It is not possible to have *industrial* zones, *commercial* zones, *pedestrian* zones
. . . but only quarters that include all the activities of urban life.

It is necessary to move toward the reduction of the built perimeter of cities and define more precisely rural zones in order to establish clearly what is town and what is countryside.

– they denounce functionalist architecture and urbanism because it has destroyed the European city in response to the exigencies of public and private capitalist industrial purposes; equally they denounce the complaisance of architects and their professional organisations in accepting the conditions of production, an attitude that has substantially contributed to the present state of things; they consider that the only possible way toward the reconstruction of the European city is the development of a labour-force with improved professional qualities and the rejection of industrial methods developed solely for the profit of their promoters.

The participants, gathered for discussion and debate on the reconstruction of the city, proclaim their conviction that the European city can be repaired, that it must be, and that the means to achieve that end are within reach.

In consequence, they resolve to pursue their work in this direction in order to cultivate the general agreement and political support of the population. (p31)

The participants of the colloquium:

Pierre Laconte (Brussels), Jaques Lucan (Paris), Jean Castex (Versailles), Antoine Grumbach (Paris), Léon Krier (London), François Loyer (Rennes), René Schoonbrodt (Brussels), Jaques Vander Biest (Brussels), Fernando Montes (Chile/ Paris), Bernard Huet (Paris), R-L Delevoy (Brussels), André Barey (Barcelona), Maurice Culot (Brussels), Philippe Panerai (Versailles), Pierluigi Nicolin (Milan/ Palermo).

Extracts. Source: *La Reconstruction de Bruxelles,* Editions des Archives d'Architecture Moderne (Brussels), 1982. © Archives d'Architecture Moderne. First published in *La Declaration de Bruxelles,* Editions des Archives d'Architecture Moderne, No 15 (Brussels), 1978, translation for this publication by Karl Kropf.

1980 MAURICE CULOT
Reconstructing the City in Stone

Over the 1970s Maurice Culot and Leon Krier took an increasingly traditional position in the architectural debate. In this short polemic they call for the use of traditional materials yet argue against capitalist means of production, combining what might be considered contrary positions.

ARCHITECTS, REFUSE TO CONSTRUCT WITH NON-TRADITIONAL MATERIALS! Capitalist construction methods do not lend themselves to the reconstruction of the European city in accordance with historical concepts of its streets and squares and the complexity of its various districts. As progressists, we also reject the production methods of modern architecture which are based on waste (large windows, large spans, etc) and upon police repression, (the need for nuclear energy to fulfil the production requirements of costly materials such as concrete, and control of world markets such as aluminium).

Construction with materials (stone, wood, brick . . .) is quite a reality today, on condition that the policy of planned scarcity is dispensed with and that production problems are treated from the public viewpoint and in accordance with the intelligent use of a given material dependent upon its properties, its use and its history. On condition too, that the promotion of natural materials is assured by public entities for use in renovation and construction programmes.

Source: *Contreprojets, Controprogetti, Counterprojects*, translator Miss S Day, Editions Archives d'Architecture Moderne (Brussels), 1980. © Maurice Culot.

1983   DEMETRI PORPHYRIOS
Classicism is Not a Style

Earning a Master of Architecture and PhD in History and Theory of Architecture from Princeton University, Demetri Porphyrios (b 1949, Greece) has pursued the Classical both through his writings and practice. As exemplified by the House in Kensington of 1987, his work achieves the Classical balance of strength and repose with precision and clarity of purpose. Porphyrios has taught at the Architectural Association, Yale University and the University of Virginia. A version of this essay was first published in Architectural Design *in 1982.*

The predicament of contemporary architecture . . . stems from our twofold inheritance: on one hand, the symbolically mute elements of industrial production inherited from Modernism, and on the other the expendable historicist and high-tech signs of industrial kitsch inherited from Modern Eclecticism. This raises, in my opinion, the crucial problem we face today: if there is an opposition between the economic priorities of mass industrial society and the yearning for an authentic culture that could sustain individual freedom in public life, under what qualifications is it possible to practise architecture at all? Paradoxically, the only possible critical stance for architecture today is to build an alliance between building construction and symbolic representation. To construct, that is, a tectonic discourse which, while addressing the pragmatics of shelter, could at the same time represent its own tectonics in a symbolic way.

It is from such a perspective that classicism should be re-evaluated today: not as a borrowed stylistic finery but as an ontology of building. Classicism is not a style. Its lesson lies in the way by which it raises construction and shelter to the realm of the symbol.

The Constructional Logic of Vernacular

Despite the superficial associations with rusticity that the word 'vernacular' brings to mind its essential meaning is different. The idea of vernacular has nothing to do with stylistics. It rather points to the universal ethos of constructing shelter under the conditions of scarcity of materials and operative constructional techniques.

By invoking vernacular, one does not seek the primitivism of pre-industrial cultures. The temptation to turn one's back on contemporary society in order to return to some pre-industrial order, when pursued, leaves us suspended amid the reverberations of Plato's ghost: 'what then?' Instead, the essential meaning of vernacular refers to straightforward construction, to the rudimentary building of shelter, an activity that exhibits reason, efficiency, economy, durability and pleasure. Certainly, varying materials and techniques attribute regionalist characteristics to vernacular. But beyond appearances, all vernacular is marked by a number of constructional *a prioris* which are universal and essentially phenomenological.

To begin with, building – by its very nature – involves the experiences of load-bearing and load-borne, the primary manifestations of which are the column and the lintel. Secondly, it involves the experience of horizontal and vertical enclosure, the primary manifestations of which are the roof and the wall. The floor, since it repeats the original ground, is flat for it is meant to be walked upon; whereas the roof is inclined since, in addition to its shedding of water, it marks the terminus and should appear as such. Finally, since all construction is construction by means of finite elements, the act of building involves necessarily the experience of demarcation, the primary manifestations of which are the beginning and ending.

When applied to making of shelter, these constructional *a prioris* give rise to a set of constructional forms: as for example the gable which marks the sectional termination of the roof and thus points to the primary experience of entry; or the engaged pilaster, which manifests the confluent experiences of load-bearing and enclosure; or the window and door, which manifest the experience of suspending enclosure locally for purposes of passage; or the colonnade, which demarcates the experience of boundary; and so on.

Classicism: The Symbolic Elaboration of Vernacular

Such constructional *a prioris* and their ensuing constructional forms can be identified – it would appear – beyond fear of interpretive dispute and could serve as the core of a common architectural knowledge.

Yet architecture cannot remain at this 'starting point'. Its vocation is to raise itself above the contingencies of building by commemorating those very contingencies from which it sprung in the first place. What distinguishes a shed from a temple is the mythopoeic power the temple possesses: it is a power that transgresses the boundaries of contingent reality and raises construction and shelter to the realm of the symbol.

This is the sense in which we can say that classicism is not a style. The classical naturalises the constructional *a prioris* of shelter by turning them into myth:

the demarcations of beginning and ending are commemorated as base and capital; the experience of load-bearing is made perceptible through the entasis in the shaft of the column; the chief beam, binding the columns together and imposing on them a common load, becomes the architrave; the syncopation of the transversal beams resting on the architrave is rendered visible in the figures of the triglyphs and metopes of the frieze; the projecting rafters of the roof, supported by the frieze, appear in the form of the cornice; finally – and most significantly – the whole tectonic assemblage of column, architrave, frieze and cornice becomes the ultimate object of classical contemplation in the ideal of the Order.

The Order sets form over the necessities of shelter: it sets the myth of the tectonic over the contingencies of construction. The power of mythical fiction presides. It is the possibility of such an act of mythical fiction that constitutes the prime aesthetic subject matter of classical thought. Classical architecture constructs a tectonic fiction out of the productive level of building. The artifice of constructing this fictitious world is seen as analogous to the artifice of constructing the human world. In its turn, myth allows for a convergence of the real and the fictive so that the real is redeemed. By rendering construction mythically fictive, classical thought posits reality in a contemplative state, wins over the depredations of petty life and, in a moment of rare disinterestedness, rejoices in the power it has over contingent life and nature.

Mythical thinking, of course, is not necessarily primitive or prelogical as common opinion might maintain today. It is true thinking for it reduces the world to order. Its truth is no less than that experimentally verified by science. Today, if it appears that the mythopoeic mind cannot achieve objectivity (and should therefore be doomed as an irrationality that can never attain consensus) this is not because it is incapable of dealing with the world, but rather because contemporary industrial life is dominated by vulgar positivism. That is why architecture today is systematically denied its mythopoeic power. The vulgarity lies not in the search for objectivity but in the immanence with which consumer culture boasts of being the mere extension of production. (pp125-127)

Extracts. Source: *Demetri Porphyrios: Selected Buildings and Writings*, Architectural Monograph no 25, Academy Editions (London), 1993. © Academy Group Ltd.

1984   LEON KRIER
Building and Architecture

> *While Krier's designs remained within a more or less Rationalist Clas-*
> *sical idiom over the late 1970s and early 80s, his rhetoric focused*
> *increasingly on the importance of tradition. In this short piece, included*
> *in a monograph of his work, he states his case with almost rabid*
> *vehemence.*

Glossarium

a) The terms classical architecture as against modernist so-called 'architecture'
   are contradictory, antagonistic and incompatible propositions: the first based on
   artisan-artistic production, the latter based on industrial modes of production.

b) The term classical denotes the best; it attains to the highest quality and belongs to intellectual culture. The term industrial denotes the necessary; it attains to profitable quantity and belongs to material culture . . .

Arche-tektonike

Architecture (Arche-tektonike) means literally *form* of *origin*. If this definition is
relevant for the architecture of any organism and structure, it is fundamental for
Architecture as the Art of Building. It is not that the principles of Architecture
reach into an immemorial past but that their origin is forever present. Architecture
reaches its highest possible form in the classical principles and orders. Even a le-
gion of geniuses cannot improve them any more than they can improve the human
figure or bone structure. They are profoundly logical, rational, simple, inevitable.
They have the same inexhaustible capacities as the principles which govern nature
and the universe itself. *Architecture* is the intellectual-artistic culture of building.
It is concerned with the imitation of the elements of building into symbolic language, expressing in a fixed system of symbols the very origins of Architecture.
The classical notions of *permanence, stability, commodity, beauty* are earthly notions, they have, furthermore, meaning only within the life span of mankind. This
is the true meaning of timeless and absolute values in Architecture.(pp118-119)

Extracts. Source: Demetri Porphyrios (ed), 'Leon Krier: Houses, Palaces, Cities', *Architectural
Design*, Profile 54, Academy Group Ltd (London) vol 54; no 7/8, 1984. © Academy Group Ltd.

1984   ROBERT AM STERN
On Style, Classicism and Pedagogy

One of the 'Grays' along with Charles Moore and Robert Venturi, as opposed to the New York Five 'Whites', Robert AM Stern (b 1939 New York City) was an early advocate of Post-Modernism. Through his writing and design he pursued the multivalent readings characteristic of the Post-Modern, making frequent references to Classical architecture. In this text he makes a more direct move toward Classicism, arguing for its timeless value as an architectural language and educational tool.

Classicism, as I see it, is the formal expression of modern (ie Post-Gothic) secular institutions in the West. Classicism inherently represents the public and institutional realm, and the vernacular may be said to represent that which is private. Classicism has traditionally been used to transcend or modify the vernacular in order to draw people together in their diversity; it brings the Republican spirit of Washington to the county courthouses of the South and Midwest, just as it in turn brought the authority of Rome to cities meant to symbolize a nation – Leningrad, New Deli, Paris and Washington. The public realm, however, extends beyond great squares, museums, and seats of government to encompass all levels of shared space. Classicism is not inherently identified with or tainted by any particular ideology, but has served rather as a distillation of the best that society can achieve. It is a tradition and a point of view . . .

Classicism is the only codified, amplified, and perennially vital system of architectural composition bringing order to the process of design. It is also the only codified, amplified, and perennially vital language of architectural form. Gothic is equally representational and widely admired, but it was a short-lived system, inextricably connected to a narrower set of associations, and without a fully developed compositional system of its own. Modernism – that is, Functionalism – set out to do away with both associative meaning and the very concept of architectural grammar. It therefore possesses only the most minimal of resources to establish or vary character, and its compositional technique was based on behaviorism and a literal-minded interpretation of construction. Classicism is at once a tradition and a language incorporating rules of syntax and rhetoric; it provides a methodology to establish composition and character . . .

Traditional 183

Students should learn the grand tradition of Classicism with all its myriad permutations and its history of anti-classical movements, including Modernism, through both historical research and investigative design . . .

It is hardly restrictive or close-minded to suggest that we expose architectural education to twenty-five hundred years of history. Now that Modernism is dead as a creative force and it is fashionable to turn to the more distant past for inspiration, it behooves us to teach the past in a logical and structured way. If we do not, the creative energies of the present moment will have the same meteorically short career as those of Modernism. A new chapter in architectural history cannot sustain itself on a superficial understanding of the past or the faddish slickness of architectural magazines.

Extracts. Source: *Precis*, The Journal of the Graduate School of Architecture and Planning, Columbia University, vol 5, Fall 1984. © The Trustees of Columbia University in the City of New York.

Robert Stern, Residence , East Hampton, New York, 1980-84

1984   HRH THE PRINCE OF WALES
RIBA Gala Speech

The notorious 'carbuncle' speech was given at the 150th anniversary gala of the Royal Institute of British Architects at Hampton Court Palace, May 1984. With that speech, HRH the Prince of Wales entered the architectural debate in no uncertain terms. After praising the reaction against the Modern Movement and promoting the Community Architecture initiative, he launched the carbuncle salvo, drawing considerable return fire over the next few weeks both in the architectural and popular press.

What, then, are we doing to our capital city now? What have we done to it since the bombing during the war? What are we shortly to do to one of its most famous areas – Trafalgar Square? Instead of designing an extension to the elegant facade of the National Gallery which complements it and continues the concept of columns and domes, it looks as if we may be presented with a kind of vast municipal fire station, complete with the sort of tower that contains the siren. I would understand better this type of High-Tech approach if you demolished the whole of Trafalgar Square and started again with a single architect responsible for the entire layout, but what is proposed is like a monstrous carbuncle on the face of a much-loved and elegant friend. Apart from anything else, it defeats me why anyone wishing to display the early Renaissance pictures belonging to the gallery should do so in a new gallery so manifestly at odds with the whole spirit of that age of astonishing proportion. Why can't we have those curves and arches that express feeling in design? What is wrong with them? Why has everything got to be vertical, straight, unbending, only at right angles – and functional? . . .

In this 150th anniversary year, which provides an opportunity for a fresh look at the path ahead and in which by now you are probably regretting having asked me to take part, may I express the earnest hope that the next 151 years will see a new harmony between imagination and taste and in the relationship between the architects and the people of this country. (p43)

Extracts. Source: Charles Jencks, *The Prince, the Architects and New Wave Monarchy*, Academy Editions (London), 1988. © HRH The Prince of Wales.

1986 ALEXANDER TZONIS & LIANE LEFAIVRE

Critical Classicism: The Tragic Function

Historians and educators, Alexander Tzonis and Liane Lafaivre have written widely on both contemporary and historical architecture. In their article 'The Grid and the Pathway' published in 1981, they coined the phrase 'critical regionalism', an idea later elaborated by Kenneth Frampton. This extract is taken from the concluding chapter of Classical Architecture: The Poetics of Order *in which Tzonis and Lafaivre set out an explication and critique of Classical Architecture and put forward the notion of critical Classicism.*

A classical building, a temenos, a world within a world factored by the rule-based actions of its architect, contains a set of abstract general relations that represents a large number of phenomena of reality. Taxis, genera, symmetry, and their numerous schemata can set up representations in an 'analoglike' manner whose chains, matrices, lattices, and even more complex pattern of reasoning are implicit in the formal patterning of the work. Thus, although the formal patterns of classical buildings might have originated in depictions of specific events and specific objects, in the end classical buildings through formal patterns embody abstract relations of quantity and space, out of which one can infer by analogy statements about many other facets of reality: the reality of nature, the reality of thinking, the reality of human associations, and the reality of future artifacts.

Good classical architectural compositions are ingenious essays in stone, intelligently argued dialectics and hermeneutics. This is true of most ancient Greek temples and most buildings, for example, by Alberti or Palladio. In these buildings partitioning, ornament, and rhythm, in the sense we have been using here, form a conceptual structure for implementing a major part of the program of classical architecture: to create representations of reality; to explore through the formal relations of the building the architecture of reality; to identify in reality independence, equivalence, subalternation, contrary, symmetry, transitivity, correlation, identity, whole, continuity; to study how space works, how we can work in space, how our mind works, and how we can work together as a society.

A classical building also relates to reality in a diametrically different way from the way it does when it reproduces it mimetically. We call this relation *foregrounding* and *estrangement*. The world of the building in this case is not only about truth and epistemology but also about goodness and morality . . . (pp275-276)

Aristotle, in his *Poetics*, had already remarked that 'by deviating in exceptional cases from the *normal* idiom, the language will gain distinction' (ch XXII, para 4). He had even used the notion of 'strange' (*xenikon*) (ch XXII, para 1) for words that had been rendered phonetically, grammatically, syntactically, or semantically deviant. In his *Art of Rhetoric* the notion of 'strange' (distant, remote) is linked with 'removing from the ordinary' and with august dignity of poetic discourse (bk III, ch II, para 2, 3). The foregrounding of certain aspects of a building that one observes in classical architecture can be seen as such necessary deviations from the 'normal idiom' to achieve distancing from established social perceptions and practices. Brecht's theory of 'estrangement' (in the original German *Verfremdung*) in drama comes to remarkably similar conclusions. Worldmaking in this sense is strangemaking . . .

In a building as in tragedy, it is difficult to disentangle how much the use of the classical canon leads to strangemaking and how much leads to imitation, to, one is tempted to say, 'samemaking', how much through formalization the building confronts reality and how much it represents it. It is equally difficult to specify the degree to which formalization, generalization, and strangemaking separate the work from the world without concurrently engaging it critically with reality. It all depends on how the work is being used, on our intentions as much as on the structure of the work itself.

It is even more difficult to ascertain the interpretation that classical formal patterns might have when applied in ways outside the canon. Let us take a chance and venture, although this is rightly the topic of a new study, that there are three major applications of partial use of the classical canon: (1) 'Citationism' of classical motifs, or so-called free-wheeling classicism; (2) syncretism; and (3) the use of classical fragments in architectural 'metastatement'.

Under citationism belongs the 'classicism' of kitsch, of consumer products, of propaganda, and of even more ambitious cultural objects, 'prestige' buildings and in several occasions *some* of the so-called post-modernist buildings . . . (pp277-279)

Let us return to the two other partial applications of the classical canon: syncretism and metastatement. Unlike citationism, they do not cause nostalgia or illusion. They can be pessimistic or ironic, polemical or adversarial, but always critical. In the case of syncretism more than one canon is used simultaneously in the same design, even if these are at odds and produce non sequitur effects. In the second case, that of metastatement, a world of higher visual statements is built that refers to the classical canon. Classical segments are used to say something about classicism . . .

In both cases – syncretism and metastatement – fragments of the classical canon are used as means of questioning a dogmatic or quasi-automatic, routine application of the classical order . . . (p281)

The world of classical architecture today is a world of scattered forms that in their incompleteness can be seen as icons of decomposition. But they can also be seen as unfinished pictures of a promised world, like the suspended golden hour in the landscapes of Claude Lorrain to be taken as part of the nightfall or the dawn. The time direction of the classical fragments that still surround us points to two diametrically opposed paths. We have taken the one leading away from the joyful pessimism of that grand hotel, Abyss.

The critical potentials of classicism might arise from the fact that we belong to a generation of crisis, and frequently, of counterfeit culture, in which there is a disintegration of human relations at every level of association and in which the threat of total war, of total annihilation, is real. Children of happier times might find, in the obsessive efforts of classicism to align, partition, measure, relate, and finish, a discipline of the mind. They might discover in these countless redefinitions of the game of interspacing and termination, superimposition and repetition, an imperative to generate a work free of contradiction. Perhaps they will recognize in classicism a thinking that struggles for consistency and completeness. They might see in this imperative for order and rationality a quest in the domain of thinking – but also what Thomas Mann (1957) called 'the highly cherished idea of a perfected humanity.' (pp281-287)

Extract. Source: Alexander Tzonis and Liane Lefaivre, *Classical Architecture: The Poetics of Order*, MIT Press (Cambridge, Mass), 1986. © 1986 by The Massachusetts Institute of Technology.

1987   HRH THE PRINCE OF WALES
Mansion House Speech

After three years and five major speeches promoting Community Archi-tecture, Classicism and conservation, Prince Charles returned to the subject of Modernism in the Mansion House speech. As in the Car-buncle speech, he was less than complimentary and again provoked a strong reaction within the architectural profession.

I was in Germany a few weeks ago, and returned greatly impressed by the way in which Munich has been so carefully restored after the ravages of the war.

You have, Ladies and Gentlemen, to give this much to the Luftwaffe: when it knocked down our buildings, it didn't replace them with anything more offensive than rubble. *We* did that. Clausewitz called war the continuation of diplomacy by other means. Around St Paul's, planning turned out to be the continuation of war by other means.

What went wrong? Your predecessors bought the fashionable post-war ortho-doxy that arose from the 1947 Town and Country Planning Act and the Ministry guidelines, only too appropriately entitled 'The Redevelopment of Central Areas' . . .

Is it right that the people, their elected representatives, the Secretary of State himself, can take no initiative of their own? Is it sensible that they can only react to developers' proposals? There must be something wrong with a system which involves public opinion at so late a stage that the only course left open to the public is to obstruct the development through whatever means the planning system allows. If the planning system is to blame, if the rules are at fault, then why don't we change them? To be specific, here are three major shortcomings in our system:

First, control over design of buildings next to major monuments is fuzzy and, in practice, unenforceable . . .

Second, and closely related to this . . . the Department of the Environment does not encourage planning authorities to set firm aesthetic guidelines in development . . .

Third, that skyline [London's], once the envy of other cities: let's admit that the approach adopted for protecting it over the past forty years has simply not worked. The rules are too woolly . . .

To sum up: because there is this broad discretionary element in our planning legislation, as well as an absence of aesthetic control, architects and developers have the wrong kind of freedom – the freedom to impose their caprice, which is a kind of tyranny. Competitions even encourage them to come up with the voguish innovations and fashionable novelties that appeal to nobody but other architects. One prominent architect recently confessed, airily and with no apparent sign of shame, that some of his own earlier buildings have ceased to interest him, now that the thrill of creativity has worn off.

Well, what kind of creativity is that? To put up a building which other people have to live with, and leave them to live with it while you wander off saying you're tired of it, and then to put up another one which you will presumably get tired of too, leaving yet more people to live with the all-too-durable consequences of your passing fancy. There is a terrible fecklessness to all this, when grown men can get whole *towns* in the family way, pay nothing towards maintenance, and call it romance . . . (p47-49)

Extracts. Source: Charles Jencks, *The Prince, the Architects and New Wave Monarchy*, Academy Editions (London), 1988. © HRH The Prince of Wales.

Paternoster Associates, Paternoster Square proposal, London, 1993 – the scheme that Prince Charles pushed through as a counter-scheme to the winning Arups' competition (drawing: Carl Lubin)

1989 DUANY + PLATER-ZYBERK

Traditional Neighbourhood Development Ordinance

Trained as architects, Andreas Duany and Elizabeth Plater-Zyberk studied at Princeton and Yale Universities, at the latter under Charles Moore. With Seaside, designed in 1982, they combined Moore's sense for American vernacular with the anti-Modernist urbanism of Leon Krier and European notions of typology. The result, as realised at Seaside and later developments, is the Traditional Neighbourhood Development (TND) based on a regulating plan and a set of building codes or ordinance.

Intent

This ordinance is designed to ensure the development of open land along the lines of traditional neighbourhoods. Its provisions adopt the urban conventions which were normal in the United States from colonial times until the 1940s.

Traditional neighbourhoods share the following conventions:

— Dwellings, shops and workplaces, all limited in size, are located in proximity to each other.

— A variety of streets serve equitably the needs of the pedestrian and the automobile.

— Well-defined squares and parks provide places for informal social activity and recreation.

— Well-placed civic buildings provide places of purposeful assembly for social, cultural and religious activities, becoming symbols of community identity.

— Private buildings are located along streets and squares forming a disciplined edge unbroken by parking lots.

Traditional neighbourhoods achieve certain social objectives:

— By reducing the number and length of necessary automobile trips, traffic congestion is minimized and commuters are granted increased personal time.

— By bringing most of the needs of daily living within walking distance, the elderly and the young gain independence of movement.

— By walking in defined public spaces, citizens come to know each other and to watch over their collective security.

— By providing a full range of housing types and workplaces, age and economic class are integrated and the bonds of an authentic community are formed.

— By promoting suitable civic buildings, democratic initiatives are encouraged and the organic evolution of society is secured.

Until the advent of postwar zoning ordinances, traditional neighbourhoods were commonplace in the United States. Many survive as examples of communities which continue to be practical and desirable today.

Extracts. Source: *Architectural Design* vol 59; no 5/6, 1989. © Foundation for Traditional Neighbourhoods

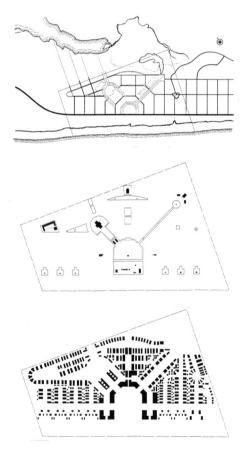

Duany + Plater-Zyberk, Seaside – zoning maps of public and private space, monuments and major avenues

1989   QUINLAN TERRY
Architecture and Theology

Significantly referring to AWN Pugin in this essay, Quinlan Terry (b 1937, London) takes a similar position to Pugin in claiming a connection between religious faith and architectural style. It might be more correct to say tradition rather than style as for Terry that tradition is the Classical (as opposed to Pugin's Gothic). Educated at the Architectural Association, whose Modernist bias he rejected, Terry worked with Raymond Erith from 1962, continuing to practise under the name Erith and Terry after the latter's death in 1973.

My subject is architecture and theology, or rather Art and Faith, the place where architecture and religion meet. The two great authorities on this subject from the last century were Pugin, who designed the Houses of Parliament, and Ruskin, the celebrated artist and writer. Both started their lives as devout Christians, and ended their days in a mental asylum. Perhaps this is a warning to tread carefully and not to expect too much from Art, and certainly not to look at art for the supreme truth and consolation that Faith alone provides . . .

We are the victims of a voracious technology, ruthlessly consuming the resources of the earth. A Pandora's box has opened which no one can close. Everyone realises that for all their benefits these things will bring about huge collective disasters. The march of progress has crushed gentler species of animal and plant to extinction beneath its feet.

But the gentlest and rarest species are the creative gift of Art and the fear of the Creator; both of which, speaking generally, have disappeared. 'The fear of the Lord is the beginning of wisdom'; we have lost this fear and so we have become foolish.

I do not know how to explain this phenomenon, except by relating this lack of creative gift to the Creator. The building of the Tabernacle showed that when mankind rejects the belief in the Creator, then his creative ability disappears. Never before in the history of the world has man been ablew to reject God so completely and successfully.

Even the Ancient Roman at his most evil had a fear of God which we have discarded. He realised that his life depended on the one who gives rain and sunshine. If there was famine he prayed to Ceres, the goddess of corn; if he was sick he brought libations to Aesculapius, the god of healing; when he was childless he prayed to the goddess of fertility; and he acknowledged his dependence on the goddess Fortuna for good luck. But the pride of technological man has no limits, and is infinitely greater than that of his Roman counterpart.

Whereas the heathen feared the creator and bowed down to wood and stone, modern man fears no God and has no hope beyond technology. Ancient man harnessed nature and expressed this in his art; modern man finds himself tragically opposed to nature and has expressed this defiance in his art. Thus the creative artistic gift must disappear.

This process has occurred in architecture. In the past we were confined to the disciplines of natural materials – brick, stone, timber, slate and stucco. My own village is a good example. The height was controlled by our ability to climb stairs and the depth was controlled by natural light and air. In our cities the same disciplines applied. But now steel, glass, concrete and plastics, electric lifts, artificial light and air, have given us an unbridled and unlimited freedom which we are unable to control. Cheaper, temporary construction and maximum profit have become our gods. In the 18th century Canaletto painted a view of the city of London from Somerset House. It was a beautiful city with St Paul's dominating the skyline. Today the same view shows St Paul's dwarfed by the temples of Mammon: the banks which live off usury and insurance companies which fix their stakes on our misfortunes. In the old days people built as Hawksmoor built in Oxford's Radcliffe Camera. Nobody can fail to notice the exquisite proportions, the genial use of the Classical Orders, the natural materials, human scale and accomplished harmony and how it fits in with its surroundings. Today we build skyscrapers which look like oil refineries eschewing natural materials, working with no sense of proportion and with no harmony or grace. Buildings like these cannot be compared with the buildings of our forefathers. The ability to design and build beautiful buildings has ceased . . .

So is our position today without hope? Are we of all men the most miserable? By no means! As in theology so in architecture, there is always a remnant whose sights are fixed on another world. And as we toil below, through this short and uncertain earthly life, we can at least attempt to recreate something of His Creation. Every commission, however small, is an opportunity to keep the lamp of traditional architecture flickering and is a chance not only for the architect, but also for the workman, to practise the skills he was born to use: to create with his hands the thing that is good, be it a Corinthian capital in stone or a scroll in an iron railing, or a leaf carved in wood or even a fine rubbed arch in a brick wall. All these raise a man from a mere wage earner to a craftsman:

Who lest all thought of Eden fade
Bringst Eden to the Craftsman's brain
Godlike to muse o'er his own trade
And manlike to stand with God again.
And though in our fallen state we do dimly grope after perfection, it is this quest for beauty that makes both their work and mine so worthwhile. As in theology, so in architecture. However, it is necessary to bear all the ridicule and scorn that are deployed by the Darwinian misconception that evolution and progress are mandatory. We are coerced into believing that every age must bring something new. But here again, as in theology, so in architecture – there is nothing new worth having. As Solomon said:

The thing that hath been is that which shall be, and that which is done is that which shall be done and there is no new thing (worth having) under the sun. Is there anything whereof it may be said, See this is new? It hath already been before us in old times. (Ecclesiastes, Chapter 1, verses 9-10.) (pp136-138)

Extracts. Source: *Quinlan Terry: Selected Works*, Architectural Monographs No 27, Academy Editions (London), 1993. © Academy Group Ltd.

Quinlan Terry, Richmond Riverside, London, 1984-88

1989   HRH THE PRINCE OF WALES
A Vision of Britain

On 28 October 1988, BBC1 broadcast Prince Charles' programme A Vision of Britain. In one sense a culmination of his architectural activism and in another a point of departure for further activity, the programme gave substance to the ideals hinted at in his previous speeches. The companion book was published a year later and detailed the principles the Prince seeks to promote.

Ten Principles we can build upon

It isn't up to me to rewrite the planning laws, but I do think it might help if we sat back for a moment and looked at the whole process. It seems to me that we are lost in a maze of regulations; perhaps the way out is simpler than we think. I'm sure that the man in the street knows exactly what he wants, but he is frustrated by form-filling and the mystique that surrounds the professionals. I want to see laymen and professionals working together; developers, architects and craftsmen understanding each other. I want to demolish the barriers of bureaucracy, and discover that common ground we seem to have lost. There is nothing wrong with simplicity.

The Place

We must respect the land. It is our birthright and almost every inch of it is densely layered with our island history . . .

Hierarchy

There are two kinds of hierarchy which need concern us here. One is the size of buildings in relation to their public importance. The other is the relative significance of the different elements which make up a building . . .

Buildings should reflect these hierarchies, for architecture is like a language. You cannot construct pleasing sentences in English unless you have a thorough knowledge of the grammatical rules. If you abandon these basic principles of grammar the result is discordant and inharmonious. Good architecture should be like good manners and follow a recognized code . . .

Scale

Man is the measure of all things. Buildings must relate first of all to human proportions and then respect the scale of the buildings around them. Each place has a characteristic scale and proportion: farmhouses in Nottinghamshire may be tall and thin and in Northumberland they may be low and squat. It is high, and out-of-scale buildings that are the most damaging . . .

Harmony

Harmony is the playing together of the parts. Each building that goes beside another has to be in tune with its neighbour. A straggling village street or a wide city avenue which may consist of buildings belonging to many different periods can look harmonious . . .

Enclosure

One of the great pleasures of architecture is the feeling of well-designed enclosure. It is an elementary idea with a thousand variants and can be appreciated at every level of building from the individual room to the interior of St Paul's Cathedral, or from the grand paved public square to the walled garden . . .

The secret of enclosed spaces is that they should have few entrances; if there are too many the sense of security disappears. If the space contains something to love such as a garden, a sculpture or a fountain, it is more likely to be cherished and not vandalised. A community spirit is born far more easily in a well formed square or courtyard than in a random scattering of developers' plots. The squares, almshouses, universities and inns of court of our past that we love so well have always answered our needs. Their virtues are timeless, still providing privacy, beauty and a feeling of total safety.

Materials

Britain has to revive and nurture its rural and individual urban characteristics based upon local materials. Perhaps there is even a case for reopening some of our great stone quarries. We must also encourage our traditional craftsmen – our flint-knappers, our thatchers, our blacksmiths – and involve them in the building of our future. This will in time engender an economic revival which is not dependent on centralised industries but which is locally based . . .

Decoration

We need to reinstate architecture as the mistress of the arts and crafts. I would suggest that the consumers are ahead of the professionals here. They seem to feel, as I do, that living in a factory-made world is not enough. Beauty is made by the unique partnership of hand, brain and eye. The results should be part of all new architecture, helping to enrich our spirits.

Art
Artists and architects might as well be educated on different planets. The principles by which art and architecture are taught need to be revised. There should be common disciplines taught to all those engaged in the visual arts. Life drawing and a study of nature is as essential for architects as it is for any artist. Remembering common roots can nourish both these great arts for their mutual benefit and our delight.

Signs and Lights
Far too many of the marks of 20th-century progress take the form of ugly advertising and inappropriate street lighting, apparently designed only for the motor car. The car and commerce are both vital to the well-being of the country, but it is the junk they trail with them that we have to tackle . . .

Good lettering must be taught and learned; its qualities are timeless and classical in the broadest sense . . .

Our towns should be beautifully lit at night. Safety is not a matter of light intensity but of the overall quality of the surroundings. Many great cities of the world have retained a magic quality at night due to incandescent lighting. We should bury as many wires as possible and remember that when it comes to lighting and signs the standard solution is never enough.

Community
People should be involved willingly from the beginning in the improvement of their own surroundings. You cannot force anyone to take part in the planning process. Legislation tries to make it possible for people to share some of the complex processes of planning, but participation cannot be imposed: it has to start from the bottom up . . .

There must be one golden rule – we all need to be involved together – planning and architecture are much too important to be left to the professionals. (pp78-97)

Extracts. Source: HRH The Prince of Wales, *A Vision of Britain: A Personal View of Architecture*, Doubleday (London), 1989. Copyright 1989 AG Carrick Ltd. Permission granted by Sheil Land Associates.

1992   THE URBAN VILLAGES GROUP
Urban Villages

With a membership made up of developers, housebuilders, and representatives of funding institutions as well as architects, planners and environmentalists, the Urban Villages Group was set up in 1989 on the instigation of HRH the Prince of Wales. The goal of the group is to investigate and promote mixed-use and mixed-tenure development. In 1992 they published a report and the extracts here were drawn from a summary. As explicitly noted in the report, the urban village concept is based on the work of Leon Krier, other consultees including Christopher Alexander, Sir Andrew Darbyshire, Rob Krier, Elizabeth Plater Zyberk, John Thompson and Francis Tibbalds.

The Main Points

1   The report proposes that a new category of development, the mixed-use 'urban village', or Structured Planned Urban Development (SPUD), should be recognized and widely developed wherever suitable sites exist.

2   It recommends this to government, planning authorities, landowners, developers, funding institutions, and a wider public, as a means of creating more civilised and durable urban environments.

3   In the 1990s, still less in the 21st century, our changing society should not cling to outdated 'monoculture' zoning, or the dubious assumption that tidy, single-use development is a more durable investment. We need to set our minds and resources to creating a more flexible, sustainable kind of urban neighbourhood: the urban village . . .

13   To succeed, a planned mixed-use development needs to achieve critical mass. It must be big enough to support a wide range of uses and amenities; to attract firms and individuals who give it life and prosperity. But it must be small enough for all its buildings to be within easy walking distance . . .

14   The ideal size for an urban village is probably about 100 acres (40 hectares). We envisage it having a combined working and resident population of around 3,000-5,000. It should cater for daily shopping, basic health facilities, primary and nursery schooling, and some recreational/cultural needs . . .

16   The mix of uses should occur within each street block as well as within the village as a whole; houses and flats should balance workspace so as to achieve

a theoretical 1:1 ratio between jobs and residents able and willing to work . . .

17 The mixture of uses should be accommodated with a variety of sizes and types of building . . .

18 An urban village should be flexible, so that both buildings and uses can change with changing needs and conditions without the need for clean-sweep redevelopment.

19 There should be a mixture of tenures both for housing and employment uses, ranging form owner-occupation through equity-sharing to easy-in/easy-out licences for small businesses, and housing association flats and houses . . .

21 . . . Early and full public involvement will be crucial to success. If the development is to foster a real sense of belonging, the community must participate at the earliest possible moment . . .

25 As important as the buildings are the spaces between them – the whole layout of streets, squares, lanes, pedestrian ways, green spaces, hard spaces, and the paving and street furniture that they contain. Ecological balance, public art and convenient access for disabled and physically encumbered people are also essential.

26 Existing buildings of architectural quality, historical interest or strong and pleasing character strengthen the sense of place and historical continuity; they should be exploited as visual and psychological assets.

27 These and other characteristics of the urban village need to be laid down in a master plan, supported by detailed codes governing the nature and provision of infrastructure, urban form, architectural language, and public spaces . . .

33 Though the size and layout of the urban village make it easy and agreeable to reach any place within it on foot, it must cater for motor vehicles. But it must not allow them to take over. Its design must prevent motor vehicles from destroying or eroding environmental quality . . .

35 It should therefore be sited and planned so as to have good public transport links . . .

Extracts. Source: The Urban Villages Group, Summary, *Urban Villages: A Concept for Creating Mixed-Use Developments on a Sustainable Scale*, The Urban Villages Group (London), 1992, unpaginated. Text by Tony Aldous. © The Urban Villages Group.

1994   ALLAN GREENBERG
Why Classical Architecture is Modern

Allan Greenberg (b 1938, Johannesburg) is perhaps best known for his US State Department offices and reception rooms, Washington, DC, 1989, which he realized in an unequivocally Classical idiom. Greenberg studied at Yale University and worked in the offices of Jørn Utzon in the 1960s. Inspired by the work of Sir Edwin Lutyens and others, he turned to Classicism, exploring its possibilities through his many designs for courthouses. He teaches and continues in private practice in Washington, DC.

Classical architecture is the cutting edge of architecture for the 21st century because it is the most comprehensive and the most challenging approach to architectural design and city planning. Because it is rooted in the physiology and psychology of the individual human being, the Classical language of architecture is always modern. To be truly modern means more than responding to some unique circumstances of the moment; it means finding the optimal balance between eternal human values on the one hand and the particular demands of the present on the other. Classical architecture has a proven track record, covering nearly 3,000 years, illustrating its ability to achieve this balance. It remains the most comprehensive language of architecture for serving the diverse needs of human beings and the societies they create . . .

Classicism's Communication

A Classical approach to design fulfils architecture's most basic responsibility: to communicate to citizens the mission of our civic, religious, and educational institutions. Classical architecture is based on a language of form capable of communicating these ethical and political ideals. This is particularly important in the United States, where our system of government is based not on ideals of blood, tribe, or land, but on the natural rights that the Declaration of Independence tells us belong to all human beings. Our government is the people.

Classical architecture, which developed in Ancient Greece simultaneously with the ideal of democratic government, is particularly suited to expressing democratic ideals because it is based on the belief that human beings are the measure of all things . . .

Human Based Elements

Because Classicism is founded on anthropomorphism, human form and personality may be attributed to Classical buildings, parts of buildings, and even groups of buildings. Even the transitions among the parts of a Classical building are modelled on human joints like knees and ankles. The tripartite division of the human form – legs, torso, head – parallels the differentiation of walls, columns and whole buildings into base, middle and top . . .

Classical architecture is distinguished from all other kinds of architecture by its basic commitment to the sacred importance of each individual and to democratic republics as the ideal form of government. It is a language of architecture that facilitates rational discourse about government and architecture, an essential ingredient in a democratic society whose citizens constitute the government and participate in public affairs.

Architectural Coexistence

The point I wish to make is that Classical architecture is essentially modern. We should adopt a more comprehensive view that includes all of the 20th-century's architectural output. The Bauhaus's worldview has taught us that there is an unbridgeable chasm between Classical and Modern ideals; the former, irrelevant. Such ideology distorts our view of 20th-century architecture.

Classicism has been present throughout the 20th century, and we need a history that recognises the genius of Arthur Brown, John Russell Pope, Henry Bacon, Charles Platt, Edwin Lutyens, and others. Such a history should also explain the coexistence of their buildings with those of Frank Lloyd Wright, Le Corbusier, Mies van der Rohe, and Alvar Aalto. Let's try to stand Mies on Schinkel's shoulders so that we who stand on Mies's shoulders will be able to see farther. We will learn that Mies's architecture, as well as that of Wright, Le Corbusier, and Aalto, becomes much more potent and significant when seen in the context of Classical architecture.

By recognising that all 20th-century architecture is important and must be studied, that we can learn from both the Lincoln Memorial and the Villa Savoye, that both Classical and Modern architecture have produced masterpieces, that both have deficiencies and strengths, we can understand the best of both. Only then will we see that Classicism is essentially modern, and that, in its noblest elements, Modern architecture is essentially Classical. (pp57-63)

Extracts. Source: *Architecture*, vol 83; no 11, November 1994. © BPI Communications.

1994   ROGER SCRUTON
Architectural Principles in an Age of Nihilism

A professor of philosophy who has written on a wide range of sub-
jects, Roger Scruton has focused on architecture in a number of es-
says as well as in the book The Aesthetics of Architecture. *The title*
here plays on that of Rudolf Wittkower's well-known work, Architectural Principles in the Age of Humanism. *The play is, of course, that*
Scruton offers an 'aesthetic discipline' of fundamental principles as
an antidote *to the nihilism, rather than a means for expressing it.*

The search for some kind of co-ordination of tastes is forced on us by our nature as social beings. This search may not lead to a single set of principles; neverthe-less it involves a common pursuit of an acceptable solution . . .

What was principally wrong with modernism was not its rigidity, its moralis-ing, its puritanical zeal – although these were repulsive enough. Modernism's respect for discipline was its sole redeeming feature: but it was a discipline about the *wrong things*. It told us to be true to function, to social utility, to materials, to political principles. It told us to be 'of our time', while enlisting architecture in those insolent experiments for the re-fashioning of man which have threatened our civilisation with such disaster. At the same time, modernism threw away, as a worthless by-product of the past and a symbol of its oppressive rituals, the *aesthetic* discipline embodied in the classical tradition . . .

Post-modernism is a reaction to modernist censoriousness. It 'plays' with the classical and gothic details which were forbidden it by its stern parent, and so empties them of their last vestiges of meaning. This is not the rediscovery of history, but its dissolution . . .

Such a practice marks a new departure of the nihilistic spirit which is foreshad-owed in modernism, and which there takes the belligerent form of a doctrine. In-stead of the unbending rectitude of modernism, we are given the self-service life-styles of the moral playground . . .

Nevertheless, all is not lost. It is possible for a civilisation to 'mark time' in the absence of the spirit which engendered it . . .

Our civilisation continues to produce forms which are acceptable to us, be-cause it succeeded in enshrining its truth in education. An astonishing effort took place in nineteenth-century Europe and America to transcribe the values of our culture into a secular body of knowledge, and to hand on that knowledge from generation to generation without the benefit of the pulpit or pilgrimage.

Nowhere was this process more successful than in the field of architecture . . .

I wish to record and endorse some of the principles which informed the education of the nineteenth-century architect . . . My procedure will be to lay down eleven *fundamental* principles, and then throw down a challenge to those who would reject them. Finally, I shall add eleven more specific principles, whose authority is less obvious.

1 Architecture is a human gesture in a human world, and, like every human gesture it is judged in terms of its meaning.

2 The human world is governed by the principle of 'the priority of appearance'. What is hidden from us has no meaning. (Thus a blush has a meaning, but not the flux of blood which causes it.) To know how to build, therefore, you must first understand appearances.

3 Architecture is useful only if it is not absorbed in being useful. Human purposes change [. . .] Buildings must therefore obey the law of the 'mutability of function'.

4 Architecture plays a major part in creating the 'public realm': the place in which we associate with strangers. Its meaning and posture embody and contribute to a 'civic experience', and it is against the expectations created by that experience that a building must be judged . . .

5 Architecture must respect the constraints which are imposed on it by human nature. Those constraints are of two kinds – the animal and the personal. As animals, we orient ourselves visually, move and live in an upright position, and are vulnerable to injury. As persons we live and fulfil ourselves through morality, law, religion, learning, commerce and politics . . .

6 The primary need of the person is for values, and for a world in which his values are publicly recognised. The public realm must permit and endorse either a recognised public morality, or at least the common pursuit of one.

7 The aesthetic experience is not an optional addition to our mental equipment. On the contrary, it is the inevitable consequence of our interest in appearances . . .

8 The aesthetics of everyday life consists in a constant process of adjustment, between the appearances of objects, and the values of the people who create and observe them. Since the common pursuit of a public morality is essential to our happiness, we have an overriding reason to engage in the common pursuit of a public taste . . .

9 A beautiful object is not beautiful in relation to this or that desire. It pleases us because it reminds us of the fullness of human life, aiming *beyond* desire, to a state of satisfaction . . .

10 Taste, judgement, and criticism are therefore immovable components of the aesthetic understanding . . .

11 All serious architecture must therefore give purchase to the claims of taste. It must offer a public language of form, through which people can criticise and justify their buildings, come to an agreement over the right and wrong appearance, and so construct a public realm in the image of their social nature . . .

12 The problem of architecture is a question of manners, not art . . . Our problem is this: by what discipline can an architect of modest ability learn the aesthetic decencies? The answer is to be found in aesthetic 'constants', whose values can be understood by whomsoever should choose to build.

13 The first constant is that of scale. To stand in a personal relation to a building, I must comprehend it visually, without strain, and without feeling dwarfed or terrorised by its presence . . .

14 Buildings must therefore have façades, able to stand before us as we stand before them. It is in the façade that the aesthetic effect is concentrated . . .

15 It follows that the first principles of composition concern the ordering of façades. But to establish such principles we must break with the tyranny of the plan . . .

16 Composition requires detail, and the principles of composition depend upon the sense of detail . . .

17 The true discipline of style consists, therefore, in the disposition of details . . .

18 The art of combination relies for its effects on regularity and repetition. The useful details are the ones that can be repeated, the ones which satisfy our demand for rhythms, sameness, and symmetry. To invent such details, and at the same time to endow them with character and life, is not given to every architect at every period. On the contrary, it is here that the *great discoveries* of architecture reside. The value of the classical tradition is crystallised in the theory of the Orders, in which beauty is transfigured into a daily discipline . . .

19 As the Orders make clear, the true discipline of form emphasises the vertical, rather then the horizontal line . . .

20 To endow a façade with vertical order, it is necessary to exploit light, shade and climate, to divide the wall space, and to emphasise apertures. In other words, it is necessary to use mouldings . . . In a nutshell, mouldings are the *sine qua non* of decency, and the source of our mastery over light and shade.

21 The building of a human face in architecture depends not only on details, but

also on materials. These should be pleasant to the touch, welcoming to the eye and accommodating to our movements . . .

22 The discipline of [the ordinary] builder consists in the ability to perceive, to draw, to compare and to criticise details; and thereafter to combine those details in regular and harmonious forms, whatever the shape of the site in which he works, and without doing violence to the surrounding order. (pp74-84)

Extracts. Source: Roger Scruton, *The Classical Vernacular: Architectural Principles in an Age of Nihilism*, Carcanet (Manchester), 1994. © Roger Scruton.

Charles Vandenhove, Renovation in Hors Chateau, Liege, 1978-85

LATE MODERN

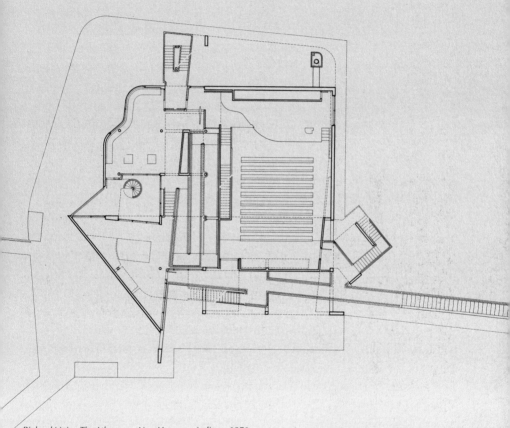

Richard Meier, The Atheneum, New Harmony, Indiana, 1976

1954   PHILIP JOHNSON
The Seven Crutches of Modern Architecture

*Philip Johnson (b 1906, Cleveland, Ohio) helped to introduce Euro-
pean Modernism to American not as an architect but as Director of
the Department of Architecture at the Museum of Modern Art in
New York where, with Henry-Russell Hitchcock, he organised the International style exhibition in 1932. Only later, at the age of 38, did he
become an architect, working for a time with Mies van der Rohe on
the Seagram building and establishing his own reputation with his
Meisian Glass House (New Canaan, Connecticut, 1949). Always
focusing more on the aesthetic – rather than the social – aspects of
Modernism, Johnson was, by the mid-1950s, beginning to tire of its
formal strictures, an attitude that emerges in this text of a talk he
gave at Yale University in 1959.*

Art has nothing to do with intellectual pursuit – it shouldn't be taught in a university at all. Art should be practised in gutters – pardon me, in attics.

You can't learn architecture any more than you can learn a sense of music or
of painting. You shouldn't talk about art, you should do it.

If I seem to go into words it's because there's no other way to communicate.
We have to descend to the world around us if we are to battle it. We have to use
words to put the 'word' people back where they belong.

So I'm going to attack the seven crutches of architecture. Some of us rejoice
in the crutches and pretend that we're walking and that poor other people with
two feet are lightly handicapped. But we all use them at times, and especially in
the schools where you have to use language. . .

The most important crutch in recent times is not valid now: the Crutch of
History. In the old days you could always rely on books. You could say 'What
do you mean you don't like my tower? There it is in Wren.' Or, 'They did that
on the Subtreasury Building – why can't I do it?' History doesn't bother us very
much now.

But the next one is still with us today, although, here again, the Crutch of
Pretty Drawing is pretty well gone . . .

It's a wonderful crutch because you can give yourself the illusion that you
are creating architecture while you're making pretty drawings. Fundamentally,

architecture is something you build and put together, and people walk in and they like it. But that's too hard. Pretty pictures are easier.

The next one, the third one, is the Crutch of Utility, of Usefulness. This is where I was brought up, and I've used it myself; it was an old Harvard habit.

They say a building is good architecture if it works. Of course, this is poppycock. All buildings work. This building [referring to Hunt Hall] works perfectly – if I talk loud enough. The Parthenon probably worked perfectly well for the ceremonies that they used it for. In other words, merely that a building works is not sufficient. You expect that it works. You expect a kitchen hot-water faucet to run hot water these days. You expect any architect, a graduate of Harvard or not, to be able to put the kitchen in the right place. But when it's used as a crutch it impedes. It lulls you into thinking that that is architecture . . .

If the business of getting the house to run well takes precedence over your artistic invention the result won't be architecture at all; merely an assemblage of useful parts . . .

That's not as bad, though, as the next one: the Crutch of Comfort. That's a habit that we come by, the same as utility. We are all descendants of John Stuart Mill in our thinking. After all, what is architecture for but the comforts of the people who live there? But when that is made into a crutch for doing architecture, environmental control starts to replace architecture . . .

The Crutch of Cheapness. That is one that you haven't run into as students because no one's told you to cut $10,000 off the budget, because you haven't built anything. But that'll be your first lesson. The cheapness boys will say: 'Anybody can build an expensive house. Ah, but see, my house only cost $25,000.' Anybody who can build a $25,000 house has indeed reason to be proud, but is he talking about architecture or his economic ability? Is it the crutch you're talking about or architecture?. . .

Then there's another very bad crutch that you will get much later in your career. Please, please, watch out for this one: the Crutch of Serving the Client. You can escape all criticism if you can say, 'Well, the client wanted it that way'. . .

Where do you draw the line? When do the client's demands permit you to shoot him and when do you give in gracefully? It's got to be clear, back in your own mind, that serving the client is one thing and the art of architecture another.

Perhaps the most troublesome of all is the Crutch of Structure. That gets awfully near home because, of course, I use it all the time myself. I'm going to go on using it . . .

Structure is a very dangerous thing to cling to. You can be led to believe that clear structure clearly expressed will end up being architecture by itself. You can say: 'I don't have to design any more. All I have to do is make a clean structural order.' I have believed this off and on myself. It's a very nice crutch, you see, because, after all, you can't mess up a building too badly if the bays are all equal and all the windows the same size.

Now why should we at this stage be that crutch-conscious? Why should we not step right up to it and face it: the act of creation. The act of creation, like birth and death, you have to face by yourself . . .

You can't escape it any how, why fight it? Why not realize that architecture is the sum of inescapable artistic decisions that you have to make. If you're strong you can make them . . .

I like the thought that what we are to do on this earth is to embellish it for its greater beauty, so that oncoming generations can look back to the shapes we leave here and get the same thrill that I get in looking back at theirs – at the Parthenon, at Chartres Cathedral . . .

I am a traditionalist. I believe in history. I mean by tradition the carrying out, in freedom, the development of a certain basic approach to architecture which we find upon beginning our work here. I do not believe in perpetual revolution in architecture. I do not strive for originality . . .

We have very fortunately the work of our spiritual fathers to build on. We hate them, of course, as all spiritual sons hate spiritual fathers, but we can't ignore them, nor can we deny their greatness. The men, of course, that I refer to: Walter Gropius, Le Corbusier and Mies van der Rohe. Frank Lloyd Wright I should include – the greatest architect of the nineteenth century . . .

Never in history was the tradition so clearly demarked, never were the great men so great, never could we learn so much from them and go our own way, without feeling constricted by any style, and knowing that what we do is going to be the architecture of the future, and not be afraid that we wander into some little bypath, like today's romanticists where nothing can possibly evolve. In that sense I am a traditionalist. (p240)

Extracts from a speech made at Yale University, February 5, 1954. Source: *Philip Johnson: Writings*, Oxford University Press (New York), 1979. © Philip Johnson.

1955 ALISON AND PETER SMITHSON AND THEO CROSBY

The New Brutalism

Inspired by a range of things from Le Corbusier's use of concrete, Japanese architecture and American advertising, the Smithsons (Alison, b 1928, Sheffield, d 1993; Peter, b 1923, Stockton-on-Tees) were re-acting against the then current British orthodoxy of 'people's detailing', a vaguely Scandinavian inspired version of Modernism. The result of the reaction was Brutalism, which was, as the Smithsons noted else-where, an attempt 'to be objective about "reality" – the cultural objectives of society, its urges, its techniques and so on.' This text appeared in Architectural Design, *with an introduction written by Theo Crosby acting in his position as editor.*

In 1954 a new and long overdue explosion took place in architectural theory. For many years since the war we have continued in our habit of debasing the coinage of M. Le Corbusier, and had created a style – 'Contemporary' – easily recognis-able by its misuse of traditional materials and its veneer of 'modern' details, frames, recessed plinths, decorative piloti (sic). The reaction appeared at last in the shape of Hunstanton School (by Alison and Peter Smithson) an illustration of the 'New Brutalism'. The name is new: the method, a re-evaluation of those advanced buildings of the twenties and thirties whose lessons (because of a few plaster cracks) have been forgotten. As well as this, there are certain lessons of the formal use of proportions (from Professor Wittkower) and a respect for the sensuous use of each material (from the Japanese). Naturally, a theory which takes the props from the generally accepted and easily produced 'Contemporary' has generated a lot of opposition. All over the country we have been asked to explain the new message. In the hope of provoking as many readers as possible to think more deeply about the form and purpose of their art, we asked the Smith-sons, as prophets of the movement, to supply a definition or statement which, somewhat edited, appears below. Theo Crosby

Our belief that the New Brutalism is the only possible development *for this moment* from the Modern Movement, stems not only from the knowledge that Le Corbusier is one of its practitioners (starting with the 'béton brut' of the Unité)

but because fundamentally both movements have used as their yardstick Japanese architecture, its underlying idea, principles and spirit.

Japanese architecture seduced the generation spanning 1900, producing, in Frank Lloyd Wright, the open plan and an odd sort of constructed decoration; in Le Corbusier the purist aesthetic – the sliding screens, continuous space, the power of white and earth-colours; in Mies, the structure and screens as absolutes. Through Japanese architecture the longings of the generation of Garnier and Behrens found FORM.

But, for the Japanese, their FORM was only part of a general conception of life, a sort of reverence for the natural world and, from that, for materials of the built world.

It is this reverence for materials – a realisation of the affinity which can be established between buildings and man – which is at the root of the so-called New Brutalism.

It has been mooted that the Hunstanton School, which probably owes as much to the existence of Japanese architecture as to Mies, is the first realisation of the New Brutalism in England.

This particular handling of materials, not in the craft sense of Frank Lloyd Wright, but in intellectual appraisal, has been ever present in the Modern Movement, as, indeed, familiars of the early German architects have been prompt to remind us.

What *is* new about the New Brutalism among movements is that it finds its closest affinities, not in past architectural style, but in peasant dwelling forms. It has nothing to do with craft. We see architecture as the direct result of a way of life.

1954 has been a key year. It has seen American advertising rival Dada in its impact of overlaid imagery; that automotive masterpiece the Cadillac convertible, parallel-with-the-ground (four elevations) classic box on wheels; the start of a new way of thinking by CIAM; the revaluation of the work of Gropius; the repainting of the villa at Garches? (p1)

Source: *Architectural Design*, vol 25, January 1955. © Alison and Peter Smithson.

1956   PAUL RUDOLPH
The Six Determinants of Architectural Form

Studying under Gropius at Harvard Graduate School of Design in the early 1940s, Paul Rudolph (b 1918, Elkton, Kentucky) went on to become one of the most prolific and influential figures in post-war American Architecture. His formalist and monumentalising approach resulted in buildings such as the Yale Art and Architecture Building (New Haven, 1963) and urban schemes with similarities to the work of the Japanese Metabolists such as the Graphic Arts Center project (New York, 1967).

Many of our difficulties stem from the concept of functionalism as the prime or only determinant of form. There are certainly as many as six determinants of architectural form, and though their relative importance varies with the individual problem, each is important, each must be heeded.

The first determinant is the environment of the building, its relationship to other buildings and the site . . .

A truly successful building must be related to its neighbours in terms of scale, proportions and the space created between the buildings. Most important of all, it must define and render eloquent its role in the whole city scheme. Buildings such as government structures, religious buildings, palaces devoted to entertainment, gateways to the city, should serve as focal points in our cities and could undoubtedly indulge in certain excesses, while buildings for commerce, housing, finance, administration should not dominate our environment . . .

The second determinant of form is the functional aspect. I will not discuss this except to say that most of our buildings look like assemblages of workable parts from Sweet's Catalogue, with little regard for the whole, the idea expressed, or the human response. This is not to say one is not passionately concerned with how the building works.

The third determinant of form is the particular region, climate, landscape and natural lighting conditions with which one is confronted. The great architectural movements of the past have been precisely formulated in a given area, then adapted and spread to other regions, suiting themselves more or less to the particular way of life of the new areas.

We now face a period of such development. If adaptation, enlargement and enrichment of basic principles of twentieth-century architecture were carried out, related always to the main stream of architecture and the particular region, the world would again be able to create magnificent cities. Unfortunately, little progress has yet been seen. We continue to ignore the particular . . .

There are several conditions which tend to limit regional expression. First there is industrialization; second, ease of travel and communication; third, the rising cost of traditional materials and skilled labour; fourth, the influence of the architectural press; fifth, the worship of that which is popular and our desire to conform; sixth, the 'do it yourself' 'according to the manufacturer's instruction' movement; and seventh, the abstract qualities inherent in the new concept of space.

The fourth determinant of form is the particular materials which one uses. Each material has its own potential and one seeks the most eloquent expression possible. We are currently going through a structural exhibitionism stage, but this will pass . . .

Buckminster Fuller domes, the latest space frames, the newest plastics, etc, are only new kinds of bricks which broaden our means of expression. Only buildings which need great visual emphasis should utilize such devices, and structure should always remain merely a means to an end. Many young architects fail to appreciate this basic principle. However, regular structural systems are usually a better method of organizing our designs than the axial arrangement of much traditional architecture.

The fifth determinant of form is the peculiar psychological demands of the space. Such necessities are met primarily through the manipulation of space and the use of symbols. We are particularly unsure of this aspect, partly because the revolution threw out much which still has validity. We must learn anew the meaning of monumentality. We must learn anew how to create a place of worship and inspiration; how to make quiet enclosed, isolated spaces; spaces full of hustling, bustling activities pungent with vitality; dignified, vast, sumptuous, even awe inspiring spaces; mysterious spaces; transition spaces which define, separate, and yet join juxtaposed spaces of contrasting character. We need sequences of space which arouse one's curiosity, give a sense of anticipation, beckon and impel us to rush forward to find that releasing space which dominates, which promises a climax and therefore gives direction.

The sixth determinant of form is concerned with the spirit of the times. This one is perhaps the most difficult of all; here is the call to genius . . . We need not be ashamed of our own passion for certain forms today, although the layman does not always share our enthusiasm. Interestingly enough, the layman usually reacts favourably to that which is truly great.

These six determinants of architectural form might lead toward richer architectural expression. At the same time one cries for greater expressiveness, one must also heed Rudolph Wittkower. He said, 'When architects depend on their sensibility and imagination architecture has always gone downhill'. There are few geniuses and most of us need guidance and discipline . . .

At this moment architecture so sorely needs its plagiarists that the value of not being a genius needs stating afresh . . .

In one sense any classical building with its columns, capitals, porticoes and window architraves, is a collections of clichés. The cantilever, the superstructure perched on pilotis, the glass enclosed staircase tower, the ribbon window, are legitimate expressions of our structural methods that in the last thirty years added so much to the architect's repertoire. The clichés in their proper rôle, are not merely a means of appearing up-to-date, but a means of insuring a civilized standard of design – even in the absence of genius – by providing the architect with a range of well-tried, culturally vital forms and motifs to convert the passive act of plagiarism into the creative act of building up and systematically enriching an architectural language appropriate to our times . . .

In every cultural effort of each generation it is the very disciplines which we so anxiously want to cross out that help us find and determine our basic values. These of course change with each generation because society is dynamic. But for the clarity of its dynamic force it needs discipline. Otherwise it becomes chaotic.

Great architectural precepts – still valid – would surely suggest other determinants of form than the fashionable or the functional. Perhaps they would suggest also some disciplines, to keep us from being carried away by our new freedoms. Modern architects fought hard against the restraints of outworn styles; the day is won; but the visual disorder of our cities still abounds. Can we enlarge our vision sufficiently to meet this challenge? It is the architect's responsibility. (p149-150)

Extracts. Source: *Architectural Design*, vol XXVII, May 1957. © Paul Rudolph and *Architectural Record*. First published in *Architectural Record*, vol 120, October 1956, pp183-190.

1960 REYNER BANHAM
Theory and Design in the First Machine Age

Associated with the Independent Group of Pop theorists based at the Institute of Contemporary Arts in London, Reyner Banham was one of the foremost historians of the Modern Movement. Like Siegfried Giedion, Banham was an operative historian, but unlike him, was not so convinced by the architecture of the Modern Masters, much less their rhetoric, a position he makes clear in Theory and Design in the First Machine Age.

While we yet lack a body of theory proper to our own Machine Age, we are still free-wheeling along with the ideas and aesthetics left over from the first. The reader may therefore, at any turn, find among these relics of a past as economically, socially, and technologically dead as the city-states of Greece, ideas that he is using every day of his life. Should he do so, may he ask himself two things; firstly, are any of his ideas as up-to-date as he thinks them to be, this is the Second Machine Age not the First; and secondly, how outmoded in truth are the ideas he dismisses as mere fashions of the Jazz Decades, for one Machine Age is more like another Machine Age than any other epoch the world has ever known. The cultural revolution that took place around 1912 has been superseded, but it has not been reversed . . . (p12)

It may well be that what we have hitherto understood as architecture, and what we are beginning to understand of technology are incompatible disciplines. The architect who proposes to run with technology knows now that he will be in fast company, and that, in order to keep up, he may have to emulate the Futurists and discard his whole cultural load, including the professional garments by which he is recognised as an architect. If, on the other hand, he decides not to do this, he may find that a technological culture has decided to go on without him. It is a choice that the masters of the Twenties failed to observe until they had made it by accident, but it is the kind of accident that architecture may not survive a second time – we may believe that the architects of the First Machine Age were wrong, but we in the Second Machine Age have no reason to be superior about them. (pp329-330)

Extracts. Source: *Theory and Design in the First Machine Age*, The Architectural Press, (London) 1960. © Architectural Press.

1962   CEDRIC PRICE
Activity and Change

*An advocate of Fulleresque 're-think', expediency and expendability,
Cedric Price (b 1934, Stone, Staffordshire) has few extant building to
his name as a matter of principle. He favours non-architectural solutions to the accommodation of human activities and denigrates the
limitations of permanent and monumental buildings. Price contributed to Archigram, in which this text appeared.*

An expendable aesthetic requires no flexibility in the artifact but must include
time as an absolute factor.

Planned obsolescence is the order within such a discipline – shoes; motor
cars; magazines.

The validity of such an aesthetic is only achieved if replacement is a factor of
the overall design process. The mobile home presupposes a continuance of production of such units . . .

In all such cases the artifact at any one time is complete in itself and the overall design problem requires a solution to the organization of such units – flowers
in a bowl; caravans on a site.

In allowing for change, flexibility, it is essential that the variation provided
does not impose a discipline which may only be valid at the time of design.

It is easier to allow for individual flexibility than organisational change – the
expandable house; the multi-use of fixed volumes; the transportable controlled
environment. The massing of living units in single complex [sic] presupposes the
continuance of physically linked activity complexes . . .

Physical forms as known are often the by-product of social, economic, technical conditions no longer relevant. Planning for activities must allow for change
not only in content but in means of operation. Disciplines can only be based on
foreseeable change and thereafter only order and not direction of change should
be established.

Extracts. Source: Peter Cook (ed), *Archigram 2*, Archigram (London), undated, unpaginated.
© Cedric Price.

1962 ALISON AND PETER SMITHSON
Team 10 Primer

After CIAM X in Dubrovnik in 1956 – and the dissolution of CIAM – Team 10 continued as a 'gradually changing caucus' until 1963. The Smithsons were central figures of the Team along with Jacob Bakema, George Candilis, Giancarlo de Carlo, Aldo van Eyck and Shadrach Woods. Reacting against the functionalist reductionism and indifference to time and place of CIAM's Athens Charter on urbanism, Team 10, and the Smithsons in particular, sought a new way of seeing and new solutions to the problems of the contemporary city.

The aim of urbanism is comprehensibility, ie clarity of organization. The community is by definition a comprehensible thing. And comprehensibility should therefore be a characteristic of the parts . . .

In general, those town-building techniques that can make the community more comprehensible are:

1 To develop the road and communication systems as the urban infrastructure. (Motorways as a unifying force.) And to realize the implication of flow and movement in the architecture itself.

2 To accept the dispersal implied in the concept of mobility and to re-think accepted density patterns and location of functions in relation to the new means of communication.

3 To understand and use the possibilities offered by a 'throw-away' technology, to create a new sort of environment with different cycles of change for different functions.

4 To develop an aesthetic appropriate to mechanized building techniques and scales of operation.

5 To overcome the 'cultural obsolescence' of most mass housing by finding solutions which project a genuinely twentieth-century technological image of dwelling – comfortable, safe and not feudal.

6 To establish conditions not detrimental to mental health and well-being . . . (pp48-52)

A community should be built up from a hierarchy of associational elements and . . . express these various levels of association (THE HOUSE, THE DISTRICT, THE CITY)

It is important to realize that the terms used: street, district, etc, are not to be taken as the reality, but as the idea, and that it is our task to find new equivalents for these forms of house-groupings, streets, squares, greens, etc, as the social reality they presented no longer exists.

In the complex of associations that is a community, social cohesion can only be achieved if ease of movement is possible, and this provides us with our second law, that height (density) should increase as the total population increases, and vice versa. In the context of a large city with high buildings, in order to keep ease of movement, we propose a multi-level city with residential 'streets-in-the-air'. These are linked together in a multi-level continuous complex, connected where necessary to work places and to those ground elements that are necessary at each level of association. Our hierarchy of associations is woven into a modulated continuum representing the true complexity of human associations.

This conception is in direct opposition to the arbitrary isolation of the so-called communities of the 'Unité' and the 'neighbourhood'.

We are of the opinion that such a hierarchy of human associations should replace the functional hierarchy of the 'Charte d'Athenes'. (pp76-78)

Extracts. Source: Alison Smithson (ed), *Team 10 Primer*, Studio Vista (London), 1968. © Alison Smithson. Originally published in magazine form in *Architectural Design*, December 1962. Reprinted in August 1965 in square paperback format by the Whitefriars Press.

1964 CHRISTOPHER ALEXANDER
Notes on the Synthesis of Form

Alexander studied architecture and mathematics at Cambridge University. Fusing the disciplines, he applied a scientific rigour to the development of design methods. He sought to achieve a clear, rational design process free from the cultural preconceptions that cloud the view of the designer and lead to a lack of 'fitness' between the form and its purpose. Remaining a fundamentally experimental and theoretical architect, Alexander's ideas have undergone a metamorphosis since the publication of 'Notes' as evident in such works as The Timeless Way of Building.

Goodness of Fit

The ultimate object of design is form . . .

The following argument is based on the assumption that physical clarity cannot be achieved in a form until there is first some programmatic clarity in the designer's mind and actions; and that for this to be possible, in turn, the designer must first trace his design problem to its earliest functional origins and be able to find some sort of pattern in them. I shall try to outline a general way of stating design problems which draws attention to these functional origins, and makes their pattern reasonably easy to see.

It is based on the idea that every design problem begins with an effort to achieve fitness between two entities: the form in question and its context. The form is the solution to the problem; the context defines the problem. In other words, when we speak of design, the real object of discussion is not the form alone, but the ensemble comprising the form and its context . . .

An object like a kettle has to fit the context of its use, and technical context of its production cycle . . .

The rightness of the form depends . . . on the degree to which it fits the rest of the ensemble . . . (pp15-17)

The Source of Goodness of Fit

We must now try to find out how we should go about getting good fit. Where do we find it? What is the characteristic of processes which create it successfully?

It has often been claimed in architectural circles that the houses of simpler civilizations than our own are in come sense better than our own houses. While these claims have perhaps been exaggerated, the observation is still sometimes correct. I shall try to show that the facts behind it, if correctly interpreted, are of great practical consequence for an intelligently conceived process of design . . .

It is inconceivable that we should succeed in organizing an ensemble as complex as the modern city until we have a clear enough view of simpler design problems and their implications to produce houses which are physically clear as total organizations.

Yet at present, in our own civilization, house forms which are clearly organized and also satisfactory in all the respects demanded by the context are almost unknown.

If we look at a peasant farmhouse by comparison, or at an igloo, or at an African's mud hut, this combination of good fit and clarity is not quite so hard to find . . .

Let us ask, therefore, where this success comes from.

To answer this question we shall first have to draw a sharp and arbitrary line between those cultures we want to call simple, for the purposes of argument, and those we wish to classify with ours. I propose calling certain cultures unselfconscious to contrast them with others, including our own, which I propose to call selfconscious . . . (pp28-32)

If forms in an unselfconscious culture fit now, the chances are that they always did. We know of no outstanding differences between present states and past states of unselfconscious cultures; and this assumption, that the fit of forms in such cultures is the result of gradual adjustment (that is, improvement) over time, does not illuminate what must actually be a dynamic process in which both form and context change continuously, and yet stay mutually well adjusted all the time . . .

Roughly speaking, I shall argue that the unselfconscious process has a structure that makes it homeostatic (self-organizing), and that it therefore consistently produces well-fitting forms, even in the face of change . . . (pp37-38)

The Program

Here is the problem. We wish to design clearly conceived forms which are well adapted to some given context. We have seen that for this to be feasible, the adaptation must take place independently within independent subsystems of variables. In the unselfconscious situation this occurs automatically, because the individual craftsman has too little control over the process to upset the pattern of adaptation implicit in the ensemble. Unfortunately this situation no longer exists; the number of variables has increased, the information confronting us is profuse and confusing, and our attempts to duplicate the natural organization of the unselfconscious process selfconsciously are thwarted, because the very thoughts we have, as we try to help ourselves, distort the problem and make it too unclear to solve . . . (p73)

The program, which represents a functional decomposition of the problem, is a way of identifying the problem's major functional aspects. But what kind of physical form, exactly, is the designer likely to realize with the help of such a program? Let us look at the form problem from the beginning.

The organization of any complex physical object is hierarchical. It is true that, if we wish, we may dismiss this observation as an hallucination caused by the way the human brain, being disposed to see in terms of articulations and hierarchies, perceives the world. On the whole, though, there are good reasons to believe in the hierarchical subdivision of the world as an objective feature of reality. Indeed, many scientists, trying to understand the physical world, find that they have first to identify its physical components, much as I have argued in these notes for isolating the abstract components of a problem . . .

Designers try to shape the components of new structures. The search for the right components, and the right way to build the form up from these components, is the greatest physical challenge faced by the designer. I believe that if the hierarchical program is intelligently used, it offers the key to this very basic problem – and will actually point to the major physical components of which the form should consist.

When we consider the kinds of constructive diagrams which are likely to be suggested by sets of requirements, at first it seems that the nature of theses diagrams is very various. Some diagrams seem to define overall pattern properties of the form, like being circular, being low rather than high, being homogeneous. Other diagrams seem to be piecelike rather than patternlike. They define pieces of which the whole form is made, like the diagram defining the street as a piece of the city, or the handle as a piece of the kettle, and so on.

This is the general rule. Every aspect of form, whether piecelike or patternlike, can be understood as a structure of components. Every object is a hierarchy of components, the large ones specifying the pattern of distribution of the smaller ones, the small ones themselves, though at first sight more clearly piecelike, in fact again patterns specifying the arrangement and distribution of still smaller components.

Every component has this twofold nature: it is first a unit, and second a pattern, both a pattern and a unit. Its nature as a unit makes it an entity distinct from its surroundings. Its nature as a pattern specifies the arrangement of its own component units. It is the culmination of the designer's task to make every diagram both a pattern and a unit. As a unit it will fit into the hierarchy of larger components that fall above it; as a pattern it will specify the hierarchy of smaller components which it itself is made of.

The hierarchical composition of these diagrams will then lead to a physical object whose structural hierarchy is the exact counterpart of the functional hierarchy established during the analysis of the problem; as the program clarifies the component *sources* of the form's structure, so its realization, in parallel, will actually begin to define the form's *physical* components and their hierarchical organization. (pp129-131)

Extracts. Source: Christopher Alexander, *Notes on the Synthesis of Form*, Harvard University Press (Cambridge, Mass), 1964; distributed in Great Britain by Oxford University Press (London). © The President and Fellows of Harvard College.

1964   ARCHIGRAM
Universal Structure

*The ideas of movement and expendability underlying Archigram 1
were taken from the level of the building and expanded to the level
of the city in Archigram 4 and 5. Peter Cook's Plug-in-City, Dennis
Crompton's Computer City and Ron Herron's Walking City are amal-
gamations of familiar products of technology resulting in apparently
alien urban organisms. Contributing to the notion of megastructure,
the images of these projects proved both compelling and disturbing
and brought Archigram international attention.*

A major problem of the organization (and the imagery-control) of large areas of
city is the achievement of a consistency running through parts with widely different functions and sizes. Add to this the problems of absorbing growth and avoiding the piecemeal one-offness of block-to-block relationship, the answer is obviously
found in a large-scale structural idea, which is anyhow a necessity of a consistent
building . . .

Source: Peter Cook (ed), *Archigram 5*, Archigram (London), 1964. © The individual authors.

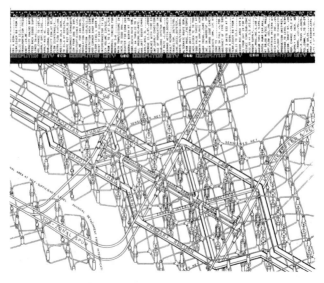

Dennis Crompton, Computer City, Archigram 5, London, 1964

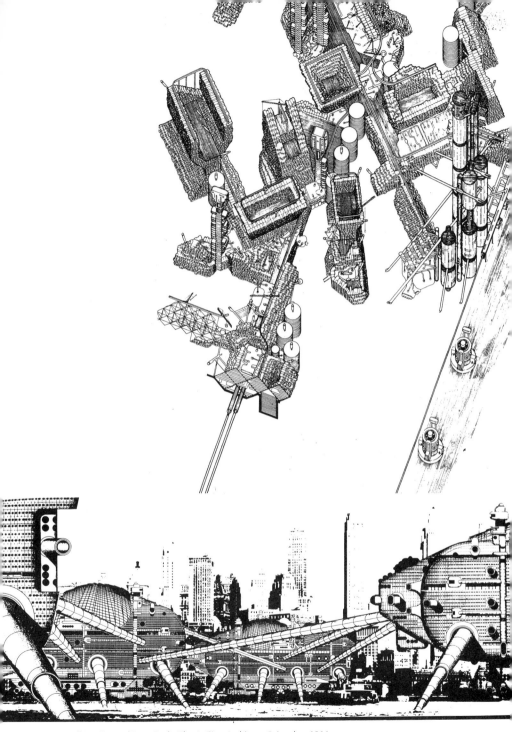

Ron Herron, Walking City, and Peter Cook, Plug In City, Archigram 5, London, 1964

Late Modern *225*

1964   JOHN HEJDUK
Statement

At once cryptic and poetic, John Hejduk (b 1929, New York City) has built relatively few buildings but through his projects, drawings and teaching has had an immense impact on American architecture. He taught at the University of Texas and Cornell University before becoming Professor and later Dean of Architecture at the Cooper Union in New York where he has been since 1964. The projects to which the text refer were begun after Hejduk's time in Texas and are notable for their clarity of structure.

The realisation that the hand and mind are one, working on first principles, and filling these principles with meaning through a juxtaposition of basic relationships such as point, line, plane, and volume, opened up the possibility of argumentation. The first groupings were arbitrary; but once the arbitrary beginning was committed, the organism necessarily went through its normal evolution – and whether the evolution of form continued or stopped depended on the use of the intellect not as an academic tool, but as a passionate living element. The problems of point-line-plane-volume; the facts of square-circle-triangle; the mysteries of central-peripheral-frontal-oblique-concave-convex; of right angle and perpendicular; of scale and position; the interest in post-lintel, wall-slab, vertical-horizontal; the arguments of two-dimensional and three-dimensional space; the extent of a limited field; the meaning of implied extension; the meaning of plan, of section, of spatial expansion-spatial contraction-spatial compression-spatial tension; the direction of regulating lines, of grids; the relationships of figure to ground, or number to proportion, of measurement to scale, of symmetry to asymmetry, of diamond to diagonal; the hidden forces, the ideas of configuration; the static, the dynamic: all these begin to take on the form of a vocabulary.

The arguments and points of view are within the work, within the drawings; it is hoped that the conflicts of form in them will lead to a clarity which can be useful and perhaps transferable. (p116)

Extracts. Source: Kenneth Frampton (ed), *John Hejduk: 7 Houses*, Catalogue 12, Institute for Architecture and Urban Studies (New York), 1980. © John Hejduk.

226 Theories and Manifestoes

1964 FUMIHIKO MAKI
The Megastructure

A founding member of the Metabolist Group, Fumihiko Maki (b 1928, Tokyo) trained at Tokyo University and in the United States at Cranbrook Academy and Harvard Graduate School of Design. It was in the US as Assistant Professor at Washington University, St Louis, that he wrote Investigations in Collective Form *of which this text is a part. Maki was the first to codify the notion of megastructure, an idea that was implicit in the work of the Metabolist group and was emerging at the time in the work of architects as varied as Archigram and Paul Rudolph.*

The megastructure is a large frame in which all the functions of a city or part of a city are housed. It has been made possible by present day technology. In a sense, it is a man-made feature of the landscape. It is like the great hill on which Italian hill towns were built.

Inherent in the megastructure concept, along with a certain static nature, is the suggestion that many and diverse functions may beneficially be concentrated in one place. A large frame implies some utility in combination and concentration of function.

Urban designers are attracted to the megastructure concept because it offers a legitimate way to order massive grouped functions . . .

This suggests that the megastructure which is composed of several independent systems that can expand or contract with the least disturbance to others would be more preferable to the one of a rigid hierarchical system.

In other words, each system which makes that whole, maintains its identity and longevity without being affected by others while at the same time being engaged in dynamic contact with others. When the optimum relationship has been formed, an environmental control system can be made. The system that permits the greatest efficiency and flexibility with the smallest organizational structure is ideal . . .

One of the most interesting developments of the megaform has been done by Professor Kenzo Tange . . .

Tange's megaform concept depends largely on the idea that change will occur less rapidly in some realms than it will in others, and that the designer will be able to ascertain which of the functions he is dealing with fall in the long cycle of change, and which is the shorter . . .

The ideal is not a system . . . in which the physical structure of the city is at the mercy of unpredictable change. The ideal is a kind of master form which can move into ever newer states of equilibrium and yet maintain visual consistency and a sense of continuing order in the long run.

Although the megastructure presents . . . problems . . . it also has great promise for:

1   Environmental engineering: Megastructure development necessitates collaboration between the structural and civil engineer. Possibilities in large spans, space frames, light skin structures, prestressed concrete, highway aesthetics, and earth forming will be developed far beyond their present level. Large scale climatic control will be studied further. A new type of physical structure, environmental building, will emerge.
2   Multi-functional structures: We have, this far, taken it for granted that buildings should be designed to fulfil one specific purpose. In spite of the fact that the concept of multi-functionalism must be approached with caution, it offers useful possibilities. We can within the megaform structure, realize combinations such as those in Kurokawa's 'Agricultural City'.
3   Infra-structure as public investment: Substantial public investment can be made in infra-structures (the skeleton of megastructures) in order to guide and stimulate public structures around them. This strategy can be further extended to a new three-dimensional concept of land use where public offices will maintain the ownership and upkeep for both horizontal and vertical circulation systems. (pp8-13)

Extracts. Source: Fumihiko Maki, *Investigations in Collective Form*, a special publication, no 2, The School of Architecture, Washington University (St Louis), June 1964. © Fumihiko Maki.

1966 SUPERSTUDIO

Description of the Microevent/ Microenvironment

Exploring possibilities at their extremes, Superstudio used modern tech-nology to question modern society. They extended the Modernist notion of the emancipatory role of architecture and technology beyond the point at which architecture disappears. The group originated in Florence in 1966, and was made up of Piero Frassinelli, Alexandro Magris, Roberto Magris, Adolfo Natalini, Alessandro Poli and Cristiano Toraldo di Francia.

The proposed microevent is a critical reappraisal of the possibilities of life with-out objects. It is a reconsideration of the relations between the process of design and the environment through an alternative model of existence, rendered visible by a series of symbolic images . . .

We can imagine a network of energy and information extending to every prop-erly inhabitable area. Life without work and a new 'potentialized' humanity are made possible by such a network. (In the model, this network is represented by a Cartesian 'squared' surface, which is of course to be understood not only in the physical sense, but as a visual-verbal metaphor for an ordered and rational distri-bution of resources.) . . . (p242)

It is an image of humanity wandering, playing, sleeping, etc, on this platform. Naked humanity, walking along the highway with banners, magic objects, archaeo-logical objects, in fancy dress . . . (p243)

The model constitutes the logical selection of these developing tendencies: the elimination of all formal structure, the transfer of all designing activity to the conceptual sphere. In substance, the rejection of production and consumption, the rejection of work, are visualized as an aphysical metaphor: the whole city as a network of energy and communications . . .

[Hypotheses for Survival]

a   hypothesis for the creation and development of servoskin: personal control of the environment through thermoregulation, techniques for breathing, cyborgs . . . mental expansion, full development of senses, techniques of body control (and initially, chemistry and medicine).

b hypothesis for total system of communication, software, central memories, personal terminals, etc.
c hypothesis for network of energy distribution, acclimatization without protective walls.
d mathematical models of the cyclic use of territory, shifting of the population, functioning and non-functioning of the networks . . . (pp244-5)

The destruction of objects, the elimination of the city, and the disappearance of work are closely connected events. By the destruction of objects, we mean the destruction of their attributes of 'status' and the connotations imposed by those in power, so that we live with objects (reduced to the condition of neutral and disposable elements) and not for objects.

By the elimination of the city, we mean the elimination of the accumulation of the formal structures of power, the elimination of the city as hierarchy and social model, in search of a new free egalitarian state in which everyone can reach different levels in the development of his possibilities, beginning from equal starting points.

By the end of work, we mean the end of specialized and repetitive work, seen as an alienating activity, foreign to the nature of man; the logical consequence will be a new, revolutionary society in which everyone should find the full development of his possibilities, and in which the principle of 'from everyone according to his capacities, to everyone according to his needs' should be put into practice . . . (p245)

Journey from A to B

There will be no further need for cities or castles.
There will be no further reason for roads or squares.
Every point will be the same as any other
(excluding a few deserts or mountains which are in no wise inhabitable).
So, having chosen a random point on the map,
we'll be able to say my house will be here
for three days two months of ten years.
And we'll set off that way (let's call it B)
without provisions, carrying only objects we're fond of.
The journey from A to B can be long or short,
in any case it will be a constant migration,
with the actions of living at every point along the ideal line
between A (departure) and B (arrival).
It won't, you see, be just the transportation of matter . . . (p247)

The Encampment

You can be where you like, taking with you the tribe or family.
There's no need for shelter, since the climatic conditions
and the body mechanisms of thermoregulation have been modified
to guarantee total comfort.
At the most we can play at making shelter, or rather at the home,
at architecture.

The Invisible Dome

All you have to do is stop and connect a plug: the desired microclimate
is immediately created (temperature, humidity, etc); you plug in to the
network of information, you switch on the food and water blenders . . . (p249)

A Short Moral Tale on Design, which is Disappearing

Design, become perfect and rational, proceeds to synthesize different
realities by syncretism and finally transforms itself, not
coming out of itself, by further withdrawing into itself, in its final
essence of natural philosophy.
Thus designing coincides more and more with existence:
no longer existence under the protection of design objects but
existence as design.
The times being over when utensils generated ideas, and when
ideas generated utensils, now ideas are
utensils. It is with these new utensils that life forms freely in a
cosmic consciousness.

If the instruments of design have become as sharp as lancets and as sensitive as
sounding lines, we can use them for a delicate lobotomy . . . (pp250-1)

Extracts. Source: Emilio Ambasz (ed), *Italy: The New Domestic Landscape*, The Museum of
Modern Art, New York, in collaboration with Centro Di, Florence, (New York and Florence)
1972. © Museum of Modern Art.

1968   PETER COOK

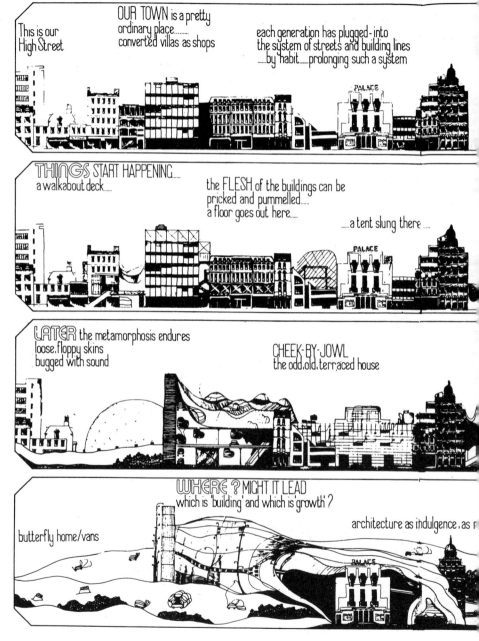

Peter Cook, *The Metamorphosis of an English Town*

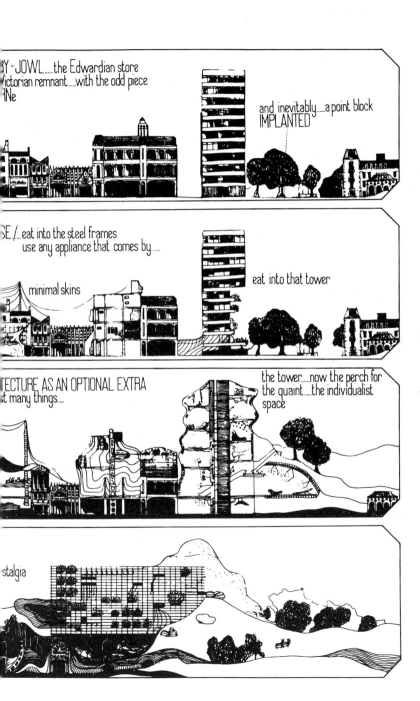

Y-JOWL......the Edwardian store
Victorian remnant.....with the odd piece
RNe

and inevitably......a point block
IMPLANTED

SE./....eat into the steel frames
use any appliance that comes by.....

minimal skins

eat into that tower

ECTURE AS AN OPTIONAL EXTRA
st many things.....

the tower.....now the perch for
the quaint.....the individualist
space

stalgia

1969　REYNER BANHAM

The Architecture of the Well-tempered Environment

In The Architecture of the Well-tempered Environment, *Banham takes up some of the preoccupations of* Theory and Design in the First Machine Age, *tracing the history of environmental control in architecture. In his characteristically sharp and trenchant manner he projects that history forward, pointing to something beyond architecture but rooted in technology, something like the visions of Buckminster Fuller and Archigram who he championed, or his own notion of the 'un-house'.*

After almost a century of . . . conscious, and consciously controlled, mechanisation of our environmental methods, we have a right to look for . . . self-confidence on the part of architects, the self-confidence to reject the obvious mechanical solution because they know a better way – and not for the usual reason that they don't know enough about the mechanical methods available to choose the right one, or that they can't find one that fits in with their prefigured ideas of how the architecture should look. Architects will certainly need this kind of self-confidence if they are to make sense of the range of choice in environmental method now open to them.

To epitomise that range, [let us simply review the examples cited in this chapter], all of about 1960 vintage, except the drive-in movie house which is a relative antique. The list covers:

Las Vegas; environment defined in light without visible structures of any consequence.

Drive-in Movie House; rally of mobile environmental structures in space defined by light and sound.

A[tomic] E[nergy] C[ommission] Mobile Theatre; space enclosed by a membrane supported on a cushion of air.

Space Capsule; rigid structure containing entirely and continuously manufactured life-support environment.

St George's School [Wallasey, Cheshire, 1961, by Emslie Morgan]; massive structure conserving environmental output of the contained activities.

The extremes of this range, as represented here, are the AEC theatre, only one step removed from pure application of power without any enclosure at all, and St George's School, only one step away from pure structure without any added power at all. Both extremes are demonstrably within the range that architects can professionally encompass – and this is not a question of visionary proposals about what architects ought to do in the future; this chapter shows that some have already done it. Nor may either of these extremes be dismissed as merely unique solutions to special problems, since all normal buildings are unique solutions to specific problems, and will remain so as long as buildings remain fixed to the ground in one place, which most of them will for a long time to come . . .

Some, perhaps most, of the buildings discussed in this book show architects evolving, or beginning to evolve, forms which are not the borrowed finery of far-out technology, but forms proper to the environmental proposition being made, whether that proposition is as mechanically advanced as [the AEC theatre], or as conservative, in the very best sense of the word, as Morgan's school. Only when such proper forms are commonly at hand will the architecture of the well-tempered environment become as convincing as the millennial architecture of the past.

Extracts. Source: Reyner Banham, *The Architecture of the Well-tempered Environment*, The Architectural Press (London), 1969. © Butterworth-Heinemann.

1969   LOUIS I KAHN
Silence and Light

Quiet and enigmatic, Louis I Kahn (b 1901, Oestel, Estonia, d 1974)was probably the most spiritual of the 'second generation' Modernists prac- tising and teaching in the United States. He extended the purism and structural logic of the first generation by turning the purity and logic into a question: 'What does the building want to be?' Kahn taught at Yale and the University of Pennsylvania, his major buildings including the Medical Research Building, Philadelphia, 1964; First Unitarian Church, Rochester, New York, 1964; Salk Institute Labora- tories, La Jolla, California, 1965 and the unfinished Dacca Assembly Building, Bangladesh, 1962-.

To me, when I see a plan I just see the plan as though it were a symphony, the realm of spaces in the construction and light. I sort of care less, you see, for the moment whether it works or not. Just so I know that the principles are respected which somehow are eternal about the plan.

As soon as I see a plan which tries to sell me spaces without light, I simply reject it with such ease, because I know that it is wrong . . .

And so, I put this on the board: Silence and Light. Silence is not *very, very quiet*. It is something which you may say is lightless; darkless. These are all invented words: *dark-less* – there is no such word. But why not? Lightless, darkless. Desire to be. To express. Some can say this is the ambient soul – if you go back, beyond and think of something in which light and silence were together, and maybe are still together, and separated only for the convenience of argument.

I turn to light, the giver of all presences. By will. By law. You can say the light, the giver of all presences, is the maker of a material, and the material was made to cast a shadow, and the shadow belongs to the light . . .

Everything you make is already too thick. I would even think that a thought is also too thick. But one can say, light to silence, silence to light, has to be a kind of ambient threshold and when this is realized, sensed, there is Inspiration . . .

In this inspiration – beside inspiration – there is a place, the Sanctuary of Art. Art being the language of man before French, you know, or German. It says: the language of man is art. It stems from something which grows out of the needing, of the desire to be, to express, and the evidence of the promise of the material to do it . . . (pp54-55)

And [the artist gets inspiration] also from another beautiful source, and that is through the experience or the Odyssey of a life that goes through the circumstances of living and what falls as important are not the dates of what happened, but in what way he discovered man through the circumstance.

The artist feels this when he makes something. He knows that he does it now, but he knows also that it has eternal value. He's not taking circumstances as it happens. He's extracting circumstances from whatever fell which revealed man to him. Tradition is just mounds of these circumstances, the record of which also is a golden dust from which you can extract the nature of man, which is tremendously important if you can anticipate in your work that which will last – that which has the sense of commonness about it. And by commonness, I mean really, the essence of silence . . .(p157)

So let's talk a little bit about a problem that comes to a man as an architect. Suppose you were assigned to say – and what a wonderful commission it would be – what is a university. And instead of being given a program . . . think in terms of *university* as though it never happened, as though it isn't here, so you have nothing to refer to, just the sense of a place of learning, an undeniable need: an undeniable desire on the part of all of us that a place be for learning . . . I gave this problem to my students . . . and one student said he believes the core of the university is the library . . . like the Acropolis. It is the offering of the mind . . . It was something about the humanities . . . another part of it was that of the professions . . .

And so the university is a sanction. The library of the sanction place, then, the places of the professions, the library of these professions are there, hooked up because there is also an offering of the mind, and this is somehow connected with the unit, with the more objective offering of the mind, which is the offering of the sanctuary of the Acropolis . . . Now if you consider this it must be put in mind differentiations of a wonderful kind. It brings in mind the difference between the garden, the court and a piazza. Because your connections are not going to be just colonnades and that sort of thing, it's going to be mental, the connection. You're going to feel it in some way . . . So the connection, then, is the realization of what is a garden, what is a court, what is an avenue, what is a piazza . . .

Playing with this so-called architecture of connection, which happens to have no rules, is a consciousness of the involvement of the land and the buildings, their association with the library. Now there are many things absent . . . there must be a place of happening . . . The Agora, for instance, was a place of happening . . . the Agora, the Stoa. The Stoa was made most marvellously . . . No partitions, just columns, just protection. Things grew in it. Shops became. People met, meet there.

It's shaded. You present a quality, architectural, no purpose. Just a recognition of something which you can't define, but must be built . . .

But that's a definite architectural quality. It has the same quality as all religious places . . . It's terrific. It's the beginning of architecture. It isn't made out of a handbook. I doesn't start from practical issues. It starts from a kind of feeling that there must be a world within a world. The world where man's mind somehow becomes sharp. (p56-59)

Extracts from a lecture given at the School of Architecture, ETH, Zurich, 12 February, 1969. The lecture officially opened an exhibition of Kahn's work. Source: Richard Saul Wurman, (ed), *What Will Be Has Always Been: The Works of Louis I Kahn*, Access Press Ltd and Rizzoli (New York), 1986. First published in Heinz Ronner and Sharad Jhaveri (eds) *Louis I Kahn: Complete Works 1935-1974*, Institute for the History and Theory of Architecture, Swiss Federal Institute of Technology (Zurich) 1977, © 1987 Birkhaüser Verlag (Basel, Boston).

Louis I Kahn, Entrance, Water, Trees, Kimbell Museum, Fort Worth, 1966-72

1969   CEDRIC PRICE
Non-Plan

Ever one to take up the counter-intuitive position and present it in its extreme, Price here suggests what in Britain even in the late 1960s was clearly the unsuggestable – total dissolution of the planning system. The idea was first put forward by Price in an article in New Society *(March 21, 1969) co-authored by Price, Reyner Banham, Peter Hall and Paul Barker.*

Planning control and legislation at present compensates for the unevenness of access, wealth, opportunity potential, and environment of various areas, and in so doing attempts to make all conditions equal – if not in appearance at least in capacity for change. Thus it would be considered more heinous to destroy a Georgian square in Gateshead than in Bristol. Non-plan is intended to destroy such a system of values. The introduction of Non-plan in four areas selected and illustrated here, would in fact encourage unevenness of development and exploitation of peculiarities. In environmental terms 'different' would supersede 'good' and 'bad'.

Under Non-plan, towns as such would no longer have to justify their inherited location and bulk by providing a centralised amenity-pad for half the area between themselves and towns of equal size. Agriculture would no longer be able to obtain protection for the dirtiest and most wasteful workshop floors on the spurious grounds that it alone could provide the necessary open-air amenity lung between settlements.

Non-plan, in reducing the permanence of the assumed worth of past uses of space through avoiding their very reinforcement, might well give society an opportunity not only to reassess such worth but to establish a new order of priorities of land, sea and air use which would be related more directly to the valid social and economic life-span of such uses.

Such a supposition, however, is bordering on moral prediction, if not planning, and this is just the situation that Non-plan is trying to avoid by encouraging unselfconscious immediacy 'at all times'. Motown must make way for 'no-town' – Utopia for non-plan . . .

The main thesis of Non-plan is that, through enabling uneven development, the particularization of occupation, habitat and appetite will be more likely to occur in places and at times best suited to it.

Non-plan, through its permissive attitude to change, is likely to increase the validity of continuous redevelopment resulting in activities and forms as yet unrealized.

The fact that the results may not be what we would expect exposes our insufficiency of planning expertise and does not necessarily negate the results.(p269)

Extracts. Source: *Architectural Design*, vol 39; no 5, May 1969. © Architectural Design.

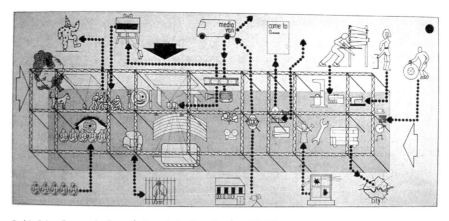

Cedric Price, Community Centre for Inter-Action Trust, London, 1972-77

1972   PETER EISENMAN
Cardboard Architecture

The book and exhibition Five Architects *brought to the attention of an international audience the urbane reappraisal of early 20th-century European Rationalism by a group of younger East Coast American architects. Of the five, Peter Eisenman (b 1932, Newark, New Jersey) was the most rigorously cerebral, earning a PhD in design theory from Cambridge University in 1963. While his interest in the work of Terragni and the early Le Corbusier is evident in houses I to IIa, Eisenman's writing reveals a rationale that repudiates functionalism. At the same time, he extends and elaborates the Modernist preoccupation with the unmediated expression of structural logic through the tactic of transformation.*

House I

House I was an attempt to conceive of and understand the physical environment in a logically consistent manner, potentially independent of its function and meaning. The thesis presented in House I, the Barenholtz Pavilion, is as follows: one way of producing an environment which can accept or give a more precise and richer meaning than at present, is to understand the nature of the structure of form itself, as opposed to the relationship of form to function or of form to meaning.

House I posits one alternative to existing conceptions of spatial organization. Here there was an attempt, first, to find ways in which form and space could be structured so that they would produce a set of formal relationships which is the result of the inherent logic in the forms themselves, and, second, to control precisely the logical relationships of forms.

There were three steps in this process in House I. First, an attempt was made to make a distinction between those aspects of form which respond to programmatic and technological requirements and those aspects of form which relate to a logical structure. In order to make this distinction, an attempt was made to reduce or unload the existing meaning of the forms. Second, a formal structure was made from these marks in the actual environment. Third, this formal structure of marks was related to another formal structure of a more abstract and fundamental nature. The purpose of this procedure was to provide an awareness of formal information latent in any environment which previously was unavailable to the individual.

One aspect of the first step was an attempt to reduce or unload the existing meaning of the forms dictated by function so that the forms could be seen as a series of primitive marks. This was attempted through a manipulation of the relationship of the color, texture, and shape of the built forms. White forms are used in House I to shift our visual perception and conception of such forms; from the perception of a real, tangible, white volumetric architecture to the conception of an abstract, colored planar space; from the 'white' of the 1920s to the neutrality of 'cardboard'.

A second aspect of the initial marking process involved the structural elements – the columns and beams. They appear initially to be rather conventional parts of a structural system. However, upon closer inspection this is found not to be the case. It is actually not possible to determine how the structure functions from looking at the columns and beams. All of the apparent structural apparatus – the exposed beams, the free-standing columns – are in fact non-structural . . .

The second intention of this work called for taking these marks and deploying them in such a way as to make a complete formal structure and to show that this structure was a primary consideration in the design of the whole building. To focus on this, required a further shift in the primary conception of an environment; this time from a concern merely for marking elements and their meaning to a concern for their relationship in a formal structure. To force this shift in House I, the formal structure was in a sense over-stressed or over-articulated so that it would become a dominant aspect of the building. One means to over-stress such a structure was to suggest two simultaneous structures which overlay and interact. These were based on a simple combination of two pairs of formal references: planes and volumes, on the one hand; frontal and oblique relationships on the other.

The two formal structures are marked by columns and beams . . . The intention was to use the columns and beams to mark two systems without giving preference to either. Together the counterpoint of these two formal systems, the frontal planar layering and the diagonal volumetric shift, overlaid and interacting with one another, make it more difficult to read a single coherent formal system directly from the physical fact. Rather they reinforce the intention that these marks in order to be understood first require disengagement of the two systems from one another, an activity which takes place in the mind . . .

If we analyze the nature of meaning in any specific context we realize it has two aspects. The first is meaning which is iconographic and symbolic and derives from the relation of the form to some reference which is external to it. For example, the particular juxtaposition of solids, columns, windows and railings in Le Corbusier's Villa Savoye is intended as a direct recall of the super-structure of the modern ocean liners, and with all the implications of the sea; discovery, newness, and ultimately man's conquest of nature. But underlying that level of meaning there is another aspect, itself a potential source of information, which conditions any iconographic interpretation; it is derived from, and is in a sense inherent in, the structure of the form. For example, the same juxtaposition of solids, voids and columns at Poissy gives us cues to entry, sequence of movement, the relationship of open to closed space, of the center to the perimeter and so forth. This information can be said to be the product of the internal structure of the form itself. While formal relationships can exist in an environment at a real, actual level, where an individual is aware of them through his senses – perception, hearing, touching, they can also exist at another level in which though not seen, they can be known . . .

If we mark both these levels in the environment they can be explicitly perceived and understood. This is the third aspect of the work – a shift in focus from an actual structure to an implied structure and to the relationship between the two . . .

This second level includes in addition to a set of irreducible formal regularities, the transformations of these regularities necessary to produce a specific environment. Transformations may be described by such formal actions as shear, compression, and rotation, to produce a new level of formal information in any specific physical environment . . .

These transformations and regularities have no substantial existence but are merely a description of this second level of formal relationships, in other words, a possible model for an architectural deep structure . . .

Any physical environment has this second or deep structural level, which not only has the capacity to convey information but does so continuously at a less-than-conscious level. It exists without being consciously designed, and there is a conceptual capacity within each individual to receive this information. Marking deep structure in the actual environment may bring it to a more conscious level. As was said above, there is no reason or meaning intended in the use of a particular formal strategy. The two overlaid systems are neither good nor bad in themselves. They are intended merely to exemplify the logic inherent in any formal structure, and the potential capacity of that logic to provide an area of new meaning. (pp15-17)

Extracts. Source: *Five Architects: Eisenman, Graves, Gwathmey, Hejduk, Meier,* Oxford University Press (New York), 1975. © Peter Eisenman.

1973 MANFREDO TAFURI
Architecture and Utopia

Professor of Architectural History at the Institute of Architecture in Venice from 1968 to 1994, Manfredo Tafuri was one of a loose group of architects – including Carlo Aymonino, Giorgio Grassi, Aldo Rossi and Giuseppe Samona – associated with the Institute in Venice and the magazine Casabella. *While some of the group were known for a general political leaning to the left, Tafuri was the most outspokenly Marxist, a position made clear in this text. His application of Marxist analysis to the production of buildings does, however, tend to result in a note of despair for the future.*

A coherent Marxist criticism of the ideology of architecture and urbanism could not but demystify the contingent and historical realities, devoid of objectivity and universality, that are hidden behind the unifying terms of art, architecture and city. It would likewise recognize the new levels attained by capitalist development, with which recognitions the class movements should be confronted.

First among the intellectual illusions to be done away with is that which, by means of the image alone, tries to anticipate the conditions of an architecture 'for a liberated society'. Who proposes such a slogan avoids asking himself if, its obvious utopianism aside, this objective is pursuable without a revolution of architectural language, method, and structure which goes far beyond simple subjective will or the simple updating of a syntax.

Modern architecture has marked out its own fate by making itself, within an autonomous political strategy, the bearer of ideals of rationalization by which the working class is affected only in the second instance. The historical inevitability of this phenomenon can be recognized. But having been so, it is no longer possible to hide the ultimate reality which renders uselessly painful the choices of architects desperately attached to disciplinary ideologies.

'Uselessly painful' because it is useless to struggle for escape when completely enclosed and confined without an exit. Indeed, the crisis of modern architecture is not the result of 'tiredness' or 'dissipation'. It is rather a crisis of the ideological function of architecture. The 'fall' of modern art is the final testimony of bourgeois ambiguity, torn between 'positive' objectives and the pitiless self-exploration of its own objective commercialization. No 'salvation' is any longer to be found

244 Theories and Manifestoes

within it: neither wandering restlessly in labyrinths of images so multivalent they end in muteness, nor enclosed in the stubborn silence of geometry content with its own perfection. For this reason it is useless to propose purely architectural alternatives. The search for an alternative within the structures that condition the very character of architectural design is indeed an obvious contradiction in terms.

Reflection on architecture, inasmuch as it is a criticism of the concrete 'realized' ideology of architecture itself, cannot but go beyond this and arrive at a specifically political dimension.

Only at this point – that is after having done away with any disciplinary ideology – is it permissible to take up the subject of the new roles of the technician, of the organizer of building activity, and of the planner, within the compass of the new forms of capitalist development. And thus also to consider the possible tangencies or inevitable contradictions between such a type of technical-intellectual work and the material conditions of the class struggle.

The systematic criticism of the ideologies accompanying the history of capitalist development is therefore but one chapter of such political action. Today, indeed, the principal task of ideological criticism is to do away with impotent and ineffectual myths, which so often serve as illusions that permit the survival of anachronistic 'hopes in design'.(pp179-182)

Extracts. Source: Manfredo Tafuri, *Architecture and Utopia: Design and Capitalist Development*, MIT Press (Cambridge, Mass), 1976. © The Massachusetts Institute of Technology. First pulished as *Progetto e Utopia*, *Guiz. Laterza & Figli* (Bari, Italy), 1973; translated from the Italian by Barbara Luigia la Penta.

1975   PHILIP JOHNSON
What Makes Me Tick

Few architects have made such a virtue of stylistic promiscuity as Philip Johnson. The elegant and sardonic urbanite, he has played a sophisticated game with architectural fashions, from the International Style (Glass House, New Caanan, Connecticut, 1949) to Post-Modernism (The AT&T Building, with John Burgee, New York City, 1978). As with many of his talks, this text, from a lecture at Columbia University, takes the form of a confessional, laying before the audience his fickleness yet his abiding concern for the formal and sensuous.

I am of the opinion that we have no faiths. I have none. 'Free at last', I say to myself. However, shapes do not emerge from a vacuum. There are currents in the air. For example, historical architecture is 'in' after almost a hundred years of neglect by the various 'moderns' of the late nineteenth and twentieth century. True, we don't build in the Gothic style or the Renaissance style, but we are not averse to inspiration at least. A Stirling with his dockyards, a Stern with his Lutyens, a Venturi with almost everybody, a Meier with his 'take' on Corbu. So what – we cannot not know history.

Philosophically, it seems to me we today are anarchistic, nihilistic, solipsistic, certainly relativist, humorous, cynical, reminiscent of tradition, myth-and-symbol-minded rather than rationalistic or scientifically minded. What makes a building satisfactory – the word 'beautiful' is more than ever treacherous – to Stern or Venturi, for instance, is bound to be different from what is satisfactory to me. *Vive la différence*, we live in a pluralistic society.

I can only talk about me. Maybe what makes me tick is unique. I don't mind, but it may be of interest to know how different my tick is from yours and yours.

Whenever I start a building design, three aspects – as I might call them – act as a sort of measure, aim, discipline, hope for my work.

First, the Aspect of the Footprint – that is, how space unfolds from the moment I catch a glimpse of a building until with my feet I have approached, entered, and arrived at my goal . . .

Second, the Aspect of the Cave. All architecture is shelter; all great architecture is the design of space that contains, cuddles, exalts, or stimulates the persons in that space. It is the design of the cave part of a building that overrides all other design questions. Like Lao-tse's cup, it is the emptiness within that is of the essence.

The third aspect, the most difficult, is the Building as Work of Sculpture. Architecture is usually thought of as different from sculpture and indeed not much great architecture is great sculpture. Pyramids, yes; Taliesin West, no. Stonehenge, perhaps; Versailles, no; the Guggenheim Museum, maybe. The Parthenon, certainly not. (Columns and entablatures see to that.) Frank Lloyd Wright roofs, arcades, colonnades, all speak architecture, not sculpture.

These three aspects, the Footprint, the Cave, the Work of Sculpture, do not in themselves give form, but they are what I think about in the night away from the boards, when I try to brush away the cobwebs of infinite possibilities and try to establish some way out. Very frustrating . . . (pp260-265)

Extracts from a lecture given at Columbia University, 5 September 1975. Source: *Philip Johnson: Writings*, Oxford University Press (New York), 1979. © Philip Johnson.

Philip Johnson, Underground Art Gallery, New Canaan, Connecticut, 1965

1975   PIANO+ROGERS
Statement

Renzo Piano (b 1937, Genoa) and Richard Rogers (b 1933, Florence, of British parents) formed a partnership in 1970 and a year later won first prize in the Place Beaubourg Competition. The building, completed in 1977 and called the Centre Pompidou, clearly demonstrates Piano and Rogers' fundamental belief in scientific enquiry as a tool, both in its application to technology and as a more general paradigm for architectural expression. Other buildings by Piano+Rogers include B & B Italia Offices (Como, Italy, 1971), Aston Martin Lagonda Offices (London, 1973) and Institut de Recerche et de Coordination Acoustique (Paris, 1977).

Ideology cannot be divided from architecture. Change will clearly come from radical changes in social and political structures. In the face of such immediate crises as starvation, rising population, homelessness, pollution, misuse of non-renewable resources and industrial and agricultural production, we simply anaesthetise our consciences. With problems so numerous and so profound, with no control except by starvation, disease and war, we respond with detachment. Today, at best, we can hope to diminish the coming catastrophe by the recognition of the existing human conditions and by rational research and practice.

The importance of technology is in the application of method to technique, whether one is talking of sophisticated or primitive technology. The aim of technology is to satisfy the needs of all levels of society. Technology cannot be an end in itself but must aim at solving long term social and ecological problems. This is impossible in a world where short term profit for the 'haves' is seen as a goal, at the expense of developing more efficient technology for the 'have nots'.

All forms of technology from low energy intensive to high energy intensive must aim at conserving natural resources while minimising ecological, social and visual damage to the environment, so that by using as little material as possible as functionally as possible to answer new briefs, we reach a self-sustaining situation where input = output. A new distribution of end and means is needed, not based purely on a limited financial evaluation of human needs. In this context it is as difficult to create a truly socially orientated brief as it is to adapt and translate it by the use of the correct technological means . . .

Much of our work has the following common factors:

a Analysing and broadening the brief to create an environment which will offer maximum freedom for man's many different activities. Reassessing traditional hierarchies and relationships between public and private, work and relaxation, child and adult, vehicular and pedestrian, worker and manager, quiet and noisy, dangerous and safe. Each overlapping realm requires special conditions to sustain and encourage it.

b Single undefined common spaces.

c Allowance for growth and change.

d No major differentiation in the section and facade except in the direction of growth as in clear span structure.

e Control of programme, quality and cost by the use of standard catalogue pieces and the elimination of craft techniques and wet trades . . .

f Maximum exploitation of minimum industrial materials.

g Use of skilled erection teams.

h Building forms and dimensions dictated by maximum economic spans and standard production limits of components.

i High thermal insulation and general environmental control by the use of sophisticated panel systems . . .

j Skin, structure and services clearly defined.

k Internal and external elements demountable and reusable.

l Use of bright colours to give order, happiness and to break down technological connotations.

m Breakdown of traditionally hierarchical planning, replaced by work flow planning. (p276)

Extracts. Source: *Architectural Design*, vol XLV; no 5, 1975. © Architectural Design.

1976 LIONEL MARCH

The Logic of Design and the Question of Value

Lionel March was a central figure at Cambridge University School of Architecture over the 1970s. He studied there under Sir Leslie Martin, and then as lecturer helped to set up the Centre for Land Use and Built Form Studies (later the Martin Centre). Under March, research at the Centre focused on the application of mathematics and analytical logic to architecture and urban design.

For the purposes of developing a vocabulary for design theory the following terms will be used: the outcome of productive reasoning is a case which is called the design or *composition* – the latter in accord with traditional architectural theory; the outcome of deductive reasoning is a *decomposition* which comprises the characteristics of the design that emerge from analysis of the whole composition – the whole is not merely the sum of these characteristics; and the outcome of inductive reasoning is a *supposition*, a working rule of some generality – that is, an hypothesis in the scientific sense and more loosely, an idea, a theory, or in their modern usage, a model, a type. To rephrase Peirce's remarks above: 'We conceive of rational designing as having three tasks – (1) the creation of a novel composition, which is accomplished by productive reasoning; (2) the prediction of performance characteristics, which is accomplished by deduction; and (3) the accumulation of habitual notions and established values, an evolving typology, which is accomplished by induction.

While it is from the collusion of specific needs and habitual notions that novelty is produced, it is productive reasoning which alone can frustrate the established order of habit and consequently inject new values. As Peirce writes: abduction, or as we have it production, 'is the only logical operation which introduces any new ideas; for induction does nothing but determine a value; and deduction merely evolves the necessary consequences of a pure hypothesis'. Thus production creates; deduction predicts and induction evaluates . . .

The survival of stereotypes in the past has been a matter of trial and error in practice: the fittest have survived as evidence of their utility. Such evidence is usually censored by a designer's judgement, collected through his experience, and in time becomes part of his intuitive response. If internalised personal judgement, experience and intuition alone are relied upon, the three modes of the PDI-model [Productive/Deductive/Inductive] become inextricably entangled and no powerfully sustained use of collective, scientific knowledge is possible. Design will remain more or less personalistic and a matter of opinion, albeit professional. If the design process is externalised and made public, as it evidently must be, for team work to be fully effective, then the three stages of the PDI-model are worth making explicit so that as much scientific knowledge can be brought to bear on the problem as seems appropriate. In this externalised process it is feasible to experiment with artificial evolution within the design laboratory using simulated designs and environments. New, synthetically derived stereotypes may emerge, and old ones may be given new potential without having to wait for practical exemplification. Design comes to depend less on a single occasion of inspiration, more on an evolutionary history, greatly accelerated as this iterative procedure can now be – a prospect opened up by recent advances in computer representation . . . (pp18-22)

Extracts. Source: Lionel March (ed), *The Architecture of Form*, Cambridge University Press (Cambridge), 1976. © Cambridge University Press.

1985 RICHARD ROGERS
Observations on Architecture

With the Lloyds of London Headquarters Building (1984), Rogers sealed the international reputation established with Beaubourg – a reputation acknowledged by a knighthood and subsequently a peerage. In this text, included in a monograph on his work, Rogers reconfirms his belief in functionalism, technology and scientific research as a foundation and tool for architecture. He also emphasises the idea that 'building form, plan, section and elevation should be capable of responding to changing needs', a capability sometimes frustrated by the exquisite sculptural – but static – qualities of his buildings.

Though a building must be complete at any one stage, it is our belief that in order to allow for growth and change it should be functionally and therefore visually open-ended. This indeterminate form must offer legible architectural clues for the interpretation of future users. The dichotomy between the complete and the open nature of the building is a determinant of the aesthetic language.

We design each building so that it can be broken down into elements and sub-elements which are then hierarchically organised so as to give a clearly legible order. A vocabulary is thereby created in which each element expresses its process of manufacture, storage, erection and demountability; so that, to quote Louis Kahn, 'each part clearly and joyfully proclaims its role in the totality. "Let me tell you the part I am playing, how I am made and what each part does", what the building is for, what the role of the building is in the street, and the city.' . . .

I believe in the rich potential of modern industrialist society. Aesthetically one can do what one likes with technology for it is a tool, not an end in itself, but we ignore it at our peril. To our practice its natural functionalism has an intrinsic beauty. The aesthetic relationship between science and art has been poetically described by Horatio Greenough as: 'Beauty is the promise of function made sensuously pleasing.' It is science to the aid of the imagination . . .

We are searching for a system and a balance which offers the potential for change and urban control; a system in which the totality has complete integrity yet allows for both planned and unplanned change.

A dynamic relationship is then established between transformation and permanence, resulting in a three-dimensional framework with a kit of changeable parts designed to allow people to perform freely inside and out. This free and changing performance of people and parts becomes the expression of the architecture . . . (pp12-13)

The architect must understand and control the machinery – the instruments that build buildings – where necessary developing and inventing new ones . . .

Only by studying and controlling the means of production and by creating a precise technological language will the architect keep control of the design and construction of the building. The correct use of building process disciplines the building form, giving it scale and grain . . .

Today problem solving involves thinking at a global scale and using science as the tool to open up the future. Science is the means by which knowledge is ordered in the most efficient way so as to solve problems . . . (p16)

The building form, plan, section and elevation should be capable of responding to changing needs. This free and changing performance will then become part of the expression of the architecture of the building, the street and the city. Program, ideology and form will then play an integrated and legible role within a changing but ordered framework. The fewer the building constraints for the users, the greater the success; the greater the success the more the need for revision and then programmatic indeterminance will become an expression of the architecture . . . (p19)

Extracts. Source: Frank Russell (ed), *Architectural Monographs: Richard Rogers + Architects*, Academy Editions (London), 1985. © Richard Rogers + Partners Limited.

Richard Rogers, Channel 4 Building, London, 1994

Late Modern 253

1990   KENNETH FRAMPTON
Rappel à l'Ordre, the Case for the Tectonic

Reacting to the extremes of both Post-Modern Classicism and the New Modernist deconstructivism, Frampton turns to a palaeo-Modernism inspired by the work of the Prussian architect and theorist Gottfried Semper and the 17th-century Italian thinker Giambatista Vico. Frampton sees in Semper's notion of the tectonic a means to get 'beyond the aprioris of history and progress and outside the reactionary closures of Historicism and the Neo-Avant-Garde'.

From its conscious emergence in the middle of the nineteenth century with the writings of Karl Bottischer and Gottfried Semper the term [tectonic] not only indicates a structural and material probity but also a poetics of construction, as this may be practised in architecture and the related arts . . .

Building remains essentially *tectonic* rather than scenographic in character and it may be argued that it is an act of construction first, rather than a discourse predicated on the surface, volume and plan, to cite the 'Three Reminders to Architects' of Le Corbusier. Thus one may assert that building is *ontological* rather than *representational* in character and that built form is a presence rather than something standing for an absence . . .

Semper was to divide built form into two separate material procedures: into the *tectonics* of the frame in which members of varying lengths are conjoined to encompass a spatial field and the *stereotomics* of compressive mass that, while it may embody space, is constructed through the piling up of identical units . . . In the first case, the most common material throughout history has been *wood* or its textual equivalents such as bamboo, wattle, and basket-work. In the second case, one of the most common materials has been brick, or the compressive equivalent of brick such as rock, stone or rammed earth and later, reinforced concrete . . .

Framework tends towards the aerial and the dematerialisation of mass, whereas the mass form is telluric, embedding itself ever deeper into the earth. The one tends towards the light and the other towards the dark. These gravitational opposites, the immateriality of the frame and the materiality of the mass, may be said to symbolise the two cosmological opposites to which they aspire: the sky and the earth . . .

It is arguable that the practice of architecture is impoverished to the extent that we fail to recognise these transcultural values and the way in which they are intrinsically latent in all structural form . . .

This brings us back to Semper's privileging of the joint as the primordial tectonic element as the fundamental nexus around which building comes into being, that is to say, comes to be articulated as a presence in itself.

Semper's emphasis on the joint implies that fundamental syntactical transition may be expressed as one passes from the *stereotomic* base to the tectonic frame, and that such transitions constitute the very essence of architecture . . .

Postscriptum: Tectonic and Critical Culture

Within architecture the tectonic suggests itself as a mythical category with which to acquire entry to an anti-processal world wherein the 'presencing' of things will once again facilitate the appearance and experience of men. Beyond the aprioris of history and progress and outside the reactionary closures of Historicism and the Neo-Avant-Garde, lies the potential for a *marginal* counter-history. This is the primaeval history of the logos to which Vico addressed himself in his *Nuova Scienza* in an attempt to adduce the poetic logic of institutional form; the self-realization of the species being *avant la lettre*. It is a mark of the radical nature of Vico's thought that he insisted that knowledge is not just the province of objective fact but also a consequence of the subjective 'collective' elaboration of archetypal myth, that is to say an assembly of those existential symbolic truths residing in the human experience. The critical myth of the tectonic points to a similar timeless but paradoxically time-bound moment, set apart from the processal continuity of time. (pp19-25)

Extracts. Source: *Architectural Design*, vol 60; no 3-4. © Academy Group Ltd.

1991 TADAO ANDO
Beyond Horizons in Architecture

'Without sentimentality, I aspire to transform place through architec-
ture to the level of the abstract and the universal.' A faith in abstrac-
tion and logic permeates the work and writing of self-taught architect
Tadao Ando (b 1941, Osaka). Recipient of the Pritzker Prize in Archi-
tecture in 1995, Ando has taught at Yale, Columbia and Harvard
Universities. His buildings include Koshino House and Studio, Ashiya,
1984; Church and Theatre on the Water, Tomamu, 1987 and the
Children's Museum, Himeji, 1989.

Architectural thought is supported by abstract logic. By abstract I mean to signify a meditative exploration that arrives at a crystallization of the complexity and richness of the world, rather than a reduction of its reality through diminishing its concreteness. Were not the best aspects of modernism produced by such architectural thinking? . . .

The most promising path open to contemporary architecture is that of a development through and beyond modernism. This means replacing the mechanical, lethargic, and mediocre methods to which modernism has succumbed with the kind of abstract, meditative vitality that marked its beginnings, and creating something thought-provoking that will carry our age forward into the twenty-first century. The creation of an architecture able to breath new vigor into the human spirit should clear a road through the present architectural impasse.

Transparent Logic

Architectural creation is founded in critical action. It is never simply a method of problem-solving whereby given conditions are reduced to technical issues. Architectural creation involves contemplating the origins and essence of a project's functional requirements and the subsequent determination of its essential issues. Only in this way can the architect manifest in the architecture the character of its origins . . .

The serious designer must question even given requirements, and devote deep thought to what is truly being sought. This kind of inquiry will reveal the special character latent in a commission and cast sharp light on the vital role of an intrinsic logic, which can bring the architecture to realization. When logic pervades the design process the result is clarity of structure, or spatial order – apparent not only to perception but also to reason. A transparent logic that permeates the whole transcends surface beauty, or mere geometry, with its intrinsic importance.

Abstraction

The real world is complex and contradictory. At the core of architectural creation is the transformation of the concreteness of the real through transparent logic into spatial order. This is not an eliminative abstraction but, rather, an attempt at the organization of the real around an intrinsic viewpoint to give it order through abstract power. The starting point of an architectural problem – whether place, nature, lifestyle, or history – is expressed within this development into the abstract. Only an effort of this nature will produce a rich and variable architecture . . .

In the Row House (Azuma Residence), Suniyoshi, I took one of three wood row houses and reconstructed it as a concrete enclosure, attempting to generate a microcosm within it. The house is divided into three sections, the middle section being a courtyard open to the sky. This courtyard is an exterior that fills the interior, and its spatial movement is reversed and discontinuous. A simple geometric form, the concrete box is static; yet as nature participates within it, and as it is activated by human life, its abstract existence achieves vibrancy in its meeting with concreteness . . .

Nature

I seek to instill the presence of nature within an architecture austerely constructed by means of transparent logic. The elements of nature – water, wind, light, and sky – bring architecture derived from ideological thought down to the ground level of reality and awaken man-made life within it.

The Japanese tradition embraces a different sensibility about nature than that found in the West. Human life is not intended to oppose nature and endeavor to control it, but rather to draw nature into an intimate association in order to find union with it. One can go so far as to say that, in Japan, all forms of spiritual exercise are traditionally carried out within the context of the human interrelationship with nature.

This kind of sensibility has formed a culture that de-emphasizes the physical boundary between residence and surrounding nature and establishes instead a spiritual threshold. While screening man's dwelling from nature, it attempts to draw nature inside. There is no clear demarcation between outside and inside, but rather their mutual permeation. Today, unfortunately, nature has lost much of its former abundance, just as we have enfeebled our ability to perceive nature. Contemporary architecture, thus, has a role to play in providing people with architectural places that make them feel the presence of nature. When it does this, architecture transforms nature through abstraction, changing its meaning. When water, wind, light, rain, and other elements of nature are abstracted within architecture, the architecture becomes a place where people and nature confront each other under a sustained sense of tension. I believe it is this feeling of tension that will awaken the spiritual sensibilities latent in contemporary humanity . . .

Place
The presence of architecture – regardless of its self-contained character – inevitably creates a new landscape. This implies the necessity of discovering the architecture which the site itself is seeking . . .

I compose the architecture by seeking an essential logic inherent in the place. The architectural pursuit implies a responsibility to find and draw out a site's formal characteristics, along with its cultural traditions, climate, and natural environmental features, the city structure that forms its backdrop, and the living patterns and age-old customs that people will carry into the future. Without sentimentality, I aspire to transform place through architecture to the level of the abstract and universal. Only in this way can architecture repudiate the realm of industrial technology to become 'grand art' in its truest sense. (pp75-76)

Extracts. Source: Harriet Schoenholz Bee (ed), *Tadao Ando*, Museum of Modern Art (New York), 1991. © Tadao Ando, Museum of Modern Art, New York.

1994   PETER RICE
The Role of the Engineer

Peter Rice (b 1935, Belfast, d 1992, London) studied civil engineering at Queens College, Belfast, and joined Ove Arup & Partners in 1956. Working on projects such as the Sydney Opera House (completed 1973), the Pompidou Centre (Paris, 1977), Lloyds' Headquarters (London 1984), and the National Museum of Science, Technology and Industry (La Villette, Paris) Rice helped to stretch the realms of the possible, making fundamental contributions to the buildings on which he worked.

To call an engineer an 'architect engineer' because he comes up with unusual or original solutions is essentially to misunderstand the role of the engineer in society. It is easiest to explain the difference between the engineer and others by comparing how each works and what they do. Designers such as the famous car stylists, like Pininfarina, or Giugiaro, work essentially by seeking to understand how they respond to the context and the essential elements of the problem: their response is essentially subjective. Different architects will respond very differently to the same problem. Their solutions will reflect their style preference and their general belief in an appropriate response to a problem . . .

The engineer when faced with a design challenge will transform it into one which can be tackled objectively. As an example, the engineer might seek to change the problem into the exploration of how to exploit a particular material completely within the context of architecture.

Thus the Lloyds building became an exploration of the use and properties of concrete. And the engineer's contribution was to try and make the structure an essay on expression in the use of concrete. But it was the properties of concrete which motivated the search and the solution.

Similarly at the La Villette 'greenhouses' in Paris. The architect defined the architectural intention, and the engineer transformed the simple architectural statement into an essay on the nature of transparency and of how to use the physical properties of glass to convey fully the concept of *transparence*. As an engineer I worked essentially with glass. It was the properties of the material which motivated the development of the design. Thus although we can say that there was originality and aesthetic choice in the way that the design developed, this way forward was directed by the need to express the properties of glass in full.

I would distinguish the difference between the engineer and the architect by saying the architect's response is primarily creative, whereas the engineer's is essentially inventive . . .

This is the positive role for the engineers' genius and skill: to use their understanding of materials and structure to make real the presence of the materials in use in the building, so that people warm to them, want to touch them, feel a sense of the material itself and of the people who made and designed it. To do this we have to avoid the worst excesses of the industrial hegemony, to maintain the feeling that it was the designer, and not industry and its available options, that decided; is one essential ingredient of seeking a tactile, *trace de le main* solution.

A building does not have to be made of brick or stone to achieve this, but rather it is the honesty and immediacy in the use of its principal materials which determines its tactile quality. That was the essential reason for the use of cast steel in Beaubourg . . .

This then is a noble role that the engineer can assume – the role of controlling and taming industry. The building industry has an enormous investment in the *status quo* and, like Iago, will use every argument to demonstrate that other choices are irrational and not very sensible. Only the engineer can withstand these arguments, demonstrate the wrongness of the position of industry and demolish its arguments. In this scenario, the engineer becomes critical and can save his soul.

In general, though, the most powerful way that an engineer can contribute to the work of architects is by exploring the nature of the materials and using that knowledge to produce a special quality in the way materials are used . . .

Extracts. Source: *An Engineer Imagines*, Artemis (London), 1994. © Sylvia Rice.

1994 IAN RITCHIE
(Well) Connected Architecture

Project architect with Foster Associates from 1972 to 1976, Ian Ritchie subsequently worked as a consultant with Michael Hopkins Architects, Ove Arup + Partners, and Peter Rice. In 1981 he formed Rice Francis Ritchie (RFR Design Engineering) with Rice and Martin Francis and in the same year also formed the independent firm of Ian Ritchie Architects. Work by the former includes the bioclimatic facades of the National Museum of Science, Technology and Industry (La Villette, Paris, 1985) and the Lintas suspended glass bridge (Paris, 1985). Buildings by Ian Ritchie Architects include Building B8 (Stockley Park 1990), Cultural Centre (Albert, France, 1990) and the Reina Sofia Museum of Modern Art (Madrid, 1990 with Castro + Onzono).

Art

Preconcepts

The prerequisite to establishing our approach to a new project is a preconcept. This is not to be mistaken for a concept informing the design and guiding the detail development of the architecture. For us, a preconcept engages the most informed holistic view we can describe, and uses expressions such as poetry to capture the essence of the project under consideration. This initial stage is the most crucial in establishing the foundation of the project. (p40)

Concepts

Our architectural concepts should emerge from the preconcept, informing and providing the framework for developing the architectural design.

The development of any one of our projects can be contained by a singular concept but also by a set of ideas which are coalesced and understood as a hierarchy of concepts, all reinforcing each other. The hierarchy of concepts for the Reina Sofia glass circulation towers, for example, were:

– solidity and transparency
– gravitas and lightness
– minimalism and complexity

and to reveal, didactically, the structural composition and behaviour. (p44)

Science and Technology
Scientific understanding
There is no doubt that our ecological awakening demands that our decisions are based on a better understanding of scientific and technical knowledge. Even today we should not have to be specialists to understand scientific language (though a reasonable grasp of numeracy is very useful) . . .

We have to establish cross-scientific links with the research and development world, industry and our fellow collaborators in project design and realisation. Fortunately, the growth in available information and knowledge is paralleled with that in data storage, retrieval and speed of communication . . .

In order to be effective as architects we have to be genuinely interested and informed, and in the process we seek enjoyment. This 'joy' comes from the enlightenment we receive through the process, the appropriate knowledge we obtain, and the success we see in integrating this new personal and shared understanding to the architectural design and its realisation. (p47)

Materials
An architecture which uses materials to reflect the conditions of society, where these materials are used in their primary state rather than as products, eg metal sheet coil, and engages craftsmen to manipulate them, with or without the use of computers, in the factory or in their site assembly, can represent a late 20th-century evolution of the Arts and Crafts tradition . . .

The kitsch and neo-traditional use of materials and products to create a veneer architecture violates our senses in a way that truly historic buildings never do.

It is crucial to remember that architecture is a very important forum for the ever evolving development of our technical culture . . . (pp52-53)

Light
Without light there is no architecture. The history of architecture has been the story of light as the essential material of architecture . . .

By understanding solar geometry we can recapture the art of carving form and the surfaces of buildings with nature's own light pen. To understand light enables us to spatially create a dynamic to tranquil range of atmospheres . . .

In our architecture, understanding the symbiotic relationship of glass and light is crucial. Having explored glass technology over the past few years our attention is now equally focused on light, its energy and colour content. (p54)

Human Purpose . . .

Compliance, conflict and reason

The design process seeks the fundamentals of a problem, often redefining them. Questioning traditional solutions, preconceived ideas, the client's practices and even the need to build at all, is a challenge for both client and architect. It is nevertheless necessary to achieve an optimum solution whether it is innovative or not . . .

Function

Form follows desire

With very few exceptions, the forms and their composition that we have created have more to do with desire than function . . .

More from less

In searching for economy, there is the real chance of producing a poetic response. A response which can express and reveal our search for economy, by providing more from less . . .

Use and Beauty

Can function be a source of art?

Beauty is a by-product of art when there is pleasure derived from it. Art is extracting an essence and translating it.

Man seeks security, thus security is a function whether physical or spiritual. Man seeks shelter, thus shelter is a function. If we consider shelter, it can be provided by walls (from the wind), by a roof on columns (from rain and sun), and by a roof on walls (from rain, sun and wind).

If we take a column, the function of which is to support a roof, and look at a metaphor in nature – the tree trunk (bypassing early Mediterranean timber architecture, the later stone architecture which apparently represented timber construction, and all the other historical references as well), we can maybe rediscover the present. Our present day ability to evoke the tree trunk, if we choose it as the familiar model for a column, gives us the opportunity to understand the beauty of a tree afresh, and to 'extract' the essential elements of it, be they visual, mathematical or technical. This should enable us to imagine, create or invent a functional form from our perception and from our scientific understanding of it. We then search for a representation of the support which raises the support function to that of potential beauty. (pp70-73)

Authenticity in Architecture . . .

Art, science and construction for human purpose

Practising architecture at the end of the 20th century requires us to restate that it is a synthetic process. Its material foundation has for the last few centuries been knowledge established largely through reductionist science. This knowledge is beginning to shift. Chaos theory and the science of complexity explored through computer simulation indicate how matter and life itself apparently synthesise from simple elements into simple systems with complex organisational and behavioural characteristics. This is a conceptual war of thinking that builds up rather than breaks down, recognising interdependence rather than independence in much the same way that we seek to produce our architecture.

This is the process of architecture we enjoy . . . (p81)

Extracts. Source: *(Well) Connected Architecture*, Academy Editions (London) – Ernst & Sohn (Berlin), 1994. © Academy Group Ltd.

NEW MODERN

Peter Eisenman, House 11a, Project for Foster House, 1978-80

1976 PETER EISENMAN
Post-Functionalism

Underlying the similarities that drew the New York Five together were forces that only a few years after the publication of Five Architects *sent them off in very different directions. Applying the ideas of literary and critical theory, Eisenman extended his notion of an autonomous architecture, leading to a new Modernism in which 'form is understood as a series of fragments – signs without meaning dependent upon, and without reference to, a more basic condition'.*

It is true that sometime in the nineteenth century, there was indeed a crucial shift within Western consciousness: one which can be characterized as a shift from humanism to modernism. But, for the most part, architecture, in its dogged adherence to the principles of function, did not participate in or understand the fundamental aspects of that change . . . This shift away from the dominant attitudes of humanism, that were pervasive in Western societies for some four hundred years, took place at various times in the nineteenth century in such disparate disciplines as mathematics, music, painting, literature, film, and photography. It is displayed in the non-objective abstract painting of Malevich and Mondrian; in the non-narrative, atemporal writing of Joyce and Apollinaire; the atonal and polytonal compositions of Schönberg and Webern; in the non-narrative films of Richter and Eggeling.

Abstraction, atonality, and atemporality, however, are merely stylistic manifestations of modernism, not its essential nature. Although this is not the place to elaborate a theory of modernism, or indeed to represent those aspects of such theory which have already found their way into the literature of the other humanist disciplines, it can simply be said that the symptoms to which one has just pointed suggest a displacement of man away from the center of his world. He is no longer viewed as an originating agent. Objects are seen as ideas independent of man. In this context, man is a discursive function among complex and already-formed systems of language, which he witnesses but does not constitute . . .

Modernism, as a sensibility based on the fundamental displacement of man, represents what Michel Foucault would specify as a new episteme. Deriving from a non-humanistic attitude toward the relationship of an individual to his physical environment, it breaks with the historical past, both with the ways of viewing man as subject and, as we have said, with the ethical positivism of form and function. Thus, it cannot be related to functionalism. It is probably for this reason that modernism has not up to now been elaborated in architecture . . .

What is being called post-functionalism begins as an attitude which recognizes modernism as a new and distinct sensibility. It can be understood in architecture in terms of a theoretical base that is concerned with what might be called a modernist dialectic, as opposed to the old humanist (ie functionalist) opposition of form and function.

This new theoretical base changes the humanist balance of form/function to a dialectical relationship within the evolution of form itself. The dialectic can best be described as the potential co-existence within any form of two non-corroborating and non-sequential tendencies. One tendency is to presume architectural form to be a recognizable transformation from some pre-existent geometric or platonic solid. In this case, form is usually understood through a series of registrations designed to recall a more simple geometric condition. This tendency is certainly a relic of humanist theory. However, to this is added a second tendency that sees architectural form in an atemporal, decompositional mode, as something simplified from some pre-existent set of non-specific spatial entities. Here, form is understood as a series of fragments – signs without meaning dependent upon, and without reference to, a more basic condition. The former tendency, when taken by itself, is a reductivist attitude and assumes some primary unity as both an ethical and an aesthetic basis for all creation. The latter, by itself, assumes a basic condition of fragmentation and multiplicity from which the resultant form is a state of simplification. Both tendencies, however, when taken together, constitute the essence of this new, modern dialectic. They begin to define the inherent nature of the object in and of itself and its capacity to be represented. They begin to suggest that the theoretical assumptions of functionalism are in fact cultural rather than universal.

Post-functionalism, thus, is a term of absence. In its negation of functionalism it suggests certain positive theoretical alternatives – existing fragments of thought which, when examined, might serve as a framework for the development of a larger theoretical structure – but it does not, in and of itself, propose to supply a label for such a new consciousness in architecture which I believe is potentially upon us.

Extracts Source: *Opposition* 6, 1976 published by the MIT Press (Cambridge, Mass), Fall 1976 © Peter Eisenman.

1977 BERNARD TSCHUMI
The Pleasure of Architecture

A graduate of the Federal Institute of Technology in Zurich, Bernard Tschumi (b 1944, Lausanne) taught at the Architectural Association from 1970 to 1975, moving to New York in 1976 where he was Visiting Lecturer at the Institute for Architecture and Urban Studies and later at Princeton University. Tschumi's work draws heavily on critical and literary theory, from Barthes and Derrida to Foucault, and, in this text, he hints at the 'pulsions' motivating and unleashed by architecture.

The architecture of pleasure lies where concept and experience of space abruptly coincide, where architectural fragments collide and merge in delight, where the culture of architecture is endlessly deconstructed and rules are transgressed. No metaphorical paradise here, but discomfort and the unbalancing of expectations. Such architecture questions academic (and popular) assumptions, disturbs acquired tastes and fond architectural memories. Typologies, morphologies, spatial compressions, logical constructions – all dissolve. Such architecture is perverse because its real significance lies outside utility or purpose and ultimately is not even necessarily aimed at giving pleasure.

The architecture of pleasure depends on a particular feat, which is to keep architecture obsessed with itself in such an ambiguous fashion that it never surrenders to good conscience or parody, to debility or delirious neurosis . . .

[Architecture] can only act as a recipient in which your desires, my desires, can be reflected. Thus a piece of architecture is not architectural because it seduces, or because it fulfils some utilitarian function, but because it sets in motion the operations of seduction and the unconscious.

A word of warning. *Architecture* may very well activate such motions, but it is not a dream (a stage where society's or the individual's unconscious desires can be fulfilled). It cannot satisfy your wildest fantasies, but it may *exceed* the limits set by them. (pp214-218)

Extracts. Source: *Architectural Design*, vol 47; no 3, Academy Group Ltd (London), 1977.
© Bernard Tschumi.

1978 COOP HIMMELBLAU
The Future of Splendid Desolation

Far from a movement, 'deconstructivism' is more a syndrome of concerns and constructional tactics pursued by various architects in parallel. One of the firms most often associated with that syndrome is Coop Himmelblau (Blue-sky Cooperative), founded by Wolf Prix (b 1942, Vienna) and Helmut Swiczinsky (b 1944 Poznan, Poland) in 1968. Starting with exhibitions and happenings, they have kindled a subversion of 'the autocrats whose motto is "efficiency, economy and expediency"' later stoked by their buildings such as the Reiss Bar, Vienna (1977), The Red Angel, Vienna (1981), and Baumann Studio, Vienna (1984).

The architectures of the future have already been built.
The solitude of squares, the desolation of the streets, the devastation of the buildings characterize the city of the present and will characterize the city of the future as well. Expressions like 'safe and sound' are no longer applicable to architecture. We live in a world of unloved objects, but we use them daily to our advantage. Today's architecture reinforces this discrepancy, until it becomes schizophrenic.

Reactionary architecture tends to conceal the problems rather than create the necessary new urban awareness. Today's architecture must be defined as a medium of expanding vitality.

Contemporary architecture will be honest and true, when streets, open spaces, buildings and infrastructures reflect the image of urban reality, when the devastation of the city is transformed into fascinating landmarks of desolation. Desolation not as a result of complacency but as a result of the identification of the urban reality will develop the desires, the self-confidence and the courage to take and hold possession of the city and to alter it. The important thing won't then be the grass you can't walk on but the asphalt you can.

But of course you have to discard everything that hinders this 'emotional act of using'. The false aesthetic, sticking like smeared make-up on the face of mediocrity, the cowardice of antiquated values, the belief that everything that is disquieting can be beautified. The autocrats whose motto is 'efficiency, economy and expediency'.

Architects must stop thinking only [of] the accommodation of their clients. Architects have to stop pitying themselves for the bad company they keep. Architecture is not a means to an end. Architecture does not have a function. Architecture is not palliative. It is the bone in the meat of the city. Architecture gains meaning in proportion to its desolation. The desolation comes from the act of using. It gains strength from surrounding desolation. And this architecture brings the message:

Everything you like is bad.

Everything that works is bad.

Whatever has to be accepted is good. (p75)

Extracts. Source: Oliver Gruenberg, Robert Hahn and Doris Knecht (eds), *The Power of the City,*Verlag der Georg Büchner Buchhandlung (Darmstadt), 1988.©Verlag der Georg Büchner Buchhandlung.

Coop Himmelblau, Video Clip Folly, Groningen, 1990

1978   REM KOOLHAAS
Delirious New York: A Retroactive Manifesto for Manhattan

Paying his way through the Architectural Association Diploma course by writing film scripts, Rem Koolhaas (b 1944, Amsterdam) moved to New York in 1972 and later became a Visiting Fellow of the Institute for Architecture and Urban Studies. His years in Manhattan, and fascination with the city, led him to a close examination of the dynamics that created it. Delirious New York and the theory of Manhattanism are the results of that study. Koolhaas founded the Office of Metropolitan Architecture (OMA) with Madelon Vriesendrop, Elia Zenghelis and Zoe Zenghelis, in 1972.

Manifesto

How to write a manifesto – on a form of urbanism for what remains of the twentieth century – in an age disgusted with them? The fatal weakness of manifestos is their inherent lack of evidence.

Manhattan's problem is the opposite: it is a mountain range of evidence without manifesto.

This book was conceived at the intersection of these two observations: it is a *retroactive manifesto* for Manhattan.

Manhattan is the twentieth century's Rosetta Stone.

Not only are large parts of its surface occupied by architectural mutations (Central Park, the Skyscraper), utopian fragments (Rockefeller Center, the UN Building) and irrational phenomena (Radio City Music Hall), but in addition each block is covered with several layers of phantom architecture in the form of past occupancies, aborted projects and popular fantasies that provide alternative images to the New York that exists.

Especially between 1890 and 1940 a new culture (the Machine Age?) selected Manhattan as laboratory: a mythical island where the invention and testing of a metropolitan lifestyle and its attendant architecture could be pursued as a collective experiment in which the entire city became a factory of man-made experience, where the real and the natural ceased to exist.

This book is an interpretation of that Manhattan which gives its seemingly discontinuous – even irreconcilable – episodes a degree of consistency and coherence, an interpretation that intends to establish Manhattan as the product of an unformulated theory, *Manhattanism*, whose program – to exist in a world totally fabricated by man, ie to live *inside* fantasy – was so ambitious that to be realized, it could never be openly stated.

Ecstasy

If Manhattan is still in search of a theory, then this theory, once identified, should yield a formula for an architecture that is at once ambitious *and* popular.

Manhattan has generated a shameless architecture that has been loved in direct proportion to its defiant lack of self-hatred, has been respected exactly to the degree that it went too far.

Manhattan has consistently inspired in it beholders *ecstasy about architecture*.

In spite – or perhaps because – of this, its performance and implications have been consistently ignored and even suppressed by the architectural profession.

Density

Manhattanism is the one urbanistic ideology that has fed, from its conception, on the splendors and miseries of the metropolitan condition – hyper-density – without once losing faith in it as the basis for a desirable modern culture. *Manhattan's architecture is a paradigm for the exploitation of congestion.*

The retroactive formulation of Manhattan's program is a polemical operation.

It reveals a number of strategies, theorems and breakthroughs that not only give logic and pattern to the city's past performance, but whose continuing validity is itself an argument for a second coming of Manhattanism, this time as an explicit doctrine that can transcend the island of its origins to claim its place among contemporary urbanisms.

With Manhattan as an example, this book is a blueprint for a 'Culture of Congestion'.

Blueprint

A blueprint does not predict the cracks that will develop in the future; it describes an ideal state that can only be approximated. In the same way this book describes a *theoretical* Manhattan, a *Manhattan as conjecture*, of which the present city is the compromised and imperfect realization.

From all the episodes of Manhattan's urbanism this book isolates only those moments where the blueprint is most visible and most convincing. It should, and inevitably will, be read against the torrent of negative analyses that emanates from Manhattan about Manhattan and that has firmly established Manhattan as the *Capital of Perpetual Crisis*.

Only through the speculative reconstruction of a perfect Manhattan can its monumental successes and failures be read.

Blocks

In terms of structure, this book is a simulacrum of Manhattan's Grid: a collection of blocks whose proximity and juxtaposition reinforce their separate meanings.

The first four blocks – 'Coney Island', 'The Skyscraper', 'Rockefeller Center', and 'The Europeans' – chronicle the permutation of Manhattanism as an implied rather than explicit doctrine.

They show the progression (and subsequent decline) of Manhattan's determination to remove its territory as far from the natural as humanly possible.

The fifth block – the Appendix – is a sequence of architectural projects that solidify Manhattanism into an explicit doctrine and negotiate the transition from Manhattanism's unconscious architectural production to a conscious phase.

Ghostwriter

Movie stars who have led adventure-packed lives are often too egocentric to discover patterns, too inarticulate to express intentions, too restless to record or remember events. Ghostwriters do it for them.

In the same way *I was Manhattan's ghostwriter*.

(With, as will be seen, the added complication that my source and subject passed into premature senility before its 'life' was completed. That is why I had to provide my own ending.) (pp6-8)

Extracts. Source: Rem Koolhaas, *Delirious New York: A Retroactive Manifesto for Manhattan*, Oxford University Press (New York), 1978. © Rem Koolhaas.

1979   DANIEL LIBESKIND
End Space

Originally a student of music, Daniel Libeskind (b 1946, Lodz, Poland) studied architecture at the Cooper Union in New York under John Hejduk and went on to teach the History and Theory of Architecture at a number of institutions including the Architectural Association and the Cranbrook Academy. During this period, Libeskind carried out a fundamentally theoretical endeavour, using text and drawings to explore the tensions between experience, intuition and formalisation, the voluntary and the involuntary.

Architectural drawings have in modern times assumed the identity of signs; they have become the fixed and silent accomplices in the overwhelming endeavour of building and construction . . .

The act of creation in the order of procedures of imagination, here as elsewhere, coincides with creation in the objective realm. Drawing is not mere invention; its efficacy is not drawn from its own unlimited resources of liberty. It is a state of experience in which the 'other' is revealed through mechanisms which provoke and support objective accomplishments as well as supporting the one who draws upon them. Being neither pure registration nor pure creation, these drawings come to resemble an explication or a reading of a pre-given text – a text both generous and inexhaustible.

I am interested in the profound relations which exist between the intuition of geometric structure as it manifests itself in a pre-objective sphere of experience and the possibility of formalisation which tries to overtake it in the objective realm. In fact, these seemingly exclusive attitudes polarise the movement of imagination and give an impression of discontinuity, when in reality they are but different and reciprocal moments – alternative viewpoints – of the same fundamental, ontological necessity . . .

Because the 'geometry of experience' is only a horizon of potential formalisation and we find it already inserted into that other horizon of desire and intuition, the task of essential clarification, as I see it, becomes the systematic and dynamic transmutation of movements; an exchange between abstract cyphers, exhausted in their own objectivity and hardened in fixed signs, and concrete contingencies responsive to the permanent solicitations of a spontaneous appeal . . .

Most of all, however, I am a fascinated observer and a perplexed participant of that mysterious desire which seeks a radical elucidation of the original pre-comprehension of forms – an ambition which I think is implicit in all architecture. If there is true abstraction here (as opposed to generalisation) it is not achieved by the elimination of contents through a gradual deployment of an increasing emptiness, but is rather an isolation of structural essence, whose manifestation in two dimensions illuminates all the sub-systems of projection (for example, three-dimensional space) . . .

The invisible ground from which it is possible to scaffold moving layers of construction enables one to recover modes of awareness quite removed from the initial hypothesis of rationality. These drawings seek to reflect, on a deeper level of consciousness, the inner life of geometrical order whose nucleus is the conflict between the Voluntary and Involuntary. Once again this duality (like that of realism-formalism) appears as an unsurpassable condition pointing to a dynamic ground which testifies to an experience receiving only as much as it is capable of giving; draws only that which allows itself to be drawn into. (pp80-81)

Extracts. Source: Daniel Libeskind, *Between Zero and Infinity*, Rizzoli (New York and London), 1981. © Rizzoli International Publications Inc and Daniel Libeskind.

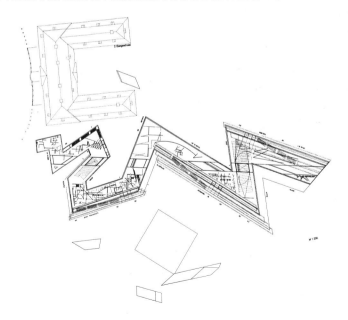

Daniel Libeskind, Extension to Berlin Museum with Jewish Museum, 1989

1980 COOP HIMMELBLAU
Architecture Must Blaze

This text accompanied an architectural happening in Graz, an actual manifestation of the blazing wing in the form of a steel frame suspended in the air incorporating flaming gas jets.

You can judge just how bad the 70s were when you look at its super tense architecture. Opinion polls and complacent democracy live behind Biedermeier-facades. But we don't want to build Biedermeier. Not now and at no other time. We are tired of seeing Palladio and other historical masks. Because we don't want architecture to exclude everything that is disquieting. We want architecture to have more. Architecture that bleeds, that exhausts, that whirls and even breaks. Architecture that lights up, that stings, that rips, and under stress, tears. Architecture should be cavernous, fiery, smooth, hard, angular, brutal, round, delicate, colorful, obscene, voluptuous, dreamy, alluring, repelling, wet, dry and throbbing. Alive or dead. Cold – then cold as a block of ice. Hot – then hot as a blazing wing.
Architecture must blaze. (p95)

Text accompanying the *Blazing Wing Action Object* (Graz) 1980. Source: Oliver Gruenberg, Robert Hahn and Doris Knecht (eds), *The Power of the City*, Verlag der Georg Büchner Buchhandlung (Darmstadt), 1988. © Verlag der Georg Büchner Buchhandlung.

Coop Himmelblau, Funder Factory, Carinthia, Austria, 1988

1981   BERNARD TSCHUMI
The Manhattan Transcripts

Along with literary and critical theory, Tschumi informs his work with theories of cinema. This is made explicit in The Manhattan Transcripts, *in which he uses a tripartite mode of notation – events, movements, spaces as well as the notions of frame and sequence – as a means both to break down habitual and conventional readings of architecture and to suggest a new order of experience. The* Manhattan Transcripts *were begun during Tschumi's time in New York as Visiting Lecturer. By the time of their publication in 1981, he had become Professor of Architecture at Princeton, later moving to the Cooper Union and finally to Columbia where he is now Dean of the Graduate School of Architecture.*

Classification

The *Transcripts* offer a different reading of architecture in which space, movement and events are ultimately independent, yet stay in a new relation to one another, so that the conventional components of architecture are broken down and rebuilt along different axes . . .

Relation

It is the *Transcripts'* contention that only the striking relationship between the three levels of event, space and movement makes for the architectural experience. Yet they never attempt to transcend the contradictions between object, man and event in order to bring them to a new synthesis: on the contrary, they aim to maintain these contradictions in a dynamic manner, in a new relation of indifference, reciprocity or conflict . . .

Notation

The purpose of the tripartite mode of notation (events, movements, spaces) is to introduce the order of experience, the order of time - movements, intervals, sequences - for all inevitably intervene in the reading of the city. It also proceeds from a need to question the modes of representation generally used by architects: plans, sections, axonometric, perspectives . . .

Articulation

The Manhattan Transcripts are not a random accumulation of events; they display a particular organization. Their chief characteristics is the sequence, a composite succession of frames that confronts spaces, movements and events, each with its own combinative structure and inherent set of rules . . .

Transformation

The Transcripts' sequences are intensified through the use of devices, or rules of transformation, such as compression, insertion, transference, etc . . .

Combination

By going beyond the conventional definition of 'function', the *Transcripts* use their combined levels of investigation to address the notion of the program – a field architectural ideologies have banished for decades – and to explore unlikely confrontations . . .

Deconstruction

Despite the abstraction of their devices, the *Transcripts* generally presuppose a reality already in existence, a reality waiting to be deconstructed – and eventually transformed. They isolate, frame, 'take' elements from the city. (Yet the role of the Transcripts is never to represent; they are not mimetic.) . . .

Sensations

If the programs used for *The Manahattan Transcripts* are of the most extreme nature it is to underline the fact that perhaps all architecture, rather than being about functional standards, is about love and death . . . (pp19-28)

Extracts. Source: Bernard Tschumi, *The Manhattan Transcripts*, Academy Editions (London), 1994. © Bernard Tschumi and Academy Editions.

1982 ZAHA HADID
Randomness vs Arbitrariness

A student at the Architectural Association in the early 1970s, Zaha Hadid (b 1950, Baghdad, Iraq) went on to become a unit master from 1977 to 1987 as well as a member of OMA (Office of Metropolitan Architecture) for several years.

Randomness: To most people there is no apparent difference either conceptually or visually between randomness and arbitrariness. It is difficult to demonstrate this basic difference scientifically. Treated as a mathematical formula, it becomes even more abstract, although the principle of distinguishing between the two is the ability to analyse the conceptual difference through abstraction.

Randomness in architecture is a visual translation of pure mathematical order and thinking which is guided by logic, whereas arbitrariness has no underlying conceptual logic – randomness is not to do with pure formalism – to demonstrate all the different aspects. It is necessary to use symbols like those of a mathematical equation – which is again obscure. So what are we saying? Aren't we just trying to justify our actions? No. So Explain.

Arbitrariness: This is difficult. It has always been a problem trying to translate because the field of 'explanation' is limited, the forces at play are not necessarily those of conventional earthly nature; it's neither spiritual nor cosmic nor religious. It is impossible to summarise the implications of the writings and manifestoes of Malevich, and the merits of his writing are not parallel to those of his paintings. This has to do with the inability to translate. He had then to resort to metaphysical and spiritual concepts to make the work comprehensible: he dressed it in a language which was familiar.

Arbitrariness has to do with a generation which has been brought up on shopping for ideas. A catalogue exists from which they freely copy anything and apply it with little relevance to any situation. But in architecture our responsibilities are far greater: we must create new dynamics of architecture in which the land is partially occupied. We must understand the basic principles of liberation.

Source: *AA Files: Annals of the Architectural Association of Architecture*, No 2, July 1982.
© Zaha Hadid and the Architectural Association.

1983   ZAHA HADID
The Eighty-Nine Degrees

In this essay, published to coincide with an exhibition of her work, Hadid makes clear her dedication to the programme of Modernity and her equal determination to take it forward into the future.

The twentieth-century triumph of technology and our accelerating and ever-changing lifestyles have created a totally new condition. These changes, despite the difficulties, have a certain exhilaration which is yet to be matched in architecture. It is that revision and the absolute need for inventiveness, imagination and interpretation that makes our role in architecture more valid. We can no longer fulfil our obligations as architects if we carry on as cake decorators. Our role is far greater than that. We, the authors of architecture, have to take on the task of reinvestigating Modernity.

An atmosphere of total hostility, where looking forward has been, and still is, seen as almost criminal makes one more adamant that there is only one way and that is to go forward along the path paved by the experiments of the early Modernists. Their efforts have been aborted and their projects untested. Our task is not to resurrect them but to develop them further. This task of fulfilling the proper role of architecture, not only aesthetically but programmatically, will unveil new territories. In every project there are new territories to be invaded and others to be conquered: and this is only the beginning.

Extracts. Source: Zaha Hadid, *Planetary Architecture Two*, Architectural Association (London), 1983, unpaginated – second facing page. © Zaha Hadid and the Architectural Association.

1983 DANIEL LIBESKIND
Unoriginal Signs

At times gnomic in his writing, Libeskind uses juxtaposition, oxymoron and paradox as heuristic devices to reach beyond the limits of the verbal. This text accompanied a series of drawings exhibited at the Architectural Association.

The recourse to surrogates is only a habit which can be given up. One can refuse to substitute, for the experience of Unoriginality, things that one has never experienced but which are known through originals. To substitute the 'essence' of Architecture for its actual non-existence would be futile and dishonest.

This work in search of Architecture has discovered no permanent structure, no constant form and no universal type. I have realised that the result of this journey in search of the essentials undermines in the end the very promise of their existence. Architecture is neither on the inside nor the outside. It is not a given nor a physical fact. It has no History and it does not follow Fate. What emerges in differentiated experience is Architecture as an index of the relationship between what was and what will be. Architecture as non-existent reality is a symbol which, in the process of consciousness, leaves a trail of hieroglyphs in space and time that touch equivalent depths of Unoriginality. (pp4-5)

Extracts. Source: Daniel Libeskind, *Chamber Works,* Architectural Association (London), 1983. © Daniel Libeskind and the Architectural Association.

1984 PETER EISENMAN

The End of the Classical: the End of the End, the End of the Beginning

Making more explicit use of literary theory, in particular that of Jacques Derrida (with whom he collaborated on the Choral Works in 1988), Eisenman presents in this essay a heated polemic against the Classical and Humanist paradigms in architecture. In their place he posits architecture as fiction, free from the weight of past or future.

The Not-Classical: Architecture as Fiction

What can be the model for architecture when the essence of what was effective in the classical model – the presumed rational value of structure, representations, methodologies of origins and ends, and deductive processes – has been shown to be a simulation?

It is not possible to answer such a question with an alternative model. But a series of characteristics can be proposed that typify this aporia, this loss in our capacity to conceptualize a new model for architecture. These characteristics, outlined below, arise from that which can *not be*, they form a structure of *absences*. The purpose in proposing them is not to reconstitute what has just been dismissed, a model for a theory of architecture – for all such models are ultimately futile. Rather what is being proposed is an expansion beyond the limitations presented by the classical model to the realization of *architecture as an independent discourse*, free of external values – classical or any other; that is, the intersection of the *meaning-free*, the *arbitrary*, and the *timeless* in the artificial.

The meaning-free, arbitrary, and timeless creation of artificiality in this sense must be distinguished from what Baudrillard has called 'simulation': it is not an attempt to erase the classical distinction between reality and representation – thus again making architecture a set of conventions simulating the real; it is, rather, more like a *dis*simulation. Whereas simulation attempts to obliterate the difference between real and imaginary, dissimulation leaves untouched the difference between reality and illusion. The relationship between dissimulation and reality is similar to the signification embodied in the mask: the sign of pretending to be *not* what one is – that is, a sign which seems not to signify anything besides itself (the sign of a sign, or the negation of what is behind it). Such a dissimulation in architecture can be given the provisional title of the *not-classical*. As dissimulation is not the inverse, negative, or opposite of simulation, a 'not-classical' architecture is not the inverse, negative, or opposite of classical architecture; it is merely different from or other than. A 'not-classical' architecture is no longer a certification of experience or a simulation of history, reason or reality in the present. Instead, it may more appropriately be described as an *other* manifestation, an architecture as is, now as a fiction. It is a representation of itself, of its own values and internal experience . . .

The End of the Beginning

While classical origins were thought to have their source in a divine or natural order and modern origins were held to derive their value from deductive reason, 'not-classical' origins can be strictly arbitrary, simply starting points, without value. They can be artificial and relative, as opposed to natural, divine, or universal. Such artificially determined beginnings can be free of universal values because they are merely arbitrary points in time, when the architectural process commences. One example of an artificial origin is a *graft*, as in the genetic insertion of an alien body into a host to provide a new result . . .

A graft is not in itself genetically arbitrary. Its arbitrariness is in its freedom from a value system of non-arbitrariness (that is, the classical). It is arbitrary in its provision of a choice of reading which brings no external value to the process. . .

The End of the End

Along with the end of the origin, the second basic characteristic of a 'not-classical' architecture, therefore, is its freedom from *a priori* goals or ends – the end of the end . . .

With the end of the end, what was formerly the process of composition or transformation ceases to be a causal strategy, a process of addition or subtraction from an origin. Instead the process becomes one of *modification* – the invention of a non-dialectical, non-directional, non-goal oriented process . . .

This suggests the idea of architecture as 'writing' as opposed to architecture as image. What is being 'written' is not the object itself – its mass and volume – but the *act* of massing. This idea gives a metaphoric body to the act of architecture. It then signals its reading through another system of signs, called *traces*. Traces are not to be read literally, since they have no other value than to signal the idea that there is a reading event and that the reading should take place; trace signals the idea to read . . .

But further, knowing how to decode is no longer important; simply, language in this context is no longer a code to assign meanings (that *this* means *that*). The activity of reading is first and foremost in the recognition of something as a language (that *it is*). Reading, in this sense, makes available a level of *indication* rather than a level of meaning or expression.

Therefore, to propose the end of the beginning and the end of the end is to propose the end of beginnings and ends of value – to propose an *other* 'timeless' space of invention. It is a 'timeless' space in the present without a determining relation to an ideal future or to an idealized past. Architecture in the present is seen as a process of inventing an artificial past and a futureless present. It remembers a no-longer future. (pp154-172)

Extracts. Source: *Perspecta: the Yale Architectural Journal*, vol 21, 1984. © Peter Eisenman.

Peter Eisenman, Wexner Centre for the Visual Arts, Columbus, Ohio, 1983-88

1986 JOHN HEJDUK
Thoughts of an Architect

Included in the New York Five for his almost Platonic geometric formulations, Hejduk nevertheless showed an idiosyncrasy that emerged more clearly in his later work. In it he investigates and plays on psychological associations resulting in a much more questioning form of architecture. This text was part of the Victims project that included several installations in Berlin and London between 1984 and 1986.

1   That architectural tracings are apparitions, outlines, figments.
They are not diagrams but ghosts.

2   Tracings are similar to X-rays, they penetrate internally.

3   Erasures imply former existences.

4   Drawings and tracings are like the hands of the blind
touching the surfaces of the face in order to understand
a sense of volume, depth and penetration.

5   The lead of an architect's pencil disappears (drawn away)

metamorphoses.

To take a site: present tracings, outlines, figments, apparitions,
X-rays of thoughts. Meditations on the sense of erasures.
To fabricate a construction of time.

To draw out by compacting in. To flood (liquid densification)
the place-site with missing letters and disappeared signatures.
To gelatinize forgetfulness.

Source: John Hejduk, *Victims*, Architectural Association (London), 1986. © John Hejduk and the Architectural Association.

1988　COOP HIMMELBLAU

The Dissipation of Our Bodies in the City

Versions of this text appeared in The Power of the City, *a mono-graph, and* The End of Architecture? *the proceedings of a symposium held in Vienna attended by many of the architects associated with deconstructivism. The text is as much a documentation of Coop Himmelblau's working method as an account of its concern for and fascination with the contemporary city.*

We love to design and make visible Cities'(invisible) real and potential force lines and force fields. Just as we also love to build buildings and their wandering shadows.

In recent years – since about 1978 – we began, without knowing where it would lead us, to densify and shorten the time of the design process. That's to say, discussions about the project are certainly held at length. But always without thinking of spatially conceivable consequences.

And then suddenly: the drawing is there. On the wall, on the table, on a piece of paper.

Somewhere.

And always and simultaneously there is the model (in no scale).

This is how it works: Coop Himmelblau is a team. There are two of us. While drawing, architecture is captured in words, the drawing is narrated into the three dimensional material of the model. (We cannot prove it, but we surmise very strongly that the more intensely the design is experienced by the designer, the better the built space will be experienced.)

Last year, we noticed that we gradually began to emphasise the verbal description of the design with gestures of our hands. And with projects for Paris and Vienna, the language of the body was the better drawing and the first model.

And when we began to work on the projects for the cities New York and Berlin, the face and body of these cities became more and more distinct.

On a team photo of Coop Himmelblau, we began to see and draw lines and surfaces of the city. Our eyes became towers, our foreheads bridges, the faces became landscapes, and our shirts site plans.

Superimposing the existing city map and the new drawing, the contours, lines and surfaces of the faces and bodies, previously so important, gradually vanished in the whirl of existing planning. Yet the lines, fields and surfaces of the new structure delineate themselves clearly, ever more clearly. They became three-dimensional and cast shadows.

Now we are going to enlarge our team photo, step by step, until just pupils of the eyes are visible. They are the plan of a tall building, and we intend to build it. (pp12-16)

Source: Oliver Gruenberg, Robert Hahn and Doris Knecht (eds), *The Power of the City*, Verlag der Georg Büchner Buchhandlung (Darmstadt), 1988. © Verlag der Georg Büchner Buchhandlung.

Coop Himmelblau, Rooftop Remodeling, Vienna, 1984-88

1988 JEFFREY KIPNIS
Forms of Irrationality

Primarily an educator and theorist, Jeffrey Kipnis has taught Theory and Design at Ohio State University in the Department of Architecture and at the Architectural Association in London. He is also a member of the firm Shirdel and Kipnis, based in Los Angeles. This text is a version of a paper first delivered to a conference on architectural theory. In it he applies a crystalline logic to a critique of rationality, seeking to identify and transcend the sources of resistance to innovation in the design process.

It seems we are presented with a dilemma. If the growing irrelevance of architecture is the result of systematic repression, then it seems that the principal vector for the persistence and dissemination of that repression has been rational design theory. This is true even when theory in that form has taken upon itself the self-reflexive problem. As we have seen, rational discourse cannot give form to the necessary question 'what is (the form of) irrationality?' Irrationality and all of its conjugates – ambivalence, multivocality, simultaneity, the mystical and so forth – are collectively that which resist and exceed the rational form of 'what is?' In short, there can be no prospect, in terms of theory of design, of an 'improved discourse', of a 'more rigorous discourse', whether such phrases mean 'more like philosophy', or 'more objective historiography', 'more sensitive to the visual/ aesthetic perception of the object', 'more sociologically responsible' or whatever other criteria might be applied . . .

In an effort to resolve this dilemma, let us begin to pay attention to a logical necessity. If no practice has ever been faithful to the model of rational discourse, if every design exceeds its principles, and if this condition is not merely historical but constitutional, then what is at fault is neither the discourse nor the practice, but the model of the relationship between the two. The rationalist model is already irrational. Thus, strictly speaking, at the moment of design, architectural discourse is not and has never been theory or history at all; once it moves to the question of design, it is nothing other than and nothing less than the morality of the design process, a gaining of permission for some forms, surfaces, and materials, a prohibition against others. In terms of design, it is therefore nothing other than and nothing less than the design process itself.

This condition, which in different words says that while the architect will always design for good reasons there are no good reasons for design, has, upon scrutiny of the history of design rationales, always persisted, from Palladio to Corb. What is proposed as different today is that we have come to a point where the ego correlates of design rationales, the good, the true and the beautiful, are themselves suspected as sources of resistance. Those correlates do not exist as such but are merely the forms by which negotiation is always already anticipated by the architect in the design process . . .

The goal for a design theory that explores the proposition in question must be to defer as long [as] possible and/or dilute as thoroughly as possible the inevitable encroachment of the ego's demands of negotiation into the design process. At the moment of design there can exist no authentic authority. No ethical nor moral imperative, no priority or precedent, no cultural or aesthetic responsibility rightfully restrains the exploration into possibilities of occupying material form. But design is always an ego process; it depends on the operation of authority through the architect and this is always already conditioned by the constraints of negotiation . . .

The task is now to overcome the double bind, to develop design processes that dilute or defer the constraints of negotiation at the level of the traditional ego correlates . . .

Currently, two classes of such design processes, which I term *absurd* and *surd*, hold out promise to accomplish this goal . . .

Both *absurd* and *surd* mean irrational, *absurd*, in the sense of utterly senseless, illogical or untrue, *surd* in the sense of incapable of being spoken . . .

In *absurd* processes, the operating principle is that, while the tradition of architectural logic is suspect in its authority, nevertheless the form of design logic can be maintained efficaciously if the sources of its motives and criteria for evaluation are displaced from the tradition of architectural decision-making. Thus pseudo-rational methods are maintained but the specific context, the sources of initial conditions and the criteria for testing progress in design, the process, is displaced from traditional architectural sources. For example, in the Eisenman Biocentrum project, the initial formal conditions were created by extruding forms drawn from biological symbols. These were then operated on with an amalgam of processes drawn from DNA replication and fractal geometry. Design progress was judged, at least initially, by the extent to which the formal manipulations analogized the borrowed processes and achieved new relationships intrinsic to those processes. As design proceeded, negotiation constraints were factored into the developing design . . .

In *surd* processes the focus is not on displacing architectural rationality in design, but on silencing it as much as possible so as to allow the entire self, rather than the rational architectural ego, to govern the design. The operating principle of *surd* processes derives from the fact that the architectural ego is but a reduced or narcissistic subset of the entire self of the architect. Thus the proposition is to construct processes that restore the architecturally disavowed aspects of the self to architectural design by suppressing the footholds for architectural rationality. The theme is objectification without rationalization under the assumption that rationalization – through geometry, for example – is but one process by which objectification can occur.

These processes typically begin either by choosing an external, non-architectural 'object' – a painting, a poem, a list of words, a way to behave or the like – and physicalizing the content of that source object. John Hejduk's work is a well-known example of such methods. Alternatively, initial objects can be 'prepared' in such a way as to remove all familiar architectural footholds. The design process can be described as the construction of a specific ritual by which the architect objectifies *surd* material. These design process[es] . . . are carried to the point of addressing negotiation constraints as well. (pp159-162)

Extracts. Source: John Whiteman, Jeffrey Kipnis and Richard Burdett (eds), *Strategies in Architectural Thinking*, Chicago Institute for Architecture and Urbanism, MIT Press, (Cambridge, Mass) 1992. © Chicago Institute of Architecture and Urbanism.

1988   MARK WIGLEY
Deconstructivist Architecture

The essay from which these extracts were taken was included in the catalogue for the exhibition of the same title, held at the Museum of Modern Art in New York in 1988. The director and guest curator was none other than Philip Johnson who, more than fifty years earlier, was co-curator of the International Style exhibition that did so much to popularise Modernism in the United States. While the Deconstructivist exhibition did not have the same impact, it did raise the visibility of the 'style' and its practitioners. Mark Wigley was Associate Curator of the exhibition.

Deconstruction is not demolition, or dissimulation. While it diagnoses certain structural problems within apparently stable structures, these flaws do not lead to the structures' collapse. On the contrary, deconstruction gains all its force by challenging the very values of harmony, unity, and stability, and proposing instead a different view of structure: the view that the flaws are intrinsic to the structure. They cannot be removed without destroying it; they are, indeed, the structure.

A deconstructivist architect is therefore not one who dismantles buildings, but one who locates the inherent dilemmas within buildings. The deconstructivist architect puts the pure forms of the architectural tradition on the couch and identifies the symptoms of a repressed impurity. The impurity is drawn to the surface by a combination of gentle coaxing and violent torture: the form is interrogated . . . (p11)

Irregular geometry is . . . understood as a structural condition rather than as a dynamic formal aesthetic. It is no longer produced simply by the conflict between pure forms. It is now produced within those forms. The forms themselves are infiltrated with the characteristic skewed geometry, and distorted. In this way, the traditional condition of the architectural object is radically disturbed.

This disturbance does not result from external violence. It is not a fracturing, or slicing, or fragmentation, or piercing. To disturb a form from the outside in these ways is not to threaten that form, only to damage it. The damage produces a decorative effect, an aesthetic of danger, an almost picturesque representation of peril – but not a tangible threat. Instead, deconstructivist architecture disturbs figures from within . . . (p16)

The more carefully we look, the more unclear it becomes where the perfect form ends and its imperfection begins; they are found to be inseparably entangled. A line cannot be drawn between them. No surgical technique can free the form; no clean incision can be made. To remove the parasite would be to kill the host. They comprise one symbiotic entity.

This produces a feeling of unease, of disquiet, because it challenges the sense of stable, coherent identity that we associate with pure form. It is as if perfection had always harboured imperfection, that it has always had certain undiagnosed congenital flaws which are only now becoming visible. Perfection is secretly monstrous. Tortured from within, the seemingly perfect confesses its crime, its imperfection.

This sense of dislocation occurs not only within the forms . . . It also occurs between those forms and their context . . . (p17)

This estrangement sets up a complicated resonance, between the disrupted interior of the forms and their disruption of the context, which calls into question the status of the walls that define the form. The division between inside and outside is radically disturbed . . .

The whole condition of enclosure breaks down.

Even though it threatens this most fundamental property of architectural objects, deconstructivist architecture does not constitute an avant-garde. It is not a rhetoric of the new. Rather, it exposes the unfamiliar hidden within the traditional. It is the shock of the old.

It exploits the weaknesses in the tradition in order to disturb rather than overthrow it. Like the modern avant-garde, it attempts to be disturbing, alienating. But not from the retreat of the avant-garde, not from the margins. Rather, it occupies, and subverts, the center. This work is not fundamentally different from the ancient tradition it subverts. It does not abandon the tradition. Rather, it inhabits the center of the tradition in order to demonstrate that architecture is always infected, the pure form has always been contaminated. By inhabiting the tradition fully, obeying its inner logic more rigorously than ever before, these architects discover certain dilemmas within the tradition that are missed by those who sleepwalk through it . . . (p18)

Extracts. Source: Philip Johnson and Mark Wigley (eds), *Deconstructivist Architecture*, The Museum of Modern Art (New York), 1988. © The Museum of Modern Art.

1991 DANIEL LIBESKIND
Upside Down X

In 1987 Libeskind won first prize for his City Edge project in the Berlin Internationale Bauausstellung (IBA) competition and in 1989 he won the competition for the Extension to the Berlin Museum. The latter is his first major design to be built. Yet as suggested by this text, included in a monograph on his work, Libeskind continues to search for something more than building.

Architecture, the very word has lost its reputation: how is it to defend itself? Both 'good and bad' days are now gone. The everyday architect is dead. His body useless unless it becomes manure or kindling for the fire which, after all, is based on what is 'no better'.

What is not alone is whole, both willing and unwilling to be named object. Once numbered and multiplied, this whole grew at the expense of zeroes into which it has stepped. One knows construction by destruction and codes ever since Eiffel changed leisure into fatigue. The road of Architecture does not have two directions but only one – meaning that eyes are better transformers than gears, when our understanding grates on matters which will be ever resistant, incomplete. Incompleteness being the trial of psyche; bridge over skill and intelligence . . .

What then is Architecture? Don't notice it. However, by supposing that force relates to looks, ie to the musical instruments still harbouring weapons, one can unhinge design of things and cities, releasing the 'more harmonious than seen' into each architectonic device whose life lies in killing. Deadly thinking: day in night time . . .

If every construction were just smoke one's perception would not be restricted. But dates themselves are senses giving and receiving each other's small insanities. How to withstand the heart's desire – since editing gets what it wants – at the soul's expense? . . .

Life is to Architecture as Earth is to a watery physical force. The architect has been locked in a trunk while Architecture is staggering mindlessly to lift the load back home. By now, or soon, the sweat will evaporate and be forever lost (cubes have always been pre-historic). Thus emerges the wonderful order of a world no longer seen as the random gathering of things significant only when clumsy. A world in which each hair-pin, arcade or tribe can no longer posture in the mother's *sensus communis*. The shapes are cold, handwritten, dry; one simply cannot find their boundary in the East or in the profound fairy detector with an always extended arm.

It shall remain Unaccountable, faintly whispering – clear of illogic and logic, sure to reason on the course of heavenly bodies, the factor π, law-abiding men trying to derive absence from songs. What penetrates fools satisfaction. Humanity reposes while mighty defenders fight madness in words, gloomy origins of the igloo, the rough millennium whose thousand-year-old ray looks like a statue of a hero gossiping behind the fallen house.

Understanding is absent-minded. The unseen Design: an inorganic sediment. The Ephasians might as well rest, letting their city be governed by children.

Without ending (since the above is neither theory nor object), I believe that even the ugliest architecture is going to be clearer than the handsomest name or the wisest visage. Because what is less wide is more beautiful. To put it simply: god at a distance looks like a construction or an edifice, but only to those who have acquired form. The calculable always equals two times god. (pp9-10)

Countersign

Only anticipation mobilises the equivocal poetry of building and in the process raises the 'Babel' motif. Beyond the immense and daring challenge of contemporary work one can sense the proliferating ascendancy of detachment. Is it possible that now *no one's 'turn' is dwelling?* More. What is built is itself an instrument of revolt. A 'turn' which cannot be entered. For who can really say again 'I have seen the hangings draped in the shape of a crescent moon but without their definitive symmetry in the quaternary?'

The ambiguous, promiscuous, violent relation one has with architecture works a tortured admission: the seal releases by sealing: the sign effaces by de-signing. The signature of architecture expropriates – can no longer be thought of as being in terms of presence. Architecture as no longer/as no/longer not. Beautiful Architecture Without Beauty. (p135)

Extracts. Source: *Daniel Libeskind: Countersigns,* Architectural Monographs No 16, Academy Editions, (London) 1991. © Academy Group Ltd and Daniel Libeskind.

1992   PETER EISENMAN

Visions' Unfolding: Architecture in the Age of Electronic Media

In his continuing attempts to foil conventional and culturally restricted interpretations of architecture, Eisenman explores in this essay the idea of endowing space 'with the possibility of looking back at the subject', a space that cannot be put together in the traditional construct of vision. To that end he takes up the concept, and tactic, of the fold, credited by Eisenman to Gilles Deleuze.

During the fifty years since the Second World War, a paradigm shift has taken place that should have profoundly affected architecture: this was the shift from the mechanical paradigm to the electronic one. This change can be simply understood by comparing the impact of the role of the human subject on such primary modes of reproduction as the photograph and the fax; the photograph within the mechanical paradigm, the fax within the electronic one . . .

The electronic paradigm directs a powerful challenge to architecture because it defines reality in terms of media and simulation, it values appearance over existence, what can be seen over what is. Not the seen as we formerly knew it, but rather a seeing that can no longer interpret. Media introduce fundamental ambiguities into how and what we see. Architecture has resisted this question because, since the importation and absorption of perspective by architectural space in the 15th century, architecture has been dominated by the mechanics of vision. Thus architecture assumes sight to be preeminent and also in some way natural to its own processes, not a thing to be questioned. It is precisely this traditional concept of sight that the electronic paradigm questions . . .

As long as architecture refuses to take up the problem of vision, it will remain within a Renaissance or Classical view of its discourse. Now what would it mean for architecture to take up the problem of vision? Vision can be defined as essentially a way of organizing space and elements in space. It is a way of looking *at*, and defines a relationship between a subject and an object. Traditional architecture is structured so that any position occupied by a subject provides the means for understanding that position in relation to a particular spatial typology, such as a rotunda, a transept crossing, an axis, an entry. Any number of these typological conditions deploy architecture as a screen for looking-at.

The idea of 'looking-back' begins to displace the anthropocentric subject. Looking back does not require the object to become a subject, that is to anthropomorphosize [sic] the object. Looking back concerns the possibility of detaching the subject from the rationalization of space. In other words to allow the subject to have a vision of space that no longer can be put together in the normalizing, classicising or traditional construct of vision; another space, where in fact the space 'looks back' at the subject. A possible first step in conceptualizing this 'other' space, would be to detach what one sees from what one knows – the eye from the mind. A second step would be to inscribe space in such a way as to endow it with the possibility of looking back at the subject. All architecture can be said to be already inscribed. Windows, doors, beams and columns are a kind of inscription. These make architecture known, they reinforce vision . . .

In order to have a looking back, it is necessary to rethink the idea of inscription . . .

Suppose for a moment that architecture could be conceptualized as a Moebius strip, with an unbroken continuity between interior and exterior. What would this mean for vision? Gilles Deleuze has proposed just such a possible continuity with his idea of the fold. For Deleuze, folded space articulates a new relationship between vertical and horizontal, figure and ground, inside and out – all structures articulated by traditional vision. Unlike the space of classical vision, the idea of folded space denies framing in favor of a temporal modulation. The fold no longer privileges planimetric projection; instead there is a variable curvature . . .

Folding changes the traditional space of vision. That is, it can be considered to be *e*ffective; it functions, it shelters, it is meaningful; it frames, it is aesthetic. Folding also constitutes a move from *e*ffective to *a*ffective space. Folding is not another subjective expressionism, a promiscuity, but rather unfolds in space alongside of its functioning and its meaning in space – it has what might be called an excessive condition or *a*ffect. Folding is a type of *a*ffective space which concerns those aspects that are not associated with the *e*ffective, that are more than reason, meaning and function. In order to change the relationship of perspectival projection to three-dimensional space it is necessary to change the relationship between project drawing and real space. This would mean that one would no longer be able to draw with any level of meaningfulness that space that is being projected. For example, when it is no longer possible to draw a line that stands for some scale relationship to another line in space, it has nothing to do with reason, of the connection of the mind to the eye. The deflection from the line in space means that there no longer exists a one-to-one scale correspondence.

My folded projects are a primitive beginning. In them the subject understands that he or she can no longer conceptualize experience in space in the same way that he or she did in the gridded space. They attempt to provide this dislocation of the subject from effective space; an idea of presentness. Once the environment becomes affective, inscribed with another logic or ur-logic, one which is no longer translatable into the vision of the mind, then reason becomes detached from vision. While we can still understand space in terms of its function, structure and aesthetic – we are still within 'four walls' – somehow reason becomes detached from the affective condition of the environment itself. This begins to produce an environment that 'looks back' – that is, the environment seems to have an order that we can perceive even though it does not seem to mean anything. It does not seek to be understood in the traditional way of architecture yet it possesses some sense of 'aura', an ur-logic which is the sense of something outside our vision. (pp21-24)

Extracts. Source: *Domus*, no 734, January 1992. © Peter Eisenman.

Peter Eisenman, Emory Centre for the Arts, Model of Folding, 1992

1993   WILL ALSOP

Towards an Architecture of Practical Delight

Will Alsop, (b 1947, Northampton) has projected a vision of archi-
tecture that goes beyond its roots in the conceptual developments of
Modernism of the 50s and 60s. He studied under Cedric Price, amongst
others, and worked in his office in the mid-70s, at the same time
lecturing at St Martin's School of Art. This text was published in a
monograph on the work of Alsop and Jan Störmer, with whom he has
worked since 1990.

The Dresden Principles
– Building both in the process of design and later under construction should be
  a celebration.
– The experience of the edifice should lift the human spirit.
– The architect should use any means possible to achieve the above.
Within the confines of these objectives, it is not possible, or desirable to become
a slave to a philosophy, style or specific procedure. Instead it is more important to
consider yourself as the consumer of products of architecture (and others) before
subjecting the world to products born of architectural debate by architects.

Rely on your own experience. Look to yourself.
Anything is possible to build, or not build, we could therefore ask the question as
to why styles and fashion and methods tend to become common practice within
our environment.

The objective is to reach the point where one is liberated from having to answer
with a justification, reason or theory. It is enough to say, honestly, 'I don't know'
and know this is correct.

Of all the arts, architecture is one in which the artist is expected to be able to
talk, reason and justify almost every move. This is because architecture is the art
of prediction. The discussions take place around approximations and speculations of a future that does not yet exist. In painting, sculpture and even science
there is a tangible result which can be appreciated for itself and therefore open to
discussion. Whatever is said, the deed has been done. Architects have nothing
concrete, only a strategy and themselves.

What is the nature of a discussion and who is it between?
Everyone has expectations. Society established codes of acceptable behaviour as a method of operating. Everything we do is an agreement, and we should never delude ourselves by thinking that we have ever acted in a completely independent manner (why should we want to?). The nature of introducing anything into the world is collaborative, therefore the nature of what we do is in its essence a compromise. If we are aware of this, we can turn the idea of compromise into a positive energy, as opposed to the common idea that all compromise is a watering down of concept. What happens if compromise is the concept? The discussion is between society and the architect and between individuals in society and the architect.

The question is then how to discuss. Each party contributing to the discussion has expectations and preconceptions. We therefore have to find ways of undermining these as much as possible. This applies to your own as well as others.

I often start by painting. The paint has a life of its own, beyond your control. It is possible to see what you cannot think. The paintings do not have the authority of traditional sealed drawings and as such can be used in discussions. This act is an invitation to misinterpret, extend and corrupt. I often describe this process as designing a conversation, not a building. People must feel relaxed and uninhibited. It is very important that all ideas, objectives and idle thoughts can be voiced and therefore considered. The conversation is open. This same principle is used with the whole team of people involved with changing the surface of the earth and/or strategies of varying known behaviours. Because change is inevitable, and always a major consideration in any proposition, it is natural that the idea of uncertainty should be built into the design process. My work is never sure of any agreement at any stage of development. It is always important to reconsider projects in part or totality right through the design and construction. This attitude accepts that the task of predicting the future is impossible and as such we can only attempt to make it as real as possible at all stages. A flash of perception ought to be acted on. It is never too late.

All fluctuations can be labelled. When they are labelled they become institutionalised. Architects spend their time worrying about the programme – usually expressed in the form of functions. I prefer the truth about behaviour as this is less specific. 'Eating' can mean anything from grazing, to picnics, to formal restaurants. If the word 'canteen' appears in your brief, it already assumes a particular type of place, which prevents thought and speculation.

Leave it loose until it feels right
Every project should be a surprise to both the client and yourself. This implies that one starts afresh with each new work. This is totally wrong. It is vital to build on the experience that you accumulate. There is no need to make the same mistake twice. The point is that all the work that we do is one work and that the development of that work is only possible through an open and direct involvement with society. The challenging of habitual behaviour resulting in an agreement between you and the world is a way forward. (p15)

Architecture: one way of exploring the world through work – it must, however, always be an exploration not a confirmation.

Extract. Source: *William Alsop and Jan Störmer*, Architectural Monographs No 33, Academy Editions (London) – Ernst & Sohn (Berlin) 1993. © Academy Group Ltd.

Alsop & Störmer, Le Grand Bleu, Marseilles, 1990-94

1993   THOM MAYNE
Connected Isolation

A graduate of the University of Southern California and Harvard Graduate School of Design, Thom Mayne (b 1944, Waterbury, Connecticut) founded the firm Morphosis with Michael Rotondi in 1976. Morphosis established itself with such buildings as 2-4-6-8 House (Los Angeles 1978), Sedlak Residence (Venice, California, 1980) and the Kate Mantilini Restaurant (Los Angeles, 1986). Typical of their work is a fusion of complexity and diversity within an ordered framework, achieving a dynamic balance 'with the aim of reflecting the richness of our pluralistic world'.

Although the relationship of architecture to its immediate political and economic context is illusive and complicated, we have no choice but to assert a position which redefines our intentions and our methods of intervention. What are the issues involved in this redefinition? First, it is important to articulate and integrate the public and the private nature of our work to develop an effective conception of *coherency (order)* as a necessary social condition. Second, it is essential to develop methods of supporting and contributing to idiosyncrasy. The importance today is to comprehend and utilise the complexity of everyday experience. Third, is our need to interpret our time *authentically*. Architecture's recent intoxication with literal historical precedent has shown us the hopelessness of such a regressive strategy in the face of the magnitude and complexity of our cities. It is necessary for architecture to be based in the present and to aspire to that presence . . .

[The] steadily growing polarity between the increasingly unwieldy 'public' sphere and the ever narrowing 'private' sphere raises questions about the fundamental fitness of groups versus individuals to resolve the problems inherent in our current circumstances. The existence of this polarity does not require a choice between one or the other . . . Architecture has an opportunity to choose to oscillate between these poles, maximising their conflicting status and their creative potential.

The physical manifestation of these destabilising forces is that our contemporary cities are no longer identifiable as entities. A coherency of place (order) is lost as is the perceptibility of an edge or boundary . . .

Our proposals question the concept of boundary as it marks or delimits an urban territory and as it oscillates between notions of inside/outside and centre/periphery and its inverse. Our earlier projects, 2-4-6-8, Venice III, and 6th Street represented a progressive investigation of surface volume relationships which attempted to maximise the tensions inherent within their conditions . . .

The potential of the modern dynamic ought to take on a particular and human form, turning people outwards. The movement away from a way of life as essentially simple and orderly to a view of life as complex and ironic is what every individual passes through in becoming mature. The essence of development as a human being is in developing the capacity for ever more complex experience . . .

Our proposals must embrace difference, they are products of the complex systems that constitute our contemporary environment. The modernist penchant for unification and simplification must be broken. This, then, is the key issue – the recognition of *diversity* is the natural evolution of things. To accept this dynamic state rather than to look for a replacement with something fixed, or stable, is to utilise the tremendous energy of the city.

Manifest in the work are organisational strategies capable of representing a high degree of differentiation within a framework of order and continuity. The coexistence, between the wilful architectural elements and the augmented landscape, expresses states of both harmony and tension. The architectural-landscape elements confront, but are simultaneously at home with, their natural setting. The solutions are characterised by their fractured natures which provide a perpetual open-endedness and unfinished quality to the projects. It is part of an accretive *making process* that allows inhabitant or observer to anticipate the next intervention. The end of our work therefore marks the beginning for the next . . .

[The] linkage of a benign architecture passively serving a status quo society is what is so apparent in our current situation. The culture of our cities is now overtaken by this frenetic reach for the *past*. This past is romanticised – seen as a place of safety and security to one who feels intrinsically unsafe . . .

This romanticising of an earlier time as 'simpler', fails to grasp that it is in the realisation of complexity and contradiction that we begin to find our way out of the psychological malaise we're currently suffering. It is embracing hazard, nurturing an eye for the idiosyncratic, the phrases left unspoken, the unfinished – that allows us to utilise the potentiality of our cities. Our work is defined by its occupation of space and by the presence of the object(s). It is about the techniques of construction which provide for a frame of reference beyond beauty and history . . .

Modern urbanism has provided the world with a vast legacy of diminished expectations, if architecture has a single objective, it is to clarify its intentions and realign its purposes with the aim of reflecting the richness of our pluralistic world. The modern, dystopian city will overlay differences rather than segment them. We will hold to that which is difficult, because it is difficult . . . and by its difficulty is worthwhile. A city is a living organism, a work-in-progress, an impasto of forms made by successive waves of habitation. One should continue to choose to do only projects which offer hope of a complex, integrated, contradictory and meaningful future. (pp7-17)

Extracts. Source: Thom Mayne/Morphosis, *Morphosis: Connected Isolation*, Architectural Monographs No 23, Academy Editions (London), 1993. © The Academy Group Ltd.

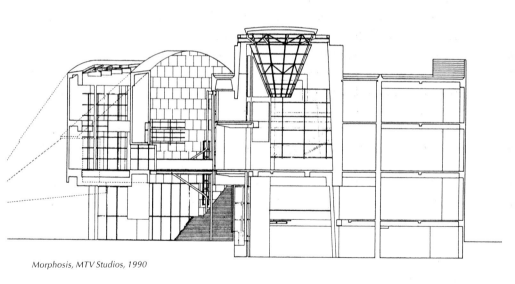

Morphosis, MTV Studios, 1990

1993 LEBBEUS WOODS
Manifesto

Having studied both engineering and architecture, Lebbeus Woods (b 1940, Lansing Michigan) turned to drawing as his primary medium. With flawless draughtsmanship he seeks to go 'beyond the limits set by conventional knowledge and practice'. Woods has taught at SCI-ARC in Los Angeles, Columbia University and The Cooper Union in New York.

Architecture and war are not incompatible. Architecture is war. War is architecture.

I am at war with my time, with history, with all authority that resides in fixed and frightened forms.

I am one of millions who do not fit in, who have no home, no family, no doctrine, nor firm place to call my own, no known beginning or end, no 'sacred and primoridal site'.

I declare war on all icons and finalities, on all histories that would chain me with my own falseness, my own pitiful fears.

I know only moments, and lifetimes that are as moments, and forms that appear with infinite strength, then 'melt into air'.

I am an architect, a constructor of worlds, a sensualist who worships the flesh, the melody, a silhouette against the darkening sky. I cannot know your name. Nor can you know mine.

Tomorrow, we begin together the construction of a city. (p405)

Source: Andreas Papadakis (ed), *Theory and Experimentation*, Academy Editions (London), 1993. © Academy Editions.

1994 REM KOOLHAAS
What Ever Happened to Urbanism?

Demonstrating a Protean ambivalence – not in the sense of indiffer-
ence – Koolhaas at once laments and exults in the conditions of con-
temporary architecture and urbanism. His experience of the Old World,
the New World and the exploding urbanism of the developing world
combines to induce hot and cold flashes of despair and exuberance.

Sous le pavé, la plage (under the pavement, beach): initially, May '68 launched the idea of a new beginning for the city. Since then, we have been engaged in two parallel operations: documenting our overwhelming awe for the existing city, developing philosophies, projects, prototypes for a preserved *and* reconstituted city and, at the same time, laughing the professional field of urbanism out of existence, dismantling it in our contempt for those who planned (and made huge mistakes in planning) airports, New Towns, satellite cities, highways, high-rise buildings, infrastructures, and all the other fallout from modernization. After sabotaging urbanism, we have ridiculed it to the point where entire university departments are closed, offices bankrupted, bureaucracies fired or privatized. Our 'sophistication' hides major symptoms of cowardice centered on the simple question of taking positions – maybe the most basic action in making the city. We are simultaneously dogmatic and evasive. Our amalgamated wisdom can be easily caricatured; according to Derrida we cannot be *Whole*, according to Baudrillard we cannot be *Real*, according to Virilio we cannot be *There*.

'Exiled to the Virtual World': plot for a horror movie. Our present relationship with the 'crisis' of the city is deeply ambiguous: we still blame others for a situation for which both our incurable utopianism and our contempt are responsible. Through our hypocritical relationship with power – contemptuous yet covetous – we dismantled an entire discipline, cut ourselves off from the operational, and condemned whole populations to the impossibility of encoding civilizations on their territory – the subject of urbanism.

Now we are left with a world without urbanism, only architecture, ever more architecture. The neatness of architecture is its seduction; it defines, excludes, limits, separates from the rest – but it also consumes. It exploits and exhausts the potentials that can be generated finally only by urbanism, and that only the specific imagination of urbanism can invent and renew. The death of urbanism – our refuge in the parasitic security of architecture – creates an immanent disaster: more and more substance grafted on starving roots . . .

If there is to be a 'new urbanism' it will not be based on the twin fantasies of order and omnipotence; it will be the staging of uncertainty; it will no longer be concerned with the arrangement of more or less permanent objects but with the irrigation of territories with potential; it will no longer aim for stable configurations but for the creation of enabling fields that accommodate processes that refuse to be crystallized into definitive form; it will no longer be about meticulous definition, the imposition of limits, but about expanding notions, denying boundaries, not about separating and identifying entities, but about discovering unnamable hybrids; it will no longer be obsessed with the city but with the manipulation of infrastructure for endless intensifications and diversifications, shortcuts and redistributions – the reinvention of psychological space. Since the urban is now pervasive, urbanism will never again be about the 'new', only about the 'more' and the 'modified'. It will not be about the civilized, but about underdevelopments. Since it is out of control, the urban is about to become a major vector of the imagination. Redefined, urbanism will not only, or mostly, be a profession, but a way of thinking, an ideology: to accept what exists. We were making sand castles. Now we swim in the sea that swept them away . . .

The seeming failure of the urban offers an exceptional opportunity, a pretext for Nietzschean frivolity. We have to imagine 1,001 other concepts of city; we have to take insane risks; we have to dare to be utterly uncritical; we have to swallow deeply and bestow forgiveness left and right. The certainty of failure has to be our laughing gas/oxygen; modernization our most potent drug. Since we are not responsible, we have to become irresponsible. In a landscape of increasing expediency and impermanence, urbanism no longer is or has to be the most solemn of our decisions; urbanism can lighten up, become a *Gay Science* – Lite Urbanism.

What if we simply declare that there *is* no crisis – redefine our relationship with the city not as its makers but as its mere subjects, as its supporters?

More than ever, the city is all we have. (pp961-971)

Extracts. Source: OMA, Rem Koolhaas, Bruce Mau, *S, M, L, XL*, Monacelli Press Inc (New York), 1995. © Rem Koolhaas and the Monacelli Press Inc.

1994   REM KOOLHAAS
Bigness: or the Problem of Large

In this essay, Koolhaas lays open one of the most nagging problems of 20th-century architecture. He unflinchingly exposes a nerve that is insensitive to style but has grown increasingly raw since the steel frame and lift were first brought together. 'The absence of a theory of Bigness is architecture's most debilitating weakness.' His own attempts to deal with bigness include the Boompjes Tower Slab project (Rotterdam, 1982), the Hague City Hall project (1986), the Bibliotheques Jussieu competition project (Paris, 1993), and the Congrexpo building (Lille, 1994).

Beyond a certain scale, architecture acquires the properties of Bigness. The best reason to broach Bigness is the one given by climbers of Mount Everest: 'because its there'. Bigness is ultimate architecture. It seems incredible that the *size* of a building alone embodies an ideological program, independent of the will of its architects.

Of all the categories, Bigness does not seem to deserve a manifesto; discredited as an intellectual problem, it is apparently on its way to extinction – like the dinosaur – through clumsiness, slowness, inflexibility, difficulty. But in fact, only Bigness instigates the *regime of complexity* that mobilizes the full intelligence of architecture and its related fields.

One hundred years ago, a generation of conceptual breakthroughs and supporting technologies unleashed an architectural Big Bang. By randomizing circulation, short-circuiting distance, artificializing interiors, reducing mass, stretching dimensions, and accelerating construction, the elevator, electricity, air-conditioning, steel, and finally, the new infrastructures formed a cluster of mutations that induced another species of architecture. The combined effects of these inventions were structures taller and deeper – Bigger – than ever before conceived, with a parallel potential for the reorganization of the social world – a vastly richer programmation.

Theorems
Fuelled initially by the thoughtless energy of the purely quantitative, Bigness has been, for nearly a century, a condition almost without thinkers, a revolution without program.

Delirious New York implied a latent 'Theory of Bigness' based on five theorems.

1 Beyond a certain critical mass, a building becomes a Big Building. Such a mass can no longer be controlled by a single architectural gesture, or even by any combination of architectural gestures. This impossibility triggers the autonomy of its parts, but that is not the same as fragmentation: the parts remain committed to the whole.

2 The elevator – with its potential to establish mechanical rather than architectural connections – and its family of related inventions render null and void the classical repertoire of architecture. Issues of composition, scale, proportion, detail are now moot.

The 'art' of architecture is useless in Bigness.

3 In Bigness, the distance between core and envelope increases to the point where the facade can no longer reveal what happens inside. The humanist expectation of 'honesty' is doomed: interior and exterior architectures become separate projects, one dealing with the instability of programmatic and iconographic needs, the other – agent of disinformation – offering the city the apparent stability of an object.

Where architecture reveals, Bigness perplexes; Bigness transforms the city from a summation of certainties into an accumulation of mysteries. What you see is no longer what you get.

4 Through size alone, such buildings enter an amoral domain, beyond good or bad.

Their impact is independent of their quality.

5 Together, all these breaks – with scale, with architectural composition, with tradition, with transparency, with ethics – imply the final, most radical break; Bigness is no longer part of any urban tissue.

It exists; at most it coexists.

Its subtext is *fuck* context . . .

Maximum

The absence of a theory of Bigness – what is the maximum architecture can do? – is architecture's most debilitating weakness. Without a theory of Bigness, architects are in the position of Frankenstein's creators: instigators of a partly successful experiment whose results are running amok and are therefore discredited. Because there is no theory of Bigness, we don't know what to do with it, we don't know where to put it, we don't know when to use it, we don't know how to plan it. Big mistakes are our only connection to Bigness.

But in spite of its dumb name, Bigness is a theoretical domain at this *fin de siècle*: in a landscape of disarray, disassembly, dissociation, disclamation, the attraction of Bigness is its potential to reconstruct the Whole, resurrect the Real, reinvent the collective, reclaim maximum possibility.

Only through Bigness can architecture dissociate itself from the exhausted artistic/ideological movements of modernism and formalism to regain its instrumentality as vehicle of modernization.

Bigness recognizes that architecture as we know it is in difficulty, but it does not overcompensate through regurgitations of even more architecture. It proposes a new economy in which no longer 'all is architecture', but in which a strategic position is regained through retreat and concentration, yielding the rest of a contested territory to enemy forces . . .

Beginning

Bigness destroys, but it is also a new beginning. It can reassemble what it breaks.

A paradox of Bigness is that in spite of the calculation that goes into its planning – in fact through its very rigidities – it is the one architecture that engineers the unpredictable. Instead of enforcing coexistence, Bigness depends on regimes of freedoms, the assembly of maximum difference.

Only Bigness can sustain a promiscuous proliferation of events in a single container. It develops strategies to organize both their independence and interdependence within a larger entity in a symbiosis that exacerbates rather than compromises specificity.

Through contamination rather than purity and quantity rather than quality, only Bigness can support genuinely new relationships between functional entities that expand rather than limit their identities. The artificiality and complexity of Bigness release function from its defensive armor to allow a kind of liquefaction; programmatic elements react with each other to create new events – Bigness returns to a model of programmatic *alchemy*.

At first sight, the activities amassed in the structure of Bigness *demand* to interact, but Bigness also keeps them apart. Like plutonium rods that, more or less immersed, dampen or promote nuclear reaction, Bigness regulates the intensities of programmatic existence.

Although Bigness is a blueprint for perpetual intensity, it also offers degrees of serenity and even blandness. It is simply impossible to animate its entire mass with intention. Its vastness exhausts architecture's compulsive need to decide and determine. Zones will be left out, free from architecture . . .

Bastion

If Bigness transforms architecture, its accumulation generates a new kind of city. The exterior of the city is no longer a collective theater where 'it' happens; there's no collective 'it' left. The street has become residue, organizational device, mere segment of the continuous metropolitan plane where remnants of the past face the equipments of the new in an uneasy standoff. Bigness can exist *anywhere* on that plane. Not only is Bigness incapable of establishing relationships with the classical city – *at most it coexists* – but in the quantity and complexity of the facilities it offers, it is itself urban.

Bigness no longer needs the city: it competes with the city; it represents the city; it preempts the city; or better still it *is* the city. If urbanism generates potential and architecture exploits it, Bigness enlists the generosity of urbanism against the meanness of architecture.

Bigness = urbanism vs architecture.

Bigness, through its very independence of context, is the one architecture that can survive, even exploit, the now-global condition of the *tabula rasa*: it does not take its inspiration from givens too often squeezed for the last drop of meaning; it gravitates opportunistically to locations of maximum infrastructural promise, it is, finally, its own *raison d'être*.

In spite of its size, it is modest.

Not all architecture, not all program, not all events will be swallowed by Bigness. There are many 'needs' too unfocused, too weak, too unrespectable, too defiant, too secret, too subversive, too weak, too 'nothing' to be part of the constellations of Bigness. Bigness is the last bastion of architecture – a contraction, a hyper-architecture. The containers of Bigness will be landmarks in a post-architectural landscape – a world scraped of architecture in the way Richter's paintings are scraped of paint: inflexible, immutable, definitive, forever there, generated through superhuman effort. Bigness surrenders the field to after-architecture. (pp494-516)

Extracts. Source: OMA, Rem Koolhaas, Bruce Mau, *S, M, L, XL*, Monacelli Press Inc (New York), 1995. © Rem Koolhaas and the Monacelli Press Inc.

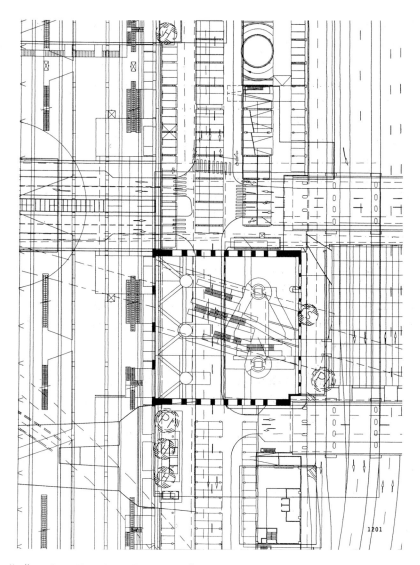

Rem Koolhaas, Espace Piranesian, TVG RR Station, Lille, France, 1993-96

EDITORS' NOTE

The task of excerpting texts, in some cases from a book down to several pages, has at times necessitated additions in order to maintain the sense of a passage. Following editorial convention, the additions are set in square brackets. Also by convention, ellipses have been omitted at the beginning of excerpted passages.

Every effort has been made to reproduce the texts as accurately as possible relative to the source cited. There may be differences relative to other versions and the editors regret any errors of transcription that remain.

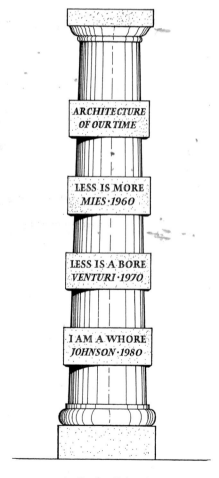

Ian Hamilton Finlay, 1984